22.75
1-18-00

Corporate
Cults

Corporate Cults

The Insidious Lure of the All-Consuming Organization

Dr. Dave Arnott

AMACOM

American Management Association

New York • Atlanta • Boston • Chicago • Kansas City • San Francisco • Washington, D. C.
Brussels • Mexico City • Tokyo • Toronto

Special discounts on bulk quantities of AMACOM books are available to corporations, professional associations, and other organizations. For details, contact Special Sales Department, AMACOM, an imprint of AMA Publications, a division of American Management Association, 1601 Broadway, New York, NY 10019. Tel.: 212-903-8316   Fax: 212-903-8083

This publication is designed to provide accurate and authoritative information in regard to the subject matter covered. It is sold with the understanding that the publisher is not engaged in rendering legal, accounting, or other professional service. If legal advice or other expert assistance is required, the services of a competent professional person should be sought.

Library of Congress Cataloging-in-Publication Data

Arnott, Dave, 1954–
    Corporate cults: the insidious lure of the all-consuming organization / Dave Arnott.
        p.   cm.
    Includes bibliographical references and index.
    ISBN 0-8144-0493-6
    1. Corporate culture.   2. Organizational behavior.   I. Title.
    HD58.7.A763   1999
    302.3'5—dc21   99-39967
                                                             CIP

Printing number

10   9   8   7   6   5   4   3   2

Contents

Preface

There is a movement among organizations to extract higher levels of commitment by treating employees as members of the family. This book warns employees about this dangerous trend, which promotes a hazardous blending of work, family, and community. I propose that employees should not involve their spirit or soul in their workplace. Those "close to the heart" elements are too important for work and should be reserved for family and community.

People often assume that corporate cults are the fault of the organization, so they expect this book to rail against the all consuming organization. While leadership certainly contributes to cultish behavior, the major part of the responsibility lies with the individual. Only the voluntary replacement of "who I am" with "what I do" can produce corporate cult membership. You're in charge, and only you can allow the insidious lure of the all-consuming organization to take over your life. Leaders do what is best for themselves and for the organization. That's what they should do. Employees should do what's best for themselves as well. Sometimes that means *being a part of* the corporate family, and sometimes it means *protecting yourself from* the corporate family.

Don't be surprised if the anecdotes and explanations of corporate cults seem to explain your workplace. The elements of corporate cults arise in all organizations as they try to squeeze more performance out of employees. There is a natural tension between labor and management in organizations. I support a certain level of tension, because it means that employees are protecting their self-interest. I get worried about organizations that seem to operate as "one big happy family," because that usually means someone has subordinated individual self-interest to the interest of the group. That's fertile ground for the growth of a corporate cult.

The first chapter of *Corporate Cults* describes the organizational actions that typify corporate cults. Chapter 2 explains the environmental effect of demographics, which produces a wider value dispersion in each succeeding generation. Organizations respond to this generational complexity by selecting employees more carefully, which is explained in the competitive advantage selection model in Chapter 3. Those who work in the hiring process will recognize the trend that I predict in this chapter.

Chapter 4 describes how work is replacing home as the source of emotional sustenance for employees. All employees will relate to some level of work-as-family. It starts with a refrigerator in the lunchroom and ends in a full-blown corporate cult. The practitioner's definition of organizational culture is "how we do things around here." That definition is expanded and analyzed via corporate cult behavior in Chapter 5.

The three elements of a cult, devotion, charismatic leadership, and separation from community, are the subject of Chapters 6, 7, and 8. It's interesting that after rating the best places to work, *Fortune* magazine summarized the three elements that produce them. The three elements were purpose, charismatic leadership, and great facilities that essentially separate the worker from the community. If you are an employee of a "best place to work," you'll be fascinated by the correlations between best places and corporate cults that are described in this section.

After reading about corporate cults, you might wonder if you're in one. The cult test in Chapter 9 answers that question by measuring the levels of devotion, charismatic leadership, and separation from community that you feel are present in your organization. If you're concerned about your level—or the level of a friend or family member—you'll want to read Chapter 10, because it describes how to remain independent of the insidious lure of the all-consuming organization.

Chapter 11 approaches the old nature vs. nurture issue, "Does corporate cult membership occur because of the way you were born, or simply at a particularly emotionally needy time in your life?" The summary answer is that it can be caused by either one.

It's frightening that everyone is susceptible to corporate cult membership. Chapter 12 leaves the reader with some advice for avoiding corporate cults in the future.

How is *your* organization a cult? You're about to find out.

Acknowledgments

Thanks to Rusty Juban who helped with the statistical analysis of the cult test and made many contributions to Chapter 9. Dean Arnott is a family counselor who provided important advice on interpersonal relationship issues. Phyllis Parker was a great encourager throughout the writing process.

Thanks to Arlie Russell Hochschild for *The Time Bind* and Carolyn Corbin for *Conquering Corporate Codependence,* both important forerunners to *Corporate Cults.*

Thanks to Larry Rottmeyer and my colleagues in the College of Business at Dallas Baptist University. I'm indebted to many of my students, who challenged my ideas and provided anecdotes of life in corporate cults.

Thanks to UTA professors Abdul Rasheed, Greg Dess, and Richard Priem for teaching me how to think strategically. Phil Hudson, Joe Mata, Frank Bauer, Kris Ankerson, and Stephanie Coray allowed me to test ideas in USDA Graduate School seminars.

Thanks to Lindsay and Lance, who had less of a father than they deserved during the writing of the book. Thanks to Harold and Ruth Arnott for telling me as a child that I was smart and could do anything. The degree to which I am and can is because of your encouragement. Thanks to Steve Stroope, Timothy Warren, and the gang at Lake Pointe.

Jim Donovan is the world's greatest literary agent and an outstanding playground basketball point guard. Sandee Smith has accurately and faithfully read my thoughts as she has produced artwork for numerous presentations and publications, including this book. Ellen Kadin at AMACOM is the best senior editor writer could ever hope to have. This book would not have been completed without the numerous and immeasurable efforts of my associate editor, Shelly Wert. Thanks to Bob Briner and Dennis Spencer for having faith in my pro sports management ability when I was underqualified. Loila Hunking taught me how to write.

Thanks to you, the survivors, escapees, and avoiders of corporate cults who truly understand the insidious lure of the all-consuming organization.

Corporate Cults

Chapter 1

When Culture Becomes a Cult

*W*ork has become too important.

People should find more value in who they are and less value in what they do. Employees to whom work has become too important have allowed their workplace to become their own corporate cult. Corporate cults are dangerous because they take more from the employee than they return. Individual identity is replaced with organizational identity. Increasing amounts of time and energy are invested in the corporation at the expense of family and community.

This book is about corporate cults. Through anecdotes, testing, and comparison, the book helps identify how "culted" you are with your organization. All organizations have some degree of "cultedness"; some have more than others. Are you in a corporate cult? This book will help you determine this.

The following is an example of a corporate cult I visited recently:

- In the first ten minutes, the visitors took a pledge to do whatever the leader said to do.

- Visitors were invited to apply washable tattoos to themselves.

- All attendees participated in a dance.

- The speaker said, "We fire for attitude."

- The first training session for new employees is done on company time; the remaining courses are taken on the workers' own time.

- The company spoke of having a diverse organization. By my estimate, eighteen of the twenty-four employees standing obediently behind the speaker were white women ages 25 to 45.

- Members of the organization often spoke of it as a "family."

- Employees were encouraged to express themselves, so the company had no written dress code. However, of the approximately fifty employees I saw that day, 100 percent of them were wearing the company shirt and either khaki shorts or blue jeans.

- Halloween was the biggest holiday.

- A "culture committee" appointed by the leaders met four times a year to determine proper and improper conduct.

- One of the organizational lore stories was about an eminently qualified specialist who was not hired because of his attitude.

- Candidates who join the organization must successfully pass multiple interviews in which the organizational screeners look for personality characteristics that allow candidates to join.

- One of the company slogans encouraged members to "Have a relationship at work."

What is this organization? A Branch Davidian compound? The Ku Klux Klan? A Baptist church? Mary Kay?

No, it's Southwest Airlines, which attributes a great deal of its much-heralded success to a unique corporate culture.

Why pick on Southwest Airlines? Throughout the book, I identify numerous corporations. I start with Southwest because it claims to encourage independence on the part of its employees. If we can find ways in which even Southwest Airlines is culted, perhaps we can find elements of corporate cultism in your organization.

It's okay to use Southwest Airlines as an example for three reasons. First, it is a public company. The actions of a public company are open to scrutiny because to some degree the fortunes of the public are affected by the success or failure of the organization. If "cultism" is a liability to the company, the public needs to know about it.

Second, Southwest Airlines is immensely successful. In business strategy, we study only the "outliers," those that lie on the extremes of the success-failure continuum. Southwest is on the success end of the continuum. It is increasingly used as a benchmark for how companies should be operated.

Third, the company doesn't take itself seriously. Everything is wrapped in humor and fun. The dance in the preceding anecdote was the macarena. It was fun. Prizes were given for the best macarena, the worst macarena, and the most spirited macarena. The tattoos were washable. But remember, *tattoo* is a verb as well as a noun. Are the employees of Southwest Airlines "tattooed"? Are you?

If you wear a pair of Nike socks, a swoosh logo appears on your lower ankle—it's woven into the sock. Some employees at Nike have the swoosh logo permanently tattooed on their ankles. Does that mean that Nike employees have been tattooed? Literally, they have been. At any rate, it makes it hard for a Nike employee to transfer to Reebok.

In this small example, we have two parties: Nike and the employee. This foreshadows the theme of this entire book: the relationship between individuals and the organizations they belong to.

The Individual vs. the Organization

Most of what we teach in organizational management tries to balance the tension between the individual and the organization, as shown in Figure 1-1. The Industrial Revolution introduced the concept of standardized manufacturing, in which efficiency became the determinant of organizational success.

Adam Smith wrote about the value of specialization and division of labor in his landmark 1776 book *The Wealth of Nations*. He

Figure 1-1. The Relationship Between Individual and Organization

cited the experience of a manufacturer of straight pins to show the value of division of labor and specialization. The pin maker was using a craft technology in which each individual pin maker performed all six functions of pin making. The pin maker would:

1. Draw the wire.
2. Cut the wire.
3. Sharpen the point.
4. Mount the head.
5. Wrap the pin in paper.
6. Place it in its box.

The system was inefficient, so an early-day consultant suggested that the pin makers specialize and divide the labor. Thus, a specialist drew wire all day, a specialist cut wire all day, etc. Production improved an astounding 4,000 percent![1]

You can predict the labor problem: B-O-R-E-D-O-M.

Since Adam Smith, academics, consultants, and management practitioners have been trying to satisfy seemingly contradictory demands: efficiency at one end of the continuum and individual value at the other. The craft process gave people value because they could see the result of their effort, and they worked on a cluster of changing activities. The specialized division of labor increased efficiency and was good for the company, but it turned the workers into automatons.

Fast-forward to the year 2000, and we find a company like Southwest Airlines, with its incredible productivity record. It seems as though it has circumvented the adage about the conflicting goals of individuals and organizations. It has made the individual and organizational goals the same by creating an organization in which individuals can become "enculted." Unfortunately, that means managers are drawn to this as a model for how to gain increased productivity from a workforce. Southwest Airlines invites business and academic leaders into the organization to tout its unique culture, in which the usually contradictory individual and organizational goals seem to be in perfect coalignment. Individuals seem to have the same goals as the organization, in contrast to the tension shown in Figure 1-1.

The culture at Southwest Airlines clearly is good for the organization. Employees are unabashedly devoted to the organization, as shown by their willingness to work extra days, stay late, and attend parties and other business functions on their own time.

That's good for the organization, but it's bad for the individual. It's bad because it takes away the individual's identity. Spending time and effort in the pursuit of organizational goals reduces the time and effort available to spend in pursuit of individual goals.

That's what this book is about. It explores the effects of corporate cults on the family and community. Employees are culted when "what I do" defines "who I am."

When "What I Do" Defines "Who I Am"

Corporate cults use individuals to achieve organizational goals. Unfortunately, there is an ample supply of cult candidates: people who gain their identity only from what they do, not from who they are. I gained value only from what I did for a long time. Here's how I finally found out I was a likely corporate cult candidate.

In the fall of 1990, I left a fifteen-year career in the sports promotions and sporting goods industry to commit four years of my life to getting a Ph.D. in business management. I dropped out of business life, exchanging a good income and promising career for the title of research assistant at a salary of $10,000 a year. Halfway through the program, my wife decided she didn't want to stay married. We got divorced, and my personal financial picture went from a few years of struggle to pending disaster. There was also academic trouble.

There are three parts of the Ph.D. program of study: coursework, comprehensive exams, and the dissertation. I wasn't too concerned about the coursework or the dissertation. I *was* worried about the second element, the comprehensive exams. Comprehensive exams are *designed* to be stressful. The student brings pencils and paper. He or she is put in a room with one sheet of questions. Typical instructions are to answer six of nine long essay questions in the next eight hours.

I received a conditional pass on my research comprehensive exam, so some research-oriented questions would be included on my management exam. That meant I could pass or fail two comprehensive exams on the same day. I made the commitment that if I passed, I would remain in the program; if I failed, I would drop out. I was going further into debt each day I remained in the program. Failing the exam would delay my graduation past the point when I would be bankrupt.

I checked my mail before taking the test. There was one letter in my box, a note from fellow Ph.D. candidate Paula Daly. Knowing that this was the day that would determine my future, she had written, "Dave, no matter what happens today, you can be proud. Not of what you've done, but of who you are. Good luck. Paula."

I was in my late thirties, halfway through a Ph.D. program, when I finally realized there was a difference between "what I do" and "who I am." I had taken great pride in completing six marathons, pedaling my bicycle across the United States, and earning a master's degree. I was raising two good kids, and I had managed the turnaround of a small manufacturing business, introduced a new sports drink, and worked in pro tennis.

My personal value was derived almost exclusively from the list of my accomplishments. Paula helped me realize that even if I didn't succeed, I was still valuable as an individual.

How We Become "Doers" Instead of "Be-ers"

For me, the value I placed on *doing* was traceable to my family. I come from a doing family. We do things. We are a bunch of "human doings." When I go to visit my parents, even as an adult, there are projects to be carried out. After the expected greetings, my dad is likely to say, "Well, David, we could take down that tree in the backyard while you're here." There is an expectation that I will jump at the chance to complete a project, because that is my family's way of being—excuse me, doing—together. We can't *be* together, so we *do* together.

My family is a throwback to the agrarian age of only 150 years ago, when families found emotional closeness through working together. Industrialization separated the work-family relationship, so social occasions—such as holiday celebrations and family meals—came to take the place of working together.[2] In the Information Age, these social relationships are moving again, this time to the workplace, where employees are forming corporate cults.

My family is not so different from many other families that produce what society calls successful people: people who accomplish things, climb social ladders, earn money, obtain high office, and make a contribution to society. These are all *doing* activities, and my family is a doing family.

I honor the doing side of my personality, and I still like to complete projects. However, knowing my family background, I have become vigilant in trying to honor my *being* side as well as my *doing* side.

My interest in this subject comes from personal experience. Before I received the note from Paula, I found too much personal value in what I did, and not enough value in who I was. I am concerned when individuals find too much value in what they do at work and cannot find value in who they are apart from work. There is a difference.

You are more than your work. It's important to know that. People who find too much value in their work sacrifice family and community for the workplace. That's good for the organization, but bad for the individual. These employees also allow their own moral and ethical codes to be violated to satisfy the demands of their organization, which they have made into a corporate cult.

What's a Cult?

In the 1976 song "Hotel California," Don Henley of the Eagles sang about membership in a drug cult. The song concluded that once the members joined they couldn't escape because they had joined of their own free will. Like the visitors to Hotel California, members of corporate cults are prisoners by choice. They enter freely; no one forces them. It's a cult of their own device. What we know as traditional cults have leaders who find prospective members who have a proclivity to be dominated. The prospective cult members have low self-esteem, so the organization is their only source of individual value. They have so little individual identity that they grasp at group identity.

The situation is very similar in corporate cults. The most likely members are employees with a "hole in their soul" that is patched by membership in the organization. This trait often takes the form of "team play" or "loyalty" when, in fact, it is a yearning to belong to anything. Members of corporate cults are prisoners of their own device.

"Hotel California" says the cult is programmed only to receive members and that members can "check out" but they can never "leave." This means they can physically go to another place, but they will remain cult members. "But I *can* leave," you insist. "I can leave this organization anytime I want." Chapter 9 of this book further analyzes specifically how "culted" you are with your organization. But for now, consider just a couple of questions:

1. Do you ever feel bad about leaving work?
2. Have you ever excused the expiration of vacation days with, "I just can't get away"?

If the answer to either question is yes, then perhaps you are more like the Hotel California guests than you realize. Can you leave?

Cults have three traits:

1. Devotion
2. Charismatic leadership
3. Separation from community[3]

Employees make their organization into a corporate cult by taking on those three traits, as explained in Chapters 6 through 8.

Are you a prisoner of your own device? Prisoners may have a better life than you do, according to the following comparison that circulated on E-mail recently:

In prison you spend a majority of your time in an 8 × 10 cell.
  At work you spend most of your time in a 6 × 8 cubicle.

In prison you get three square meals a day.
  At work you only get a break for one meal, and you have to pay for that.

In prison you get time off for good behavior.
  At work you get rewarded for good behavior with more work.

In prison a guard unlocks and opens the doors for you.
At work you must carry a security card to unlock and open all the doors yourself.

In prison you can watch TV and play games.
At work you get fired for watching TV and playing games.

In prison they ball-and-chain you when you go somewhere.
At work you're just ball-and-chained.

In prison you get your own toilet.
At work you have to share.

In prison they allow your friends and family to visit.
At work you can't even speak to your friends and family on the phone.

In prison all expenses are paid by taxpayers with no work required.
At work you get to pay all the expenses to go to work and then they deduct taxes from your salary to pay for prisoners.

In prison you spend most of your life looking through the bars from the inside wanting to get out.
At work you spend most of your time wanting to get out to go to the bars.

In prison you can join many programs that you can leave at any time.
At work there are some programs you can never get out of.

In prison there are sadistic wardens.
At work the managers take care of that.

Corporate cult members can't leave their organization because they have such a high level of devotion. Can you leave? EDS is a place where employees once felt they couldn't.

A Restrictive Culture Tries to Transform Itself

Electronic Data Systems of Dallas is a large, highly successful information systems consulting company that is well known for its rigid, hard-driving, quasi-military culture. Under the tight rein of founder Ross Perot, long hair, beards, and mustaches were not allowed. Perot built a military-style organization that even prohibited wearing loafers.

Even though the Dallas billionaire sold his company to General Motors in 1984 and left two years later, the company still operates under many of the same cultural rules that were set by the founder.[4]

EDS had a well-defined organizational culture that had become a cult for many employees. In an attempt to break out of this culture, EDS hired consultants to offer training to soften the restrictive environment. A participant in the training wrote about the bad old days:

> I started my career with EDS in 1983. I remember in the interview being told all the things I should not do, or I would be fired. I took my personal life underground. We were driven to succeed, a disciplined, well-oiled machine. We grew by leaps and bounds. But we left human carnage in our wake—both customers and ourselves. We lacked balance. We were our work. I donned my gray suit and became the model EDSer. Sometimes the mold felt uncomfortable: I had to act in ways that did not feel natural to me.[5]

People whose value is drawn only from the work they do are members of corporate cults. This statement is testimony that this EDSer had allowed his organization to become his cult. That's dangerous for individuals, because they allow themselves to act in ways that aren't comfortable. What this former employee called "uncomfortableness" was his conscience—his inner value system—telling him something was wrong with what he was doing.

EDS is trying to move from "a cult of personality to a culture where the emphasis is on teams arriving at collective decisions," says EDS Vice President Gary Fernandes. CEO Les Alberthal has determined that "EDS needs a radically new identity—as the world's most sensitive services giant. The days of command and control are over."[6]

To ensure that you don't start to believe there has been a spiritual transformation at EDS, Dean Linderman, supervisor of the training program at EDS, reminds us that profit remains the goal: "They're not listening to feelings for fun; they're doing it because that's where the money is." The culture was being changed because there was more money in being sensitive. EDS was trying to break its obsession with conformity.

Obsessions Can Be Dangerous

Dallas physician Beck Weathers was obsessed with climbing the highest peaks on all continents. He succeeded when he reached the top of Mount Everest in April 1996. His seven climbing companions all died. "An obsession can be a dangerous thing," he summarized. He lost fingers, his nose, and much of his facial skin to frostbite. He lost the ability to participate in his profession as he had in the past, he lost the ability to play with his children, and he almost lost his life. Dr. Weathers is correct: An obsession can be a dangerous thing. It doesn't matter what the obsession is. Balanced living is more rewarding then obsessive living, as Dr. Weathers' experience shows.

How do we balance the requirement of work, family, and community? It's difficult, but it's possible.

The Three Organizational Circles in Balance

From an organizational point of view, people exist in three general circles: work, family, and community, as shown in Figure 1-2. A life can be analyzed from an individual point of view as well, but that requires a totally different level of analysis. For this book, we want to think of the individual as he or she interacts with others in organizations.

A person who lives a balanced life is comfortable in all three organizational circles. She or he exists as an individual who can retain a personal identity while becoming a part of work, family, and community.

Work is obvious; it's where you make your living. There is no problem with finding value in what you do at work. The problem is finding *too much* value in what you do. Students invest four years at a university to learn how to *make a living,* but the most important thing they learn is how to *live.*

It has become politically correct to defend and support the family. However, there are different definitions of *family.* In this book, I mean the nuclear family, perhaps stretched to include grandparents and grandchildren. I am talking specifically about relational families. My concern is that employees are stealing time from family to invest it at work.

The community circle is the hardest to define, but its function is clear. Community, in the sociological sense, is the source of values. It is where correction and support are encouraged. It is where individuals are held to a standard of behavior. Examples are church, YMCA, Jewish Community Center, PTA, Rotary, Red Cross, Boy Scouts and Girl Scouts, and many more.

Figure 1-2 is a picture of a balanced, emotionally stable individual who can find value in work, while still making a contribution to family and community.

Figure 1-2. The Three Organizational Circles

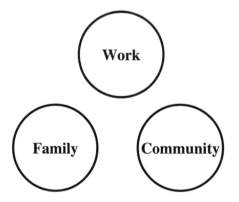

The Three Organizational Circles Out of Balance

My concern is that the lives of some people have become more like Figure 1-3. In this diagram, the individual is finding too much

Figure 1-3. Out-of-Balance Organizational Circles

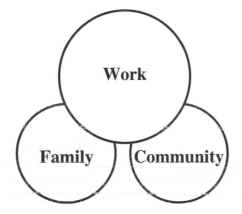

value at work. "What I do" at work is supplanting "who I am" at home and in the community.

Through culture, corporate cults have rediscovered communal ties, and they are using them to build high-commitment organizations that are very efficient.[7] This is dangerous. There is a significant difference between what you do and who you are. An individual who invests resources that should go to the family and community in the work circle is not an emotionally mature, fully functioning member of society.

The major question in the distribution of an individual's resources is whether these resources are economic or noneconomic. Economics is the study of the distribution of scarce resources. Time is clearly a scarce resource. There are twenty-four hours in a day, and try as we might, we can't make any more. Time spent at work must come from one of the other circles. This is an unquestioned trade-off.

But what about less tangible concepts, like commitment, love, and caring? If you spend more of them at work, does that mean you have less of them to spend at home and in your community?

Caring has become an economic good, used to increase production. What the Mayos discovered at the Hawthorne plant has gone terribly awry, like a horror movie. Corporate cults have claimed the human relations school of thought and made the idea of caring into a giant that is taking over the workplace.

Obviously, reasonable people hope for the proper balance: Employees who enjoy their work but are able to leave it and pursue other self-satisfying endeavors outside of the workplace. Some employees have made their workplace into a cult, and they draw value only from what they do. The workplace environment has become all three—work, family, and community—to the culted worker. Those for whom the three elements are out of balance are well acquainted with an old Tennessee Ernie Ford song.

It's okay to owe many things to the workplace. Allegiance to some degree is good. If your company has provided you with income, status, relationships, and a career, perhaps you owe the organization some allegiance. If your employer has shown commitment to you, perhaps you owe commitment in return. But I would suggest you should return to the corporation what it is paying you for: commitment of your time and talent, not your soul. You don't owe your soul or any other part of your psyche that you consider valuable to your company.

But corporate cults want more. Workplaces that invest in their employees win *emotional* allegiance from their workforce—and increasingly more of their time, which has to come from family and community commitments.[8]

Work is a contract *and* a relationship. However, when the employee comes to rely on the workplace for emotional support, for love, for care, for self-esteem, the relationship becomes unbalanced, because the organization makes a smaller commitment to the worker than vice versa.

Our college graduates are now told that during their careers, they will have numerous jobs, perhaps in several industries. They are likely to be terminated during some of those job changes. If these people find their value at work, as corporate cults encourage them to do, that means that several times in their career, when they are terminated, they will be told, "*You* are no longer of value to this organization." I think a much more acceptable phrase is, "*What you do* is no longer of value to this organization." There's a big difference. It would be easy to predict that, after the first two or three times, workers would be hurt so deeply that they would cease finding their value at work and, hopefully, retreat to finding value in their family and community relationships.

Corporate cults gain efficiency by taking increasing contributions from workers while returning decreasing financial rewards. This benefits the organization while hurting the individual.

One of the country's most important organizations is very cultish in its behavior. It's a very large organization with a very critical task.

The Military

There are two peak times for suicide among members of the military: when they join and when they leave. This is because the military is a cult. By its own admission, the military cuts the recruit's ties with family and community. The group, meaning the platoon, the troop, or the wing, becomes the family and community for members of the military.

Successful recruits accept the military as their replacement family and community and do quite well. However, those who do not succeed are lost between two worlds: the traditional family and community they left at home, and the new military one where they are failing. Lost without a family and community, they commit suicide. The other peak of suicide incidence is upon departure from the military. "I couldn't believe it," said an Air Force recruit, who was himself a military brat. "At separation from the Air Force, my dad, in his mid forties, attended a class where they actually told him what to wear to a job interview in the private sector. These are people in the middle of life," he continued, "whose lives have been so structured by the military that they don't even know how to dress themselves."[9]

A former member of the Air Force tells of a friend who was brought up on charges and severely punished for damaging Air Force property. The property he damaged was himself. He fell asleep by the pool and got a sunburn.

Most people would agree that the military is a cult. Society allows this cult to exist because the job it performs—maintaining freedom for the country—is so important. We allow the individuality of some of our citizens to be subordinated to this group so that freedom can be assured.

However, the cultedness of the military is so strong that when members leave, they have to deal with both the loss of the cult that had controlled them so stringently and the frightening notion of reentering the outside world without the secure family and community that the military offers. Many commit suicide when they are caught between the two worlds of military and civilian life.

More than a third of the homeless men who seek help at the Union Gospel Mission are veterans of military service. Vietnam and other recent veterans predominate. "The new group is tending to be people who have trouble finding their place," said the mission director. "Many recently discharged veterans are having difficulty making the transition from the order of military life. There aren't many positions available in civilian life for tank drivers."[10] The mission director was half right: They *are* having trouble making the transition—but it's not because their functional specialties don't match the needs of the civilian world. It's because they are having trouble reestablishing family and community ties after a long period of cult membership.

Every organization has some degree of cultedness. People join organizations to accomplish things that they cannot do on their own, so individuals subordinate themselves to some extent. However, in corporate cults, the organization has become work, family, *and* community for the employee. Where does this need to join groups come from? Do people join of their own volition, or is there some group effect? Chapter 2 explains the urge to merge among generational cohorts.

Notes

1. Adam Smith, *The Wealth of Nations* (London: Penguin, Reprint 1982).
2. Arlie Russell Hochschild, *The Time Bind* (New York: Metropolitan Books, 1997).
3. P. G. Zimbardo and C. F. Hartley, "Cults Go to High School: A Theoretical and Empirical Analysis of the Initial Stage in the Recruitment Process," *Cultic Studies Journal* (1985): 91–147.
4. Alan Goldstein, "Search for Success," *Dallas Morning News,* August 15, 1998.
5. David Kirkpatrick, "This Tough Guy Wants to Give You a Hug," *Fortune,* October 14, 1996.
6. Ibid.

7. Hochschild, *The Time Bind*.
8. Ibid.
9. Interview with the author.
10. *Dallas Morning News*, "Survey Finds Third of Homeless Men Seeking Shelter are Military Veterans," November 9, 1997.

Chapter 2
The Cohort Horn

*C*orporate cults come about when organizational leaders try to manage corporations filled with people who have significantly different value systems. It wasn't always that way.

Value Dispersion Among Cohorts

The cohort horn in Figure 2-1 shows the different levels of value dispersion of five different generations. The cohort horn points out the difference in value *dispersion* of the generations, not differences in the values themselves. Value dispersion is the degree to which individuals within the generation adopt different values. If individuals choose very similar values, as members of the Depression Era generation did, the generational cohort has a narrow value dispersion, as shown by the vertical axis in Figure 2-1.

The values of any particular generation are driven together by the environmental effects on the generation. When there is a strong effect, like that of the Depression, the values of the generation are forced into a very narrow band. The Depression was an event of very high impact. The entire country felt its effects, and there was a lot of individual suffering. People who grew up during the Depression could not avoid having their value systems constrained to a great extent. They all thought, acted, and reacted alike.

I Am Who I Am Because of Where I Was When

The cohort horn is based on the assumptions of Morris Massey, whose sociological theory can be summed up as, "I am who I am

Figure 2-1. The Cohort Horn of Generational Values

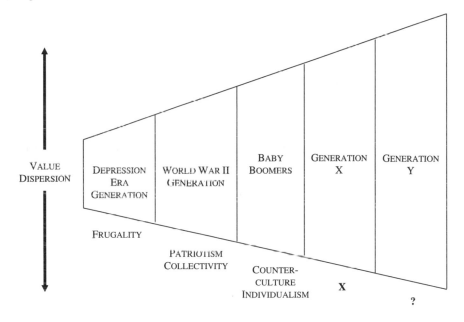

because of where I was when."[1] Most psychologists agree that values are formed by the time a child reaches age 12—some would say as early as age 6. Whether it is age 12 or age 6 makes little difference because the people working in organizations are all over age 12. (Some may not always *act* that way, but they are.) Employees arrive at an organization with a fully developed set of values. Those values change only as a result of a life-altering event.

People Don't Change

Forrest Gump said it so well: "Life is like a box of chocolates. You never know what you're gonna get." A corollary for organizations is, "Employees are like a box of chocolates. You never know what you're gonna get." But once you've got 'em, you've got 'em! The result is that people who join an organization with a particular value set will have that same value set for their entire tenure.

Some of you reading this book may have found a mate you are absolutely in love with, except for one small personality defect. You may have gotten married thinking you could fix him or her.

You didn't, did you? He or she is the same person you married and will continue to be the same person, probably for a lifetime.

Psychologist James Dobson advises parents that when the child is age 12, you're done teaching. "It's time to stop talking and start listening," says Dobson.[2] He's right. People have formed their personalities and value systems by that time.

Morris Massey is right, "I am who I am because of where I was when." We are a product of our environment. I'm not discounting people's free will and ability to change their lives when they want to. My point is they *want* to only as a result of a life-altering event, which seldom happens.

Generational Cohorts

Generational cohorts are a means of dividing a population into subgroups that are defined by the year of their birth. The technique is widely used in marketing to describe the behavioral and purchase patterns of groups of customers. I use it to describe the complexity of the employees who staff organizations and how that complexity will increase in the near future. I start the analysis by marrying Massey's edict to generational cohorts to find that generations are also "who we are because of where we were when."

The Depression Generation

The defining value of the Depression Era generation is frugality. People of this generation—born between 1912 and 1921—are often frugal because they lived through perhaps the strongest sociocultural environmental effect of modern history. The Depression caused this generation to have a very narrow value dispersion. They all think alike.

The value of frugality was impressed upon survivors of the Depression Era. They are the grandparents of much of the current-day workforce. Think about your grandparents, who probably grew up during the Depression. What did they always say? "Save for a rainy day, be cautious in your purchases, don't spend too much money." They were frugal! The amazing thing is this: If I explained my grandparents to you, you might think I was describing *your* grandparents. They were *all* frugal, because growing up during the Depression made them so.

This generation did not have credit cards, so they paid for goods using the opposite plan: lay-away. With a credit card, you take the goods home now and pay later. With a lay-away plan, you pay now and take the goods home later. This deferred gratification led to a whole different set of values for the Depression Era generation. The generation was forced to conform to this set of values; they had no choice. Credit cards didn't exist. Fitting in was very important. There were no counterculture heroes like Dennis Rodman or Easy Rider for this generation.

Also, there were fewer heroes, because fewer were needed. In a homogeneous generation, everyone had the same hero. National tastes were homogenized as well. The great flood of immigrants in this generation had the *ability* to make the population more heterogeneous, but new entrants did the opposite. They were eager to shed the culture of their country of origin and become American, like everyone else.

This desire to fit in provided a wonderfully reliable labor force for the growing industrial economy of the time. Managers could accurately predict how this group of workers would act and react in the workplace environment, and thus could reasonably predict their performance in the workplace.

The World War II Generation

The next cohort in chronological order is the World War II generation. This cohort had a significant defining event as well: World War II. The generation that was born between 1922 and 1945 has two value streams: patriotism and collectivity.

This generation believes in patriotism, the idea that one should subjugate individual interests to the interest of the whole. This value was reinforced for the World War II generation by the successful completion of the war. If individuals had not patriotically subordinated their own interests to the good of the country, the United States and its allies would not have won the war. The archetypal World War II generation hero, President John F. Kennedy, spoke for his generation when he said, "Ask not what your country can do for you, ask what you can do for your country."

The second strong value for this generation is collectivity, in this case many countries coming together to ward off a threat. These people saw during their lifetime that countries working together could produce positive outcomes.

I am providing very little description of the specific values of each generation, because they are not important in my analysis. What *is* important is the value dispersion produced by environmental events. So if you disagree that certain generations had a particular value system, I ask that you not get caught up in those details. Focus on the point of the analysis, which is that the magnitude of the environmental effect determines the value dispersion in a generational cohort.

While World War II was a major effect for this generation, its effect was somewhat weaker than the Depression's had been on the previous generation. Thus, the World War II generational cohort has more widely dispersed values than its predecessor, the Depression Era generation.

Baby Boomers

The Baby Boomers are the 78 million Americans born between 1946 and 1964. They have made their impact on society as they have moved through the various stages of life: from overcrowding elementary schools to rock and roll, from the Mustang to the Lexus. Their sheer numbers have led to noticeable changes in American culture.

Their values are quite opposite from the World War II value set. Where World War II produced patriotism and collectivity, the significant events of the Baby Boomers' formative years—Vietnam and the civil rights movement—produced a healthy criticism of big government and collectivity. These events showed Baby Boomers that government could be wrong and should not receive the blind trust showered upon it by their World War II predecessors.

But again, the cohort horn is not concerned with *what* the values are, but only with *how widely dispersed* they are. The Baby Boomers were encouraged to be free thinkers, to not trust the organizational establishment. This distrust was confirmed by the Kent State shootings, Lyndon Johnson's secretive military incursions into Laos and Cambodia, and the Love Canal fiasco. This free thinking led to a more widely dispersed set of values among the Baby Boomer cohort than was experienced by previous generations.

While the previous generations honored conformity, the Baby Boomers sought individuality. The goal of this generation is to "find myself," whatever that self may be. Postwar prosperity had a significant effect on the formative years of the Boomers. Freed from worries about external survival, they were able to turn inward, to focus on making themselves what they wanted to be.

The counterculture revolution that marked the wide dispersion of the generation was embodied in the 7-Up ad campaign that billed the drink as the "uncola." That meant that it was okay to be different. Volkswagen gently poked fun at American car makers when it targeted the bug to young Boomers with simplistic, self-deprecating, black-and-white ads. The Boomers showed their individuality by passing up branded goods in favor of store-label generic products.[3]

The growth in the size of bathrooms through the Boomers' buying years is an indication of the lavish way they have treated themselves. It's a subtle way of saying, "I am important! Even in my most private activities, I deserve space and beauty." The Boomer generation has a much wider dispersion of values than the previous generations, but it's not as wide as in the next one.

Generation X

Generation X is the cohort of people born between 1961 and 1981. The *Yankelovich Report* defines the generation as the birth years 1965 to 1978 to avoid the imprecision of having the Xers overlap the Boomers by three years.[4] I don't think an apology is necessary. Generational cohorts are inexact anyway. The last baby born in 1964 was not significantly different from the first baby born in 1965. The study of generational cohorts is a social science that has many messy edges, to say the least.

Now, name an event that happened during the formative years of Generation X that is as significant as the Depression, World War II, Vietnam, and civil rights. If you can't think of one, you're right, because there isn't one. Thus the title for this generation: X, which is the algebraic symbol for "unknown." The values of the generation are unknown, because its members have not experienced a significant life-altering event that has forced their values into a narrow band. Thus, this has become a generation of experimenters, willing to try anything that will make their lives into what *they* desire them to be. And they are ready to change that desire at a moment's notice. They see many of life's decisions as short-term commitments that can be changed with the circumstances. Seventy-nine percent say they enjoy spontaneous events. David Letterman's off-the-wall unpredictability is a keen example.

Generation Xers are accepting of many different lifestyles; 28 percent supported social pluralism by agreeing that there's no single right way to live. It's more than just the effect of being young. Only 15 percent of Boomers agreed with that statement when they were the Gen Xers' age. The *Yankelovich Monitor* summarizes, "Our research shows Xers to be, as a generation, the most socially pluralistic ever."[5] They are likely to get even more pluralistic, because this is a value that tends to get stronger as cohorts age.

In the absence of a defining generational event, members of Generation X have been given the freedom to adopt any value set they want, and they have responded by adopting a wide range of them. Thus, the values of Generation X are unknown; they are all over the map. The central tendency that marks the previous generations is seemingly missing in Generation X. They don't "tend" toward any central value system. The standard deviation for the group is greater than that for the other generations in the cohort horn.

Some would say that the defining event of the generation is the lightning-fast diffusion of computer technology. If that's so, we have to ask whether technology diffusion has driven the value dispersion narrower or wider. The answer is wider. The Internet has allowed extremely small groups composed of people with very specific interests to come together in a medium that allows them to corroborate their belief system.

So the defining event of the generation causes even greater value dispersion. Computer and Internet technology have made a wider range of choices and influences available to Gen Xers. The expansion of the TV spectrum from three to one hundred channels typifies this generation. The Internet allows Gen Xers to form an interest clique via a chat group no matter how narrow the interest.

A poll for Gen-Xer magazine *Swing* asked readers what name they preferred for their generation. Only 10 percent answered "Generation X." Almost half the answers were so eclectic that they had to be classified as "other." A Nike ad aimed at Gen Xers typifies the individualism of the generation: "I am not/A target market./I am an athlete."[6]

If the Boomers are individualists, Gen Xer's are individualists on steroids. In the book *Generation X,* author Douglas Coupland says they are "fanatically independent individuals."[7] The large value dispersion of Gen Xers means that they have to put more energy into finding a group with identical values. But since grouping is a *need,* they *do* find what *Rocking the Ages* calls "enclaves." These enclaves are tightly knit groups that share intimate lifestyles because the value bases are so narrow that the individuals can't find acceptance outside the enclave. While the individualism of the generation seems to provide them with a good set of tools for fending off cult entrapments, the "enclave" language is very cultish in nature.

If there is a value common to Gen Xers, it's their dislike for the Gen-X title. They hate it because it's been applied to them by the much larger Baby Boomer generation. They also despise the title because they are the least "groupish" of any generation in the history of the generational cohort science. They aren't a group at all; they are a collection of individuals.

Gen Xers' feelings should not be hurt by the lack of a defining sociocultural event in their cohort. This is a good thing. Any reasonable person would want to be part of a generation growing up in a time without punitive events like those faced by previous generations.

Whatever description you read of Generation X, I encourage you to question it. Descriptions of this generation are an attempt to describe the unknown—a difficult task indeed. Generation X is exactly what the X indicates: unknown.

I have read attempts to describe Gen Xers as lazy. *Some* Gen Xers are lazy; some aren't. I spend a good deal of time with high school and college students, all of them Gen Xers. I have been in the parking lot as high school was dismissed (not a good place to be, by the way) and watched as hundreds of them rushed off to work. I have college students in my classes who work two jobs

while taking a full load of classes. Yet some members of the generation seem totally unmotivated to work. Is Gen X lazy? Yes—and
no. They are X.

I have heard Gen X accused of being nonreligious. I would
invite you to visit my church on Sunday morning: There are hundreds of Gen Xers in attendance. Some Gen Xers are religious;
some aren't. Many have adopted nontraditional Eastern or New
Age religions that *seem* unreligious to the older generations that
are judging them. Some have created their own religions. And
there are those like my son and daughter, who are very religious,
but have fellowship and Bible study with a group outside of
church. Are Gen Xers religious? Yes—and no. They are X.

I have heard Gen Xers described as having no regard for
money. Well, if my teenagers are any indication, that accusation
might be correct. But again, Gen Xers are all over the map. My
nephew is a Gen X university student who worked in Alaska last
summer. He lived on the tips he received from driving a tour bus.
He sent his entire paycheck to his bank in Seattle.

We must remember Morris Massey's advice: "I am who I am
because of where I was when." Gen Xers have grown up in an era
of unprecedented wealth and affluence. They may seem uncon-
cerned about money to those of us in other generational cohorts,
but this further confirms that the environment produces value systems. Do Gen Xers have regard for money? Yes—and no. They
are X.

While the values of previous generations were driven together
by peer pressure to conform, the values of Generation X have been
pulled apart by the lack of a significant environmental effect. The
effect that has taken place—computers—*has* pulled this generation
further apart.

The widening of the value dispersion in each successive generation is borne out in *Rocking the Ages*. The authors spend twenty
pages explaining their version of the World War II generation,
twenty-seven explaining Baby Boomers, and thirty-three *trying* to
explain Generation X. Each successive cohort is harder to explain
because its value dispersion is greater than that of the previous one.

Generation X and Corporate Cults

Many Gen Xers put career first. A broad study of the generation indicated an almost universal determination that career

should precede marriage, implying that Gen Xers consider the work circle more important than the family circle.[8] This seems to indicate the generation is *more* susceptible to cults, because the affiliation and affection they do not get from family life will be found in corporate cults. The same study reported a poll showing that when compared to three other generations, Xers put the least value on patriotism and religion—where other generations found their community—and the most value on hard work, money, and self-fulfillment. These traits are effective predictors of corporate cult membership.

The information that shows that Gen X is the most individualistic generation gives rise to the hope that this generation is not cultable. However, the data indicating that they have chosen work over home and community put them in the category of very cultable. They don't need family and community when they can find both at work, at a corporate cult.

Generation Y

The next cohort has been uncreatively dubbed Generation Y. There are 57 million kids in America under age 15, so demographers have decided it's time to carve out another generation. It's too early to know much about this generation yet, but if we had to guess—and if you lead an organization, you *do* have to guess—it's easy to predict that the values of Generation Y are going to be more widely dispersed than those of Generation X.

Maslow's Hierarchy of Needs

If you've been in a college classroom in the last twenty-five years, you can approximately recite Maslow's hierarchy of needs upon demand. The hierarchy shown in Figure 2-2 has not been supported empirically, so I predict that eventually it will go out of vogue. However, it still provides us with a good structure for thinking about needs categorization and the relationship of needs to each generational cohort.

In the lower levels of Maslow's hierarchy, people are motivated to group together to satisfy physiological needs. These were

Figure 2-2. How Generational Cohorts Fit Into Maslow's Hierarchy of Needs

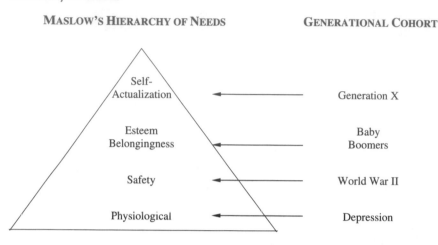

MASLOW'S HIERARCHY OF NEEDS   GENERATIONAL COHORT

Maslow's Hierarchy of Needs	Generational Cohort
Self-Actualization	Generation X
Esteem / Belongingness	Baby Boomers
Safety	World War II
Physiological	Depression

the needs addressed by the Depression Era cohort. It was difficult to provide for one's family individually, so ad hoc relationships were formed out of physiological necessity.

The nation of Israel is a good example. When the nation was formed in 1948, the region was in such poor condition that it would hardly sustain life. The natural result was the socialistic kibbutz, in which the efforts of each person were pooled to guarantee the survival of the group. As the country prospered, the kibbutzim experienced economic success, but membership dwindled. Kibbutz members have moved up the hierarchy to higher levels of need satisfaction, and are leaving kibbutzim for a more capitalist lifestyle, usually in the cities of Israel.

The kibbutz thus represents a corporate cult that was driven by economic necessity. When the economy improved, the corporate cult lost its members. If there is a move back to kibbutz membership in Israel, it will be for emotional or affiliational reasons, not economic reasons.

Safety needs were the driving force for the World War II generation. If individuals had not subordinated their individual needs to those of the group (the country), freedom from external threat would not have been secured.

Baby Boomers exemplify the belongingness and esteem needs. Baby Boomers are great joiners of organizations. They like to show their identity, not by who they are as individuals, but by who they affiliate with. The idea of mass market designer clothes was created for and by the Boomers.

Boomers have also participated in a great deal of corporate climbing throughout their careers. For members of this generation, esteem is found in a corner office, the title on the door, and association with a *Fortune* 500 company. Their esteem is more external than internal. Baby Boomers are easy corporate cult candidates because their needs for belongingness and esteem are met through organizational memberships.

Generation X has been freed from concerns about physiological, security, belongingness, and esteem needs, so they are free to self-actualize. The intention of Maslow's hierarchy of needs is to explain motivation at the individual level of analysis. However, motivation at the lower levels is expressed more through groups. As the needs progress up the hierarchy, they are increasingly individual in nature.

Self-actualization, sitting at the top of the hierarchy, is the most individual of all needs. In terms of resource availability, Gen X was practically born at the top of the hierarchy. So as a generational cohort, its members are the archetypal self-actualizers. However, this will not keep them out of corporate cults because of the emergence of the enclave concept and their desire for hard work and money.

The Effect on Corporations

This chapter has described the variance in value dispersion between generational cohorts as an individual-level construct. There is, however, an important effect for organizational functioning as well. The increasingly wide value dispersion causes problems for managers of corporations at the organizational level. It's a problem of efficiency.

Corporations thrive on efficiency. This hasn't changed much since Adam Smith encouraged specialization in *The Wealth of Nations*.[9] The American way of thinking, "If a little is good, a lot must be better," was exemplified by management guru Frederick Taylor, who at the early part of the century encouraged efficiency through precise measurement, which he called Scientific Management.[10] In any other age, Taylor would have been considered an absolutely fanatical anal retentive or would have been written off as a lunatic. But as the nation industrialized through the 1910s and 1920s, corporations came to regard Taylor's teachings as sacrosanct because they provided the support the corporations needed if they were to achieve efficiency of operation in the burgeoning factory system of the time.

We still have not shaken loose from the effects of Taylor's ideas, and the competitive market still strives for efficiency of performance. However, the increasingly wide value distribution of each successive generation works against this efficiency. Corporations want people whose actions and reactions are predictable. They want a bunch of Depression Era workers, but they can't have them because they are dying off. Increasingly, they will have to learn to be competitive with a corporation staffed by Gen Xers and their successors, members of Generation Y.

Managing a crew of Depression Era workers was easy. You could give them an assignment and leave them alone, knowing that the assignment would be completed. You could certainly predict that they would do it *frugally,* if nothing else.

Advice to managers: Don't do this with a crew of Gen Xers. Don't turn your back on them! Their value systems are widely dispersed. If you leave them alone in the workplace, some will work hard, some will loaf around, some will start a religious revival, some will rob you blind, and some will set the place on fire.

The mix of four different generational cohorts in the same workplace causes enough problems. These are intensified by the manager's dilemma of how to control an organization with an increasing population of Gen Xers, with their wide value dispersion, followed by a dose of Generation Y. What's a manager to do? This chapter was all *de*scription. Chapter 3 contains the *pre*scription.

Notes

1. Morris Massey, *People Puzzle: Understanding Yourself and Others* (Reston, VA, Reston Publishing Co., 1979).

2. James Dobson, *The New Dare to Discipline* (Wheaton, Illinois: Tyndale House Publishing, 1996).
3. J. Walker Smith and Ann Clurman, *Rocking the Ages* (New York: Harper Business, 1997).
4. Ibid.
5. Ibid.
6. Ibid.
7. Douglas Coupland, *Generation X: Tales for an Accelerated Culture* (New York, NY: St. Martin's Press, 1991).
8. Dennis Farney, "Today's Twentysomethings: Realistic, Living in Present," *The Wall Street Journal*, July 6, 1998.
9. Adam Smith, *The Wealth of Nations* (London: Penguin, Reprint 1982).
10. F. W. Taylor, *The Principles of Scientific Management* (New York: Harper, 1911).

Chapter 3

The Competitive Advantage
Selection Model

*I*n the past, most people who were hired had successfully passed through two types of screening techniques posed by their employer. First, they proved they had the ability to perform the *task* the organization required. They had the correct experiential base, the proper credentials, or the necessary level of education.

The second screen was about the *person*. In the interview, prospective employees were asked about their ability to work with people, their interests outside of work, if they had team experience, and perhaps the subject of the last book they read. Answers to these questions provided the employer with an understanding of a prospective employee as a person.

These two screening mechanisms enabled the employer to choose the correct candidate because they covered the two areas of management: tasks and people. I often tell seminar attendees: "I have a Ph.D. in the subject, but there are only two things in management: tasks and people." The traditional two-part selection procedure covers both. Competition is changing that procedure.

Two New Forms of Competitive Advantage

There are two general types of personalities: There are task people, and there are people people. Traditional corporations that mix these personality types in their employee selection process suffer a competitive disadvantage relative to new organizational forms that select only one type.

These new, more efficient models are quickly replacing the old organization model, as shown in Figure 3-1. These competitive advantage selection models are called the collection of specialists and the specialist collection.

Collection of Specialists

The movie industry exemplifies the collection of specialists. Through the 1950s and 1960s, and into the early 1970s, movies were made by studios on Hollywood production lots. If you had asked workers to show identification badges, they all would have produced a studio employment card. They worked for MGM, Universal, or whoever was making the movie.

There have been two simultaneous changes in the movie industry. First, movies are largely shot on location instead of on lots. Second, they have been almost totally outsourced. If you approached workers on a movie production set today and asked for I.D. badges, you would find that very few were employed by the studio. The studios have strategically retreated to their core competency, which is the *executive* production of movies, not the *operational* production. With the industry growing, those who work on

Figure 3-1. Competitive Advantage Selection Model

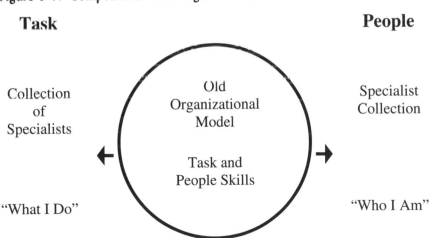

Task

People

Collection
of
Specialists

Old
Organizational
Model

Specialist
Collection

←

Task and
People Skills

→

"What I Do"

"Who I Am"

movie production have plenty of *work*, but they don't have *jobs* in the traditional sense of the word.[1] Movies are made by a collection of specialists, people who assemble for a short period of time to complete a single project, then disband. The specialists are collected only for the function they perform, not for any long-term contribution their presence will make to the organization. Members of a collection of specialists are honored for *what they do*, not for *who they are*.

Much of the computer industry exemplifies the collection of specialists lifestyle. The work people do is performed away from the company's office, often from the workers' homes. The work is done for customers the workers don't know personally, and is transmitted to the customer over the phone line. The collection of specialists corporation conducts *only* the first half of the previously mentioned selection process. It's a "just the facts, ma'am" selection process in which *only* the person's qualifications are analyzed.

The collection of specialists is efficient for three reasons. First, the corporation obtains highly trained specialists who are best in class at what they do, so operational task performance is very high. Second, the corporation doesn't "own" the employees; it simply "rents" them for the specific time period they are needed. That lowers human resources costs. Third, overhead costs are low because the employer pays no benefits. There are no sick leaves, vacation days, retirement benefits, or insurance. It's the most extreme example of pay for performance because payment is made only for task completion and nothing else.

In a competitive environment, the collection of specialists has an advantage over the old model, in which employees are selected based on both task and people skills. The collection of specialists obtains the expertise of the specialist without all the "people" baggage. And when business slows down or there is a personality conflict, the specialist is simply not hired for subsequent work.

Medicine and law both contain a high concentration of collection of specialists organizations. By their nature, medical practices must have a specialist in each of the subdisciplines of medicine: a generalist, an internal specialist, a gynecologist, an orthopedist, an eye-ear-nose-throat specialist, an x-ray specialist, etc. Because these practitioners are selected for their highly developed task speciality, there is less regard for their people skills. They work largely independent of one another, usually communicating via written medical charts or recommendations, and they get paid only for the work they do. Very few medical doctors are on salary. While medical doctors make a lot of money—the average is now just over $200,000 a year—they work in a very organizationally efficient collection of specialists.

You can imagine a medical practice adopting the old organizational model trying to compete with a collection of specialists. The competitor applying the old model would have continual struggles to maintain the exact level of expertise in a given specialty at any particular time. The costs would be enormous. The collection of specialists, however, can predict exactly what its costs will be because they are almost totally variable. When an hour of work is done, there is an equivalent hour of pay. The collection of specialists is extremely efficient.

Collection of Specialists and Corporate Cults

The employees of collection of specialist organizations must have the ability to maintain the value of who they are in their family and community because those types of "warm fuzzies" are not available at the workplace. These employees are honored for *what they do* at work because they are highly qualified camera operators, doctors, and lawyers. But they are well aware that they have been collected only for the technical expertise they contribute to the project, not for the personality contribution they make.

The collection of specialists provides a healthy corporate atmosphere because the individuals in the organization retain their own self-identity as they move from project to project. They don't have traditional long-term jobs, so they cannot be inculcated into a corporate cult.

Seventeen-year-old Doug Marcey exemplifies the new generation of specialists. He writes computer code in jeans and bare feet in his basement three days a week and earns an annual salary of $50,000 a year. As his employer, Nu Thena Systems, has discovered, the unique nature of the computer industry contributes to the growth of collection of specialists organizations because the work can be so discretely compartmentalized.[2] Each person makes her or his contribution separately, and competitive advantage is gained from the collected work of many task specialists.

The organizational culture of a collection of specialists sounds cold and contractual to some people, and they can hardly envision a society made up totally of organizations of this type. I think the corporate workplace *should* be more cold and contractual. Social economics mandates this in order to preserve two very important elements in society: the family and the community. If an employee's emotional needs are met in the corporation, he or she will not need to meet them at home and in the community. If the corporation becomes the source of emotional support, families and communities will suffer. The opposite is true as well. I recommend a cold and contractual workplace because it forces employees to meet their emotional and affiliational needs at home. I think that is a good thing. Emotional needs should *not* be supplied in the workplace setting; they should be supplied by family and community.

For those to whom the collection of specialists sounds cold and contractual, there is an option at the other end of the continuum. It's a workplace that many employees call home. I call it a specialist collection.

The Specialist Collection

An increasing number of corporations are gaining competitive advantage by selecting employees based solely on the second half of the selection process. I have given this type of corporation the title "specialist collection." These corporations collect people only for *who they are*, with little regard for *what they do*. They conduct only the last half of the traditional selection process that includes task and people abilities. Amazing as it may seem, the specialist collection doesn't care much about *task* ability; it selects employees based solely on what kind of *people* they are.

Certainly there is some limitation to this, you must be thinking. A corporation can't just hire a person because that person has a nice personality. There must be some level of task ability. Some, yes. Let's return to our example of Southwest Airlines.

Southwest Airlines is a specialist collection by personality. Southwest says it doesn't administer personality tests in its employee selection procedure. Prospective employees *do*, however, endure six interview sessions in which they are screened for their level of "spirit." What's spirit? They know at Southwest Airlines. They have to, because it's a major part of each employee's annual evaluation.

You must be thinking, "What about this task ability thing? Don't tell me they hire pilots with nice personalities who don't know how to fly!" All Southwest Airlines pilots are qualified. But the corporation *does* select among those qualified pilots for a very narrow psychographic it calls "spirit."

One of the best-known stories at Southwest is about a pilot candidate who came to interview for a job. This particular pilot was highly rated and extremely well qualified. After his rather traditional interview, the selection personnel asked the receptionist in the waiting room for her opinion of the candidate. "He was rude while waiting for his interview," she responded. "I don't think he would fit in here." Southwest didn't hire the highly qualified pilot, because he didn't fit the psychographic profile Southwest was looking for. He didn't have "spirit." It filled the position with someone who was less *task* qualified, but more *people* qualified.

Specialist collection corporations have purposely moved *down* the task qualification list so that they could move *up* the people qualification list. These corporations find efficiency in the commitment of their workforce. When employees are selected for who they are, they put more of themselves into the organization.

In and out of the workplace, every individual's self-worth is defined by "who I am." The difference for members of specialist collections is that their concept of "who I am" is defined by "what I do," as shown in Figure 3-2.

3M adopts this thinking in its hiring process. This very successful, innovative company has a strong culture that tends to pro-

Figure 3-2. Sources of Self-Worth

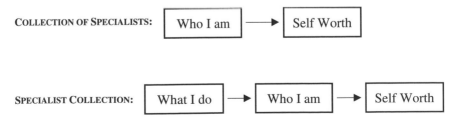

duce very long tenures among its employees. "People tend to come and make a home here," says human resources manager Dick Listad. Turnover is less than 3 percent. "Most companies can't guarantee a job for life, but at 3M that's possible, because it has a loyal, dedicated work force of members who come to work for the *company*, not a specific *division*."

"A new employee might be fully qualified to do the job for which they were hired, but we are actually hiring them to do a job beyond that," says Tom Vaaler, human resources director for the life sciences division.[3] "Beyond" means that 3M has looked past task abilities to collect employees who have a special personality or value trait that is consistent with the corporation's value statement.

Microsoft has a narrow definition of its "Softies." They are sharper than average (they hire only people with IQs well over 130) and more driven than is entirely normal.[4] By selecting only employees who are very smart and very driven, Microsoft has been able to sustain a very narrow corporate culture that prompted Douglas Coupland to dub these employees "microserfs" (the title of his book about the specialist collection). His theme is that by carefully collecting employees with just a couple of highly developed, narrowly focused traits, Microsoft has perpetuated a fiercely competitive and cultish organizational culture.

Southwest Airlines, 3M, and Microsoft are very successful companies. So far, the specialist collection sounds like a formula for success. What's wrong with this? It's good for the corporation; however, it's bad for employees.

Employees in specialist collections have "sold their souls." They are allowing themselves to be paid for "who I am," not "what I do." This is a dangerous confusing of the two issues. You should always be who you are, regardless of where you work, the function you perform, or the amount you are paid. "Who I am" should not be defined by "what I do." However, increasing numbers of workers are accepting money for "who I am," at the expense of their ultimate self-worth.

I have counseled ex-employees of corporate cults to help them understand the confusion and exile they feel after leaving the corporation. The feelings of rejection and low self-worth, the frustration and anger are closely akin to those of recent divorcées. That's because employees of specialist collections view their workplace as a corporate family. The family bonds are broken when the employee leaves the corporation, and the same feelings of familial rejection ensue.

Arlie Russell Hochschild hinted at the competitive advantage selection model in her book *The Time Bind* when she suggested three human resources strategies that produce competitive advantage.[5] The first is to cross-train workers, which is collinear with the old organizational model that mixes task and people qualifications. The second is to invest less in workers, which is done by the collection of specialists. The third is to create and manage a strong company culture. This third source of human resource competitive advantage she writes about is a specialist collection—people who are collected because they fit into the narrowly specified culture of the organization.

When Work Is a Party

The Web site of upscale sports clothing company Patagonia has a heading "Working at Patagonia" that includes photos of employees wearing shorts and sandals, surrounded by surfboards. It seems more like a playground than a workplace.[6] The organization is staffed largely by younger employees who contradict the Gen-Xers-as-slackers myth. Outside observers have noted that Patagonia employees are so committed to work that their jobs become their lives. Patagonia is further evidence of the cultability of Generation X.

In a specialist collection, work becomes home because the organization is stocked with people who are alike. They have the same interests and lifestyles, so the staff feels very comfortable together. Netscape's Web site contains Polaroids of employees jiving at a company-sponsored Jazz Festival and at the All Hands staff party.[7] The company fridge at Goldmine Software in Pacific Palisades, California, is stocked with beer. Some employees run around in stockings or bare feet, in order to feel more comfortable. Comfort is something that comes from being around people who are like you. That's what happens in specialist collections.

Generation X has the widest value dispersion of any generation ever measured, but it seems to be bimodal in nature. Perhaps more than any previous generation, this one understands the division between the two types of competitors in the marketplace: the collection of specialists and the specialist collection. Gen Xers are divided in the same way. For one group, loyalty, gratitude, and fortitude are dead. This group self-selects to a collection of specialists organization. The other group expects to find much more at work: parties, friends, entertainment, affection, and affiliation. The specialist collection provides it.

Nationsbank and Training

A Dallas Rotary Club sponsored a support clinic for underprivileged teenagers in the inner city. One of the bright young attendees asked a Nationsbank vice president, "What should I study in college to get the best job I can with Nationsbank?" The vice president didn't hesitate. "Get a liberal arts degree so you understand the world. We can teach you how to be a banker."

Since I teach at a liberal arts university, it's hard for me to disagree with this advice. However, the statement indicates that the bank is promoting a specialist collection. It seems to be saying, "We hire for *who you are,* not *what you do.*" People who are hired because of who they are will work hard because their individual ego ("who I am") is based on their performance at the bank.

Employees who are hired for "who I am" must get their functional training from the employer. Organizations favor this type of training because they have more control over it. Control is an important issue in private as well as corporate life. Corporate cults control the lives of their members, and providing specialized training allows the cult to inculcate the worker with corporate idealism and thoughts, to the exclusion of outside influences.

Gore & Associates

William Gore & Associates is a unique company. It was started by Bill Gore, a Dow Chemical engineer who invented Teflon wire insulation. Its best known product today is GoreTex, the wonderful sports fiber that allows air in but keeps moisture out. The corporation is unique in that its only hierarchy is what is mandated by incorporation laws.

When a new employee joins Gore & Associates, he or she allegedly shows up for work with no job. The introductory conversation might go something like this:

New hire: "Well, I'm here. What would you like me to do?"

Gore manager: "Whatever you want."

New hire: "Really!? Well—I have an accounting degree. Maybe I should do accounting."

Gore manager: "Why don't you try some of the other functions first? Go work in procurement for a couple of days, then try operations for a week or so. Then travel with a salesperson for a couple of weeks. See what you like."

New hire: "But if you don't have a job for me, why did you hire me?" asks the perplexed employee.

Gore manager: "We needed more people."

New hire: "But how did you select *me?*"

Gore manager: "We hired you for who you are, we thought you would fit in."

The new hire now is under a great deal of pressure to fit in. Her personal value in life is dependent upon her fitting in. If she doesn't fit in, she faces the loss of her job and of who she is—a sad thing to lose.

Beware of Specialist Collections

Specialist collections are dangerous because people who find value in who they are at work are short-changing themselves. *We are more than what we do; we are who we are.* The value of who we are is not found in what we do, it's found in who we are—who we are within our family and who we are within our community. Specialist collection employees have been given the message, "You are valuable to this company because of who you are; that's why we hired you." I don't deny that that gives the new employee a warm, wonderful feeling. But does that mean that if the person is fired—for whatever reason—the converse is true? In a firing situation, is the employee told, "You are of no value to this company because of who you are?"

The value people find at work is often related to an unwritten agreement they make with their employer. It's called the psychological contract.

The Psychological Contract in Corporate Cults

All employees are aware of the legal contract that binds them to their corporation. But another agreement, called the psychological contract, mentally and emotionally binds employees to the corporation.

The psychological contract is based on a feeling of equity. As Figure 3-3 shows, it starts out looking very much like the legal contract, in which the person states what contributions he or she will make to the corporation and what inducements are to be received from the corporation in return.

When inducements in the contract are based on quantitative performance measures, such as widgets made, sales completed, or units repaired, the psychological contract is fine. However, when inducements from the corporation take the form of emotional and affiliation elements, the workplace becomes a corporate cult for the employee.

Emotional and affiliation elements are very difficult to quantify. How many widgets made, sales completed, or units repaired earns the perpetuation of an employee's membership in the "family"? It's unlimited. The employee could labor unceasingly and still not produce enough outcome to earn membership. That's because family membership can't be earned. It's a gift we are given when we are born.

Most people would perform great acts of sacrifice for their family, and they should. They should not do the same for the corporation, because the corporation is not a family. It cannot offer the kinds of long-term sustained emotional and affiliational rewards the family can. These types of "familial" inducements are

Figure 3-3. The Psychological Contract

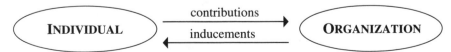

used by corporate cults to gain a level of employee commitment that delivers competitive advantage efficiencies.

When the psychological contract gets out of balance, the employee can do one of four things to return it to equilibrium, as shown in Figure 3-4. The contract *must* be brought back into balance. Long-term out-of-balance psychological contracts produce the kind of extreme outbursts that have become known as "going postal."

The most obvious first response is to change the right-hand side of the formula by asking for a raise. (I am assuming that the employee felt the contract was out of balance in favor of the organization. I have *heard* of people who thought they were overpaid, but I have never met one.) The situation is a little different in corporate cults. The employee asks for more inducements, but not in the form of dollars or other traditional economic rewards. She or he asks for an increase in emotional and affiliation inducements. These are easy and cheap for the corporation to offer, so it does. The corporation gets more contributions from the employee, and all it costs it is a few affiliation inducements. This is a good deal for the corporation. At the time, the employee considers it a good deal as well. What the employee doesn't realize is that as the workload contributions increase incrementally and collinear with the emotional inducements, he or she is sinking deeper and deeper into a corporate cult.

The second response to a psychological contract imbalance is to reduce contributions. This really strikes at the heart of the culted employee. When "who I am" is defined by "what I do," doing less

Figure 3-4. Repairing the Psychological Contract

Increase inducements:	Ask for a raise
Decrease contributions:	Produce less work
Change your "psyche":	How you feel about the relationship
End the contract:	Quit

of "what I do" reduces the degree of "who I am." This is a dangerous and self-reinforcing negative spiral. The culted employee is
caught in a trap: She can't reduce her work contribution, because
it would decrease her value as a person. She's caught in the organizational trap of a corporate cult.

The third way to rebalance the psychological contract is not so
obvious. Since the contract is psychological in nature, the employee can equalize it by simply changing his "psyche" or feeling
about the situation. The cognitive script for the corporate cult
member goes something like, "Well, the corporation has hit upon
hard times. We lost a big contract, competition is heating up,
profits are down—I guess what I am being paid is about right."

This is extremely dangerous. By making this confession, the
employee has admitted that the organization's goals are more important than his personal goals. The entire subject of organizational
behavior rests on the fulcrum of this single relationship of the individual and the organization, shown in Figure 3-5. When the employee admits that the organization's needs are more important
than his own needs, the employee is well along the road to cultedness.

There is a fourth way to solve psychological contract imbalance: End the contract by leaving the corporate cult. This is very
difficult for culted employees to do. These employees are described in the Eagles song "Hotel California" as cult members who
can check out but never leave.

I recited those lines for Richard Schlessinger of CBS News
when he interviewed me about corporate cults. He didn't accept
the analogy. "Haven't you interviewed employees for this segment
of 48 Hours," I asked him, "who you think *couldn't* leave their corporation?" He admitted that he had interviewed people like that.

Culted employees don't have the fourth option for bringing
the psychological contract into balance. They can't cancel the contract because to do so would cancel "who I am." That's not an easy

Figure 3-5. Relationship Between Individual and Organization

action to take. Remembering that the contract is psychological in nature gives unculted employees a great deal of flexibility. They can *think* about quitting without doing it. Mentally visualizing quitting empowers the unculted employee, but it disempowers the culted employee.

Culted employees don't gain empowerment by thinking about quitting, because thinking about quitting would *reduce* their power instead of *increasing* it. Thinking about ceasing to be "who I am" disempowers the culted person. Thus, culted employees are caught in an organizational trap of their own making. Their anthem is taken from the "Hotel California," where members are prisoners who can't escape the clutches of the corporate cult.

While unculted employees use all four techniques to gain power in the organizational relationship, corporate cult members have no power in the psychological contract. They have given up their individual identities and taken on the identity of the organization. The psychological contract favors the organization over the individual, and employees are members of a corporate cult.

A Task Specialist in a People Organization

Ernest Gordon entered an Eaton Corporation plant with a decade of experience in the auto industry. His gruff behavior earned him a mandatory visit to the company psychologist, from which he bolted. When he was fired because of the incident, he complained, "They should have judged me on my job performance, not on how I interact with teammates."[8]

Gordon was simply a task-oriented worker misplaced in a people-oriented organization. Some people are more easily culted than others. He was not amenable to the high-intensity team requirements at Eaton. After being unceremoniously shown the door, he went back to a union shop where there are more clearly delineated organizational roles. Being a naturally task-oriented person, he was happier in the union environment.

Tying the Cohort Horn to the Specialist Collection

The cohort horn described a problem: the increasing value dispersion of each successive generation. The specialist collection prescribes what managers can do about it. Their response to a wide value dispersion is to narrowly prescribe the type of person they select to enter their corporation. By doing so, they achieve the same efficiency effect that was achieved with the Depression Era generation, as shown in Figure 3-6.

By accepting only employees whose values are within a narrow band, managers can produce a highly committed workforce that has a competitive advantage based on efficiency of output. This narrow constriction is defined differently by each organization that practices stringent selection procedures. At Microsoft, employees are considered "Softies" or "Microserfs." They have two distinct characteristics: They are smart, and they are very committed.

While being smart and committed might be good qualities for any selection system, they are unnaturally distinct at Microsoft. Because the corporation is very successful, it can be extra particular about who it accepts. This direct correlation between success and size of the applicant pool allows successful corporations to be even more particular when selecting candidates. As the corporation's selection procedure becomes more narrow, the organization's

Figure 3-6. The Cohort Horn—Restriction as a Response to Value Dispersion

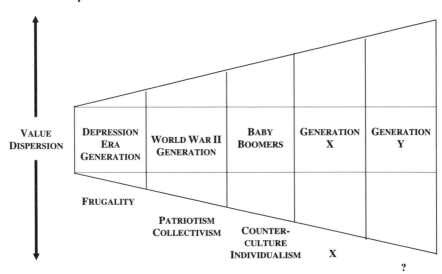

workforce becomes increasingly more homogeneous, by whatever measure the organization prefers. This narrow selection procedure produces a specialist collection: a workforce of people selected because of who they are, not what they do.

Self-esteem arising from this dangerous mixture is toxic from the start of the individual's tenure with the corporation, because he or she feels rewarded by surviving the selection process. The further employees get into the corporation, the more they find people with values, personalities, and lifestyles that mirror their own. This reinforces self-esteem from a bad source. Employees feel they are valuable because they are being paid for who they are.

It's a dangerous continual spiral in which workers are enculted by replacing "who I am" with "what I do." Eventually, "what I do" so fully replaces "who I am" that the individual ceases to exist separate from the corporation, and the person is a member of a corporate cult.

The McDonald's Hybrid

McDonald's maintains strict control over restaurant operation by maintaining very specific franchise rules. Those elements may seem cultish, but McDonald's is a hybrid that can be described at two very different levels.

The top level of McDonald's management has the traits of a specialist collection. Many members of top management began their careers flipping burgers in a McDonald's. Fewer than half of the company's corporate officers graduated from college. This signifies McDonald's very narrow culture for corporate success: loyalty, dedication, and service. The top level of management at McDonald's thus has many of the elements of a specialist collection that lead to the characteristics of a corporate cult.

At the individual store level, McDonald's is a very different organization. *People* are secondary to the *task* to be performed. The success of the restaurant chain is based on the ability to replicate highly efficient procedures in each of its restaurants worldwide. The tasks involved in the scientific process are penultimate at the store level, so there is a culture of a collection of specialists.[9] With distinctly different cultures at headquarters and the stores, there is a major gap between the two elements of the corporation. Hamburger University helps to pass on the famed culture of fast, friendly service and clean stores. It also serves as a means of selecting candidates for upward movement within the corporation. There is a very narrow entryway into the upper ranks, and the gate is Hamburger University. Those who fit the definition of the specialist collection are moved up; those who don't are moved out. Entry into a specialist collection is limited to the few who have the very narrow definition called for in the culture of the corporate cult.

McClelland's Needs

McClelland's well-known organizational theory effectively explains the source of motivation for involvement in the workplace. The theory is honored in the academic world for its precision and simplicity, because it states that people are motivated by only three outcomes: achievement, power, and affiliation. McClelland's theory fits very nicely into the competitive advantage selection model, as shown in Figure 3-7.

The old organizational type satisfies the power need. In that model, empire builders gain and sustain power in organizations

Figure 3-7. Competitive Advantage Selection Model With McClelland's Needs

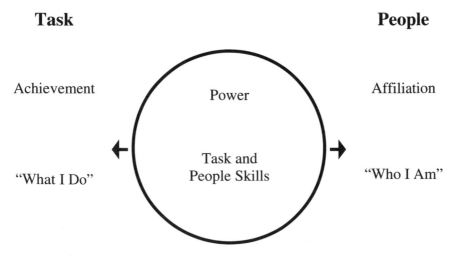

by setting the intricate rules that govern the organization. The hierarchies that protect the upper echelons of organizations built on these systems are complex because the hiring process contains two screens: task skills and people skills.

The achievement needs in McClelland's framework are satisfied by the task-oriented collection of specialists. These organizations exist only to achieve results, so achievement-oriented people naturally gravitate to them. These are the organizations made up of doers who are not concerned about the "being" side of life. They measure success by quantifiable units, such as work completed, products manufactured, sales made, or tests completed.

McClelland's affiliation needs are satisfied in the specialist collection. These are "people people." They are happiest when they are surrounded by others. The Myers-Briggs Type Indicator seeks to answer a major question, "Do you gain energy from being *with people* or being *alone?*" Specialist collection members can't imagine gaining energy from being alone. They are the first ones to organize a party and the last to leave.

Affiliation-needy people are the subject of Arlie Russell Hochschild's *The Time Bind*. She reports about people who are happier at work than at home. One of the major reasons they are happier at work is their emotional and affiliational relationships with their workmates.

People who are affiliation-needy are ideal candidates for corporate cult membership. Their need for affiliation draws them to the corporate cult. They are so happy in the cult that they can't imagine doing anything else. These people have their affiliation needs satisfied in the corporation and nowhere else. As they gain recognition for their work, they begin a self-reinforcing spiral that draws them deeper and deeper into the organization until they are totally culted. "What I do" replaces "who I am" because "what I do" *is* "who I am."

Men and Women

Yes, there *are* some generalizable differences between men and women. Men are more achievement-oriented and like task completion. Women are more affiliation-oriented and like people. Reaffirming bonds of friendship and building community are more common activities for women than for men.[10] Men find self-esteem in work; women find it through relationships and family.[11]

From these generalizations, we could conclude that collection of specialist organizations are led by men, and specialist collection organizations are led by women. Mary Kay Cosmetics comes to mind.

It's a good thing Mary Kay Ash didn't come to me for advice before starting what she now calls "the best-selling brand in America." I'm a man. I would have looked at her business plan from the task-oriented, collection of specialists point of view. My advice would have been something like, "This idea of independent reps is good. You've got individual motivation, owning your own business, all those good things. But associates will never go for it. They will sit down with pencil and paper and figure out that they would make more per hour by flipping hamburgers."

My man-perception would have kept me from seeing the real brilliance of the plan. Women *like* spending time with one another. They don't see time together as a monetary *cost*, they see it as a *gain*. Mary Kay associates look at the plan and say, "You mean I can have all this fun and make money at the same time?" That's because women, in general, enjoy affiliation; they enjoy being to-gether.

If I were chauvinist, I would say they also enjoy spending money, but even that brings up a gender difference. Women shop, men hunt. The Mary Kay plan allows the customer to handle a lot of samples, try them on, pass them around, see how they look on other women. It's a whole affiliation thing. It's a *family* thing.

Men often become leaders in task-oriented groups.[12] Women tend to emerge as leaders in organizations that have complex inter-personal relationships.[13] This could easily lead to speculation that organizations should have two leaders: one to manage the task, and the other to manage the interpersonal relationships.[14] I dis-agree. It seems to me that the organization should simply decide whether its business is task- or people-oriented. Organizations that gain their competitive advantage from task orientation should fol-low the collection of specialists formula. Those that gain their com-petitive advantage through people orientation should adopt the specialist collection model—but with the warning that specialist collections are collinear with corporate cults.

Success vs. Significance

In *Half Time,* Bob Buford tells his own personal story of midlife
change to encourage others to stop seeking success and instead
search for significance.[15] Buford says most people spend the first
half of their lives chasing success and the second half chasing significance. He's not so righteous as to claim that what he does is
the only source of significance. Instead, he describes a process for
finding significance.

Buford's midlife change process raises an interesting challenge to my assumption that people don't change very much during their lives. I have assumed that an employee's personality and
values constitution would predestine him or her for the task-
oriented collection of specialists or the people-oriented specialist
collection. I would attribute an individual's move from one type to
another as an early career misalignment.

Buford says that success is for self, and significance is for others. Success is found in the task environment of the collection of
specialists. Significance is found in the people-oriented specialist
collection. His suggestion that people seek success early in their
careers and significance later encourages people to change from
one type to another. *Half Time* exemplifies how a person can
change from one type to another, but only as a result of a life-
altering event, which Buford explains at length. After "seeing the
light," he encourages others to change their lives as he did. This
book describes employees' self-selection into competitive advantage selection types, whereas Buford has prescribed how they
should change their lives.

Downsizing

As companies downsize, rightsize, and "capsize," the collections
of specialists and specialist collections will become more pro-
nounced. Companies using the old organizational model in the
middle of the diagram are realizing their competitive disadvantage
and are downsizing to become more competitive. As they do, they
outsource more work to contractors and consultants, which are
typically collections of specialists.

These consulting organizations are staffed with people who

were downsized out of old organizational model companies. They have less loyalty to companies and more loyalty to themselves. Having been thrown out by large old organization models, they have taken a huge step toward independence and uncultedness by joining consulting and outsourcing firms of the collection of specialists variety.

The media love to overgeneralize, and they cover the above-mentioned trends ad infinitum, in stories that are replete with anecdotes and stuffed with mounds of layoff data. By trying to describe "average" commitment levels, they tend to the statistical mode, which is the event that occurs the most. They are correct in reporting that the movement to the collection of specialists is currently the major trend. But they fail to report the other end of the spectrum, which is the subject of this book. The employer-employee commitment relationship is moving *both* ways at the same time, thus vacating the middle. As the standard deviation becomes greater, the average becomes less meaningful, and it makes more sense to look at the bimodal nodes on either side of the average. On the left side of the average is the collection of specialists type. On the right side is the specialist collection type.

Downsizing moves commitment relationships to both ends of the continuum, to the collection of specialists at the left end and the specialist collection at the right. As the average commitment goes down, a few exceptional corporations will cull out the employees who want to be committed and will establish this commitment as a competitive advantage, way on the specialist collection end of the continuum. This small, but growing number of corporations chooses people for "who I am" (loyal) rather than "what I do" (task). They are envied for going against the grain of disloyalty, and their admirable performance is causing others to try to emulate them. This book examines them and warns individuals about the behavior of specialist collections that produces corporate cults.

The Wall Street Journal followed a small group of downsized employees and occasionally reported on their lives after the experience.[16] Two subjects in the study clearly exemplify the movement from the competitive advantage selection model's old organizational type to both ends of the continuum. One of the subjects clearly moved to a collection of specialists and one to a specialist collection.

The collection of specialists subject became a consultant, using his expertise in many different corporations. He loves the workstyle; "I'm not always doing the same thing in the same place every day," he says. That exemplifies the freedom of the collection of specialists. He is positive about the future. "Companies will eliminate bodies to look good on the books, but they'll still need to get the work done. They'll fill the need with contractors like me," he says confidently.

The other subject in the ongoing study is still unemployed, but his feelings have caused him to move to the specialist collection end of the continuum. He missed the camaraderie of the office environment. "I'm ready to go back to the work," he said sadly. He really missed the everyday comfort of friends and associates at the office. My prediction is that he will end up in a specialist collection that satisfies his desire for affiliation.

Chapter 2 explains that people's values remain largely the same over a lifetime. They change only as a result of a life-altering event. For some employees, downsizing is that event. It moves employees from the old organizational model in the middle to the ends of the competitive advantage selection model, where they feel comfortable. That's also where there is more competitive advantage for the corporation.

Effect on the Federal Government

I have shown the competitive advantage selection model to many groups of federal government employees at leadership seminars I have conducted. They instantly recognize the collection of specialists as the contractors that they increasingly rely on for services that were previously performed within the government.

They are not as quick to recognize the movement of their agency to a specialist collection, which I predict is happening at the same time. As the agency gets smaller, it is easier to define the values of the employees who are left. Simply surviving the downsizing weeds out some types of personality traits.

The federal government is perhaps the worst example of the movement to the specialist collection, because it is the largest employer in the world. However, that's exactly why I like to use it as an example. If elements of the specialist collection can be found even in this huge organization, they certainly can be found in smaller organizations. This narrowing personality band is much more evident at the agency level than it is at the very macro federal government level. My seminar attendees agree that individual agencies have well-established and distinct personality types that distinguish them from other agencies.

The Bell Curve: Intelligence and the Collection of Specialists

In *The Bell Curve*, Richard Hernstein and Charles Murray argue that the next discriminator of societal groups will be intelligence.[17] The movement of the world economy from an agrarian to an industrial then to an information society has caused an increasing positive correlation between intelligence and economic rewards.

In free societies—those without an imperial ruling class—an individual's economic returns have always been determined by the contribution he or she makes to society. In the agrarian economic culture of only 150 years ago, workers' contributions were not widely different. The variance in physical abilities was not starkly different, so there was a great mass of people who earned nearly the same economic returns.

In the Industrial Age, the workplace came to be the factory, where employees could be more closely controlled and labor could be calculated and compared more effectively. This brought about the birth of the discipline I study and teach: management. Closer control of the workplace, coupled with financial capitalism via the stock market and debt financing, encouraged the growth of huge corporations that could capitalize on economies of scale and produce profits at previously unheard-of levels. Thus, the Industrial Age encouraged a more unequal distribution of wealth. When wealth came to be determined by managerial ability, the dispersion became larger, because the skill was more unequally distributed among the population.

Now the Information Age is producing a new economic elite. As Hernstein and Murray point out, it is an economic elite driven by level of intelligence. The Information Age rewards intelligence at a higher level than the previous economic eras did. Those with higher intelligence are moving into arenas where their intelligence will produce the highest reward: Medicine, law, architecture, and engineering are just a few examples.

Hernstein and Murray's predictions are coming true in terms of the competitive advantage selection model also. Medicine, law, architecture, and engineering are all higher-intelligence disciplines that favor an organizational structure that pays high rewards: the partnership. Partnerships are clearly collection of specialists organizations, where each partner makes her contribution and has the potential of making greater returns than she would in a typical hierarchical organization.

A high-intelligence person can be viewed as making a choice between a collection of specialists, where his intelligence will produce high economic rewards, and a specialist collection, where he will have more fun. It's a clear choice between money and fun, and the intellectual elite have responded by favoring the financial rewards of the collection of specialists.

This could be seen from the opposite point of view: Intelligence is a measure not of "what I do" but of "who I am." Hernstein and Murray's great fear is that the increasing correlation between intelligence and economics will produce an intellectual elite that separates itself from the rest of the community.

I will use my family to illustrate their point. My parents graduated from a very small high school on the plains of South Dakota in 1940. They were two of the top performers in their class, and they stayed in that small community of 1,000 for most of their adult lives. This tradition of staying in the community produced an interesting mix of intelligence levels in that small midwestern town.

Now, let's compare their experience to that of my teenagers two generations later. The top academic performers in their high school graduating classes will not stay in their community. They will accept academic scholarships to prestigious universities, where they will study the disciplines that produce high economic rewards. They will marry people at the same universities who are in the same disciplines. As they move into their lucrative careers, they will move to exclusive, gated communities with others of their ilk.

While this begins to sound like the third trait of a cult, separation from community, it's not. It's actually building a community *within* the gates of the exclusive neighborhood. These people are less likely to become members of corporate cults, because they will receive greater economic rewards in collection of specialist structures that are unculted. They will work in collections of specialists because these will provide the highest financial rewards for intelligent contributions. When they fail to find emotional and affiliational rewards at work, they will be forced to find them within their families and communities.

Thus, another factor of differentiation between the collection of specialists and the specialist collection is level of intelligence that produces economic rewards. Those with higher intellects that produce higher rewards will self-select to the collection of specialists, while those with intellects that produce lower economic rewards will self-select to the specialist collection.

Products and Services

Task-oriented collections of specialists are more likely to be found in production industries, while people-oriented specialist collections are better at providing services.

There is greater competitive advantage to be gained from a collection of specialists in a production industry because the customer concentrates more on the product. This is particularly true when production is based on sequential interdependence, as is often the case in assembly line and team settings. Multiple independent experts make a specific part of the item, then pass it along to the next specialist. The current shrinking of the world via improved transportation and distribution simply means that the best producers can spread the specialized elements of production to a collection of specialists around the globe.

The rules of the collection of specialists fit very well into this type of "best-in-class" arrangement. The specialists don't have to speak the same language or have the same background, personality, or values. They don't even have to communicate! The global collection of specialists enables the corporation to simply pass the production from one worker to the next. By combining the best of all "global hands," the corporation gains a competitive advantage in terms of both quality and price.

At the opposite end of the model, the specialist collection

gains competitive advantage in service industries, because that is where the relationship with customers is so important. Professional sports is a service.[18] The spectator comes to the event with only the expectation of having a good time and leaves with only memories. Both the expectations and the memories are totally dependent on the "service" the spectator receives while at the event.

Given a choice, the sports manager would certainly prefer to have "people people" rather than "task people" working in the ballpark. Thus, we can expect service industries to contain many more specialist collections that become corporate cults. Conversely, there will be many collection of specialist types in production industries.

What's an "Associate"?

Everybody is an "associate" these days. Wal-Mart got the idea that its employees would be empowered by the new title, and now the bagboy at the grocery store, the paperboy, and secretaries are all associates. Is there cultedness in this, or is it just empowerment?

To be an associate in the traditional sense means that the person has some kind of financial stake in the business, but the spread of the term has changed its meaning. The new crop of "associates" have a greater identification with the company, but they have not gained any financial rewards to accompany the new title. The beauty of the deal for the corporation is that it gains more commitment from the employees without giving up anything in return. Corporations claim that this is a win-win relationship, but I argue that anything that brings the employee closer to the organization is good for the corporation and bad for the employee. The term *associate* does this. It brings employees into a closer relationship with their organization.

The collection of specialists uses the title associate to describe an individual's ownership of the corporation. The specialist collection uses the term to describe the corporation's ownership of the individual.

The Competitive Advantage Selection Model at the Industry Level

In his 1980 book *Competitive Strategy*,[19] Michael Porter introduced a business-level model of competitive advantage that he called generic strategies. The first two strategies he proposed are at opposite ends of a spectrum from low cost to differentiation. His exhaustive research indicated that competitors at either end of the continuum could more effectively sustain their competitive advantage than those who were "stuck in the middle."

While he defined the model at the business level of analysis, he also described how competitors jockey around one another and align themselves in niches along the low-cost-to-differentiation continuum within an industry environment. When viewed from this level, the model shows industry competitors arrayed across the spectrum of niches.

My competitive advantage selection model has many of the same traits. My prediction is that in any particular industry, we will see competitors move out of the middle (old organizational model) either to the left, where they will compete based on task proficiencies in a collection of specialists, or to the right, where they will compete based on people skills in a specialist collection.

Porter's "don't get stuck in the middle" advice applies to the competitive advantage selection model as well. Those who stay in the middle will operate at a competitive disadvantage to those who move to the ends of the spectrum. The model is built on the same assumptions as Porter's. Customers will choose the competitor at either end of the continuum who best supplies their needs. Customers who demand task specificity and expertise will buy from the collection of specialists. Customers who are more concerned with people skills and the relational aspects will buy from the specialist collection.

Some industries have already divided themselves in this manner. Almost all competitors in the software industry are on the collection of specialists side of the model, where employees jump between companies with great regularity. But one of the most successful, Microsoft, is clearly a specialist collection, where employees tend to stay for relatively long periods. The annual turnover rate for "Softies" is only 7 percent.

The auto industry hasn't changed much from the days when Henry Ford used to complain, "I hire people just to use their hands, but they keep bringing their minds with them." The auto industry wants task specialists to do a narrowly prescribed job for a union-negotiated number of dollars in a collection of specialists. Most divisions of General Motors, Ford, and Chrysler fit the mold. So when GM wanted to create a "different kind of car company," it put Saturn at the specialist collection end of the competitive advantage continuum. Saturn is a people company in a task industry; thus it is different.

Most consulting firms can be described as collections of specialists whose "hired guns" perform specific tasks. McKinsey is the contrarian that competes as a specialist collection.

In the airline industry, American and United seek the best-qualified *task* specialist for their collection of specialists. Southwest Airlines hires the *person* who fits best into its specialist collection.

At the store level, fast-food competitors McDonald's, Burger King, and Wendy's promote or fire managers based on quantitative goal achievement, as good collection of specialist competitors do. Chick-fil-A managers are part of a family in a specialist collection.

When the Baby Bells were tossed out of the incubator, most of them changed from a clubby, close-knit group to an intracompetitive, slash and burn culture that is indicative of the collection of specialists. Southwestern Bell has staunchly sat at the people end of the continuum and retained much of the camaraderie and loyalty of long-term employees that is typical of the specialist collection.

Figure 3-8. Summary of the Differences Between Collection of Specialists and Specialist Collection in the Competitive Advantage Selection Model

Collection of Specialists	Specialist Collection
Task	People
Success	Significance
Men	Women
Money	Fun
What I Do	Who I Am
Achievement	Affiliation
High Intelligence	High Involvement
Products	Services
Associates as Owners	Associates as Owned

Technology companies like Texas Instruments are reliant on research and development, so there is a constant movement of employees *between* competitors to find the right researcher-company fit for any particular innovation. This exemplifies the collection of specialists. In the 3M family, researchers are moved around *within* the company, so it is a specialist collection. Figure 3-8, on the previous page, summarizes the difference between the collection of specialists and the specialist collection.

The successful cooptation of the term *family* is perhaps corporate cults' greatest success. How the term has been hijacked by many organizations that are not families is the subject of Chapter 4. What does family mean to you? It means something totally different in corporate cults.

Notes

1. William Bridges, *Job Shift* (Reading, Mass.: Addison-Wesley, 1994).
2. Eric Wee, "Young Guns," *Washington Post*, June 15, 1998.
3. "3M's Staffing Strategy Promotes Productivity and Pride," *Personnel Journal*, February 1995.
4. *The New York Times*, May 26, 1998; Douglas Coupland, *Microserfs* (New York: HarperCollins, 1996).
5. Arlie Russell Hochschild, *The Time Bind* (New York: Metropolitan Books, 1997).
6. Nina Munk, "Organization Man," *Fortune*, March 16, 1998.
7. Ibid.
8. Timothy Aeppel, "Not All Workers Find Idea of Empowerment as Neat as It Sounds," *The Wall Street Journal*, September 8, 1997.
9. "McDonald's: A Prime Example of Corporate Culture," *Public Relations Quarterly*, Winter 1995.
10. Hochschild, *The Time Bind*, 168.
11. Carolyn Corbin, *Conquering Corporate Co-Dependence* (Englewood Cliffs, N.J.: Prentice-Hall, 1993).
12. P. H. Andrews, "Sex and Gender Differences in Group Communication: Impact on the Facilitation Process,"*Small Group Research* 23 (1992): 74–94.
13. A. H. Eagly and S. J. Karau, "Gender and the Emergence of Leaders: A Meta-analysis," *Journal of Personality and Social Psychology* Vol. 60(5) (1991): 685–710.
14. J. Kevin Barge and Lawrence R. Frey, *Managing Group Life: Group Communication*, (Boston, Mass.: Houghton Mifflin College, 1996).
15. Bob Buford, *Half Time* (Grand Rapids, Mich.: Zondervon, 1996).

16. *The Wall Street Journal*, June 26, 1998, p. A9
17. Richard Hernstein and Charles Murray, *The Bell Curve: Intelligence and Class Structure in American Life*, (New York: The Free Press, 1994).
18. Dave Arnott, "How Do You Sell What You Can't See?" *SportsBusiness Journal*, August 17, 1998.
19. Michael Porter, *Competitive Strategy: Techniques for Analyzing Industries and Competitors*, (New York: The Free Press, 1980).

Chapter 4

When Work Becomes a Family

*A*merican corporations have taken over the meaning-making process for individuals that was once supplied by family and community. But corporations cannot deliver on their promise to fulfill so many multifaceted needs in the employee's life. The notion that organizations can hijack an existential vacuum in their employees' lives and harness it for corporate gain is a false seduction of the employee.[1] There are many ways in which work replaces family en route to the formation of a corporate cult.

Odysseus was excited about setting off for the Trojan War. The only problem was, he had to leave his family. He promised to return soon. But then one thing led to another, and the next thing he knew, many years had passed.

In the legend of Odysseus, we find the same conflict so many employees face in today's work-is-life culture. Slaying dragons and working with beautiful people are exciting, but employees also want to be home. Odysseus' work group became his family because he was gone for so long. Is your life any different? You're gone a lot, too. Has work become your family? Some say it should, but I disagree.

Odysseus moved around a lot, like many present-day corporate cult members. The United States is a country whose generations are scattered over the geographic landscape. However, the movement of workers to different parts of the country does not remove their need for family. By definition, needs must be satisfied. The work family of the Information Age has a greater need for community because people in families are geographically separated from their loved ones and extended families. Also, the erosion of neighborhood ties has contributed to fewer connections in the community.[2] One in six Americans moves every year. With that much moving around, it's hard to establish community ties outside the corporation. Several people have told me that multiple moves force the family to become a tighter, more interdependent unit. That may be good for the family, but the reason the family is closer is that its members have no community *outside* the family. After multiple moves, the corporation becomes the only family that vagabond employees know on a long-term basis.

The one-in-six figure is down from one in four in the 1950s and 1960s. That would be good, *if* the decrease in moves could be attributed to employees' desire to stay closer to extended family units. But it can't; the spouse's job prevents movement.[3] In the corporate cults of a couple decades ago, employees moved to keep jobs; now they are not moving to keep jobs. The job does not seem to be losing its grip on American families and culture. Corporate cults are winning the relocation battle in the work-family war.

Balance Is a Good Thing

Research seems to suggest that the extreme commitment level of corporate cult employees is not always best for the corporation. In one study, workers who spent less time at the office because they took advantage of family-friendly policies, like maternity and paternity leave and job sharing, were among the best performers and the least likely to have disciplinary problems.[4] Employees who are frustrated over not having a life outside work aren't very effective.[5]

This suggests that there is something other than a direct correlation between time spent at the office and performance levels. Balanced people are not only happier but more productive.

Corporate Cults Are Like Dysfunctional Families

Corporate cults are like dysfunctional families in which there are no boundaries between the individual member and the family. The family is the individual, and the individual is the family. Each person's private business is everybody's business. The dynamics of those relationships lack the natural barriers that people need in order to protect themselves.

The word *dysfunctional* describes a situation in which less powerful members of a family or other group suffer invisible emotional damage at the hands of more powerful members.[6] This happens to corporate cult members when the employee allows "what I do" to replace "who I am."

In functional families, members are valued for being themselves not for following the rules. This sense of self-expression carries through to corporations as well. Those that honor and allow freedom of expression are functional, healthy groups. Those that overtly or covertly force conformance with company culture are corporate cults.

In a dysfunctionally controlled family, members feel that their privacy and independence are violated. Siblings seek out and uncover other family members' greatest fears. Parents don't let children have their "own stuff" and constantly snoop through their rooms and question their friends for evidence of untruthfulness. Those family traits take away the "person" from a child and cause her or him to be more vulnerable to the same techniques in a corporate cult as an adult. This too-close family relationship is repeated by corporate cult members as they seek the kind of familial relationships they had in their developmental years.

Companies can be easily viewed as distinct family units, with each department forming a member of the corporate family. A close look at the dynamics in those departments reveals a structure of power and authority that is learned in family dynamics.[7]

Being a new hire at an organization is a lot like being born into a family. As people mature in their biological family, they learn the rules for survival and prosperity. The corollaries for corporate life are explained in Figure 4-1. Employees learn the same kind of rules as they adapt to the culture of their corporation. One author openly acknowledges the family-corporate similarity when he encourages managers to "be the best parent you can be."[8]

The normative triangle in Figure 4-2 shows how relationships should be hierarchically arranged. The top level of the triangle indicates that we should have very few, but very intimate relationships within the family. The second level indicates we should have a middle number of somewhat less intimate relationships in the

Figure 4-1. List of Corollaries

Family	Corporation
Marriage	Hire
Honeymoon	Honeymoon
Children	New Hire
Father	Mentor
Death	Firing

community. The third level, at the bottom of the triangle, indicates that we should have the greatest number of distant relationships at work.

The order has been reversed for corporate cult members, as shown in the second triangular hierarchy. They have a few intimate friends at work and many distant relationships with family.

This upside-down world of relationships and intimacy is good for the organization and bad for the individual. It separates the employee from her or his community and family while replacing those relationships with corporate intimacy and emotional reliance.

Figure 4-2. Hierarchical Arrangement of Relationships

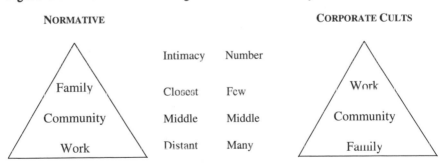

NORMATIVE			CORPORATE CULTS
	Intimacy	Number	
Family	Closest	Few	Work
Community	Middle	Middle	Community
Work	Distant	Many	Family

How About a Hug?

"The average human being needs eight to ten hugs a day," says Harley King, customer service director for Health Care & Retirement Corp in Toledo, Ohio.[9] King not only encourages hugging at the company but has mandated an eleven-hour training session in the practice. This seems to ensure that he will get specialist collection employees and will scare off the collection of specialist breed. King's employees certainly won't be average on the hugging scale. The company will select huggers, and hugging employees will self-select to the organization.

Let's assume that this average person who needs ten hugs a day exists. If he gets ten at work, how many does he need at home? That's how applying social economics to the workplace falsifies the corporate cult claim that work should replace home. Work should *not* replace home, but it does when a person gets emotional and affiliational gratifications, like hugs, at work.

A family of 1,500 ants was displayed in a six-by-four-foot sealed glass case in the lobby of Steelcase's New York City headquarters as a metaphor for how families live and work together. "For more people, work and non-work are blending," says Steelcase's Dave Lathrop in defense of the display. "Ants live to work and work to live," he continued.[10] People do too, when work becomes a family in a corporate cult.

A Deal You Can't Refuse

There are many different definitions of family. When the boundaries between work and family become blurred, there is often conflict for the individual involved.[11]

Families are life-span groups, meaning that they are maintained throughout the life of the individual. Work groups are limited to the task to be performed. It's quite clear that people join work groups to accomplish the task at hand; when the task is done, the group disbands—unless the group has other, more deep-seated motives.

The Mafia exemplifies a very close-knit family. The three circles of work, family, and community are all stacked upon one another. Weaving work, family, and community into one tightly wrapped strand produces incredible levels of member commitment, which is very good for the Mafia. It's very bad for the individual Mafia members. The blending of work, family, and community is a dangerous mixing of allegiances that produces overcommitment to work at the expense of family and community.

Gangs are a minor-league version of the Mafia-style community. While the obvious reason for joining gangs is physical protection, research shows that gang life is more about the emotional and psychological issues of solidarity, support, and family than it is about crime, violence, and death.[12] Gangs provide young people with all three of the very important support groups—work, family, and community—in one organization. Gang members think it's convenient for them, because they get all three in the same group. That's also why people join corporate cults.

The need for family *must* be satisfied in the lives of individuals. The need is being satisfied by various and often-changing definitions of the term *family*. There are single-parent families, blended families, and friends as family.[13] These innovative ways of thinking about family are called the constructionist approach. That means that when the current rules and roles of society don't satisfy needs, there is a conflict. Since needs can't change, the definitions of terms like *family* must. Corporate cults extend the definition of family to the organization. The need for family that is unsatisfied in many employee's lives is satisfied by the work family at the corporate cult.

Until the end of World War II, the family was traditionally seen as the refuge from the harshness of the outside world.[14] Since that time, families have to some extent disintegrated and to a much larger extent have thrown off the role of protector. Corporations have found that filling the role of protector through corporate cults provides an incentive that ties the employee to the workplace with a familial strand that has great strength.

"More often now, the work environment is the only place that's functional to employees, and they just won't leave," says Tom Bardwell, president of Worx, an organizational development consulting firm in Caro, Michigan. "Their support group is shifting from the family to the work environment."[15]

One-Stop Emotional Shopping Is Not Advised

Corporate cults are dangerous because employees are given the false assurance by their corporation that they will always be taken care of. In a specialist collection, people are hired and promoted for who they are, but their continued employment is based on what they do. That's why the paradoxical promise of the corporate cult is so dangerous. Mixing the two produces an employee who does "what I do" to maintain "who I am." That's a dangerous mix of signals. Corporate cults purposely mix the two because it benefits the corporation at the employee's expense. You might think the corporate cult lifestyle is limited to large companies, but it's not.

It Happens in Small Companies

I showed the three circles of work, family, and community to Beth Wright-Smith, the co-owner of World Balloon Corporation in Albuquerque, New Mexico. "They're all the same," she responded without hesitation. "I have no life other than World Balloon and Taylor (her daughter)." In that particular statement, she didn't mention her husband, Paul, whom she lives with but doesn't see three or four days a week. As executive director of the Albuquerque International Balloon Fiesta, he often gets home late in the evening. She goes to bed early so that she can get up at 4:30 to give balloon pilot lessons at sunrise.

While Wright-Smith claims to have some family life—Paul drops Taylor off at day care and she picks her up—clearly the work, family, and community circles are all the same to her. "Do you foresee this changing?" I asked. "Not this year," she said emphatically. Somehow, I doubt that it will change for a long time.

Small sole-proprietorship companies can be the worst at taking over the family and community circles. I ran a small business for two years and it consumed my family and community life. Don't let it happen to you.

You Can't Lose Your *Real* Family

It scares me sometimes, but I continue to tell my two teenagers that they can *never* do anything that will end our relationship. I will *always* be their father. I am sometimes disappointed with their choices and behavior—what they do—but I always love them for who they are—my children—and that will never change.

Corporate cults try to say that to employees via lifetime employment, but it's a lie! Corporations that say they have no-layoff policies are telling a lie. They cannot guarantee continued employment. Public companies can't make the guarantee because the managers don't have unfettered control over the vast amount of resources it would take to make such a guarantee. Even if they did, they have no guarantee that they will be around long enough to fulfill the promise.

Private companies can't fulfill the promise either. Managers in private companies can't control or even predict the future environment in which they will operate to the extent that would be necessary to ensure that the company will survive for the working tenure of its employees. Yet corporate cults continue to make covert promises to provide everything the individual needs. Sometimes the satisfaction of needs even extends to death.

One study reported that on average, when an employee's mother dies, the employee receives more helpful resources from fellow workers than from his or her spouse or religious organization.[16] If the corporate cult is more important than family and religion, how does it rate relative to money?

Recognition Is More Effective Than Money

The more psychic rewards and self-actualization are included in a motivational plan, the more productive—and culted—the employees become. Managers have known for a long time that recognition is more effective and cheaper than financial rewards. That's because financial rewards must be spent *outside* the organization, virtually anywhere the employee chooses. This separates the employee from the organization. Recognition rewards have to be spent *inside* the organization because that's the only place where they have any value. People outside the organization don't have enough information to recognize the value of intraorganizational rewards.

The Best Companies to Work For Are Corporate Cults

Fortune magazine seemed to think work-as-family was a good thing when it delivered its first annual report on "The 100 Best Companies to Work For."[17] The magazine found that at least 40 of the 238 companies it surveyed do dry cleaning for employees.

Cleaning employees' clothes seems to be an intensely personal task for a corporation to perform for employees. It's also another step in the process of separating employees from their existing community and making the corporation the employees' community. Many companies have become even more invasive—*Fortune* called it supportive—of employees' personal life by providing personal concierge service. The company concierge sends flowers and gifts for the employee and arranges vacations and parties.

Fortune didn't stop at just rating the 100 best companies to work for. It summarized its findings into three corporate traits that make a corporation one of the best places to work: a sense of purpose, inspiring leadership, and knockout facilities. Their example of "knockout facilities" was USAA Insurance in San Antonio, which is the nation's archetypal separation-from-community campus. Figure 4-3 shows how these three traits almost mirror the definition of a cult: devotion, charismatic leadership and separation from community.

When asked what type of workplace they'd be most reluctant to leave, 74 percent said, "One that promotes fun and closer work relationships with colleagues." *Fortune* unwittingly surveyed a heavy contingent of specialist collections. Its survey methodology skipped over many collection of specialist corporations whose employees don't report to offices because they do their work independently. So the 74 percent figure is not surprising. It actually confirms my prediction that organizations are dividing themselves into two groups: collections of specialists in which task-oriented employees thrive and specialist collections in which people-oriented employees thrive.

Here's what *Fortune* heard from the members of what I call specialist collections.

Figure 4-3. Characteristics of Cults vs. "Fortune's Best Places to Work"

Cult	Fortune's "Best Places to Work"
Devotion	Sense of Purpose
Charismatic Leadership	Inspiring Leadership
Separation from Community	Knockout Facilities

A Sense of Purpose—or Devotion

Fortune adopted Medtronic's motto of "Restoring patients to full life" as an exemplar of a corporation with a noble sense of purpose that makes the company one of the best places to work. Restoring patients to full life is a good thing to do, and I'm not saying Medtronic should do anything else. But, as the newscasters and x-ray technicians say, "I don't write 'em, I just read 'em." That's what I'm doing. I'm simply reading a motto such as Medtronic's and making the easy conclusion that it helps the company fulfill one-third of the equation for being a corporate cult. The construct that *Fortune* has identified as "sense of purpose" is very close to the corporate cult requirement of "devotion."

Inspiring Leadership—or Charismatic Leadership

Fortune's Exhibit A is none other than Southwest Airlines founder and CEO Herb Kelleher. Kelleher has three addictions: cigarettes, whiskey, and work. Fortunately for his employees, they must mirror only the last. I doubt if Kelleher or many of his employees could separate the three circles of work, family, and community. Work is community and family to many Southwest employees.

I asked a Southwest employee if she was involved in any charitable work outside the airline. Her immediate defense began, "Sure, we . . ." We? The plural pronoun in her answer completed that section of the interview.

Mary Kay Ash, the revered founder of Mary Kay Cosmetics, was cited in the *Fortune* article. I admire the woman a great deal. I don't have much admiration for her followers, who admittedly want to "be like Mary Kay." She's a wonderful woman. Her 475,000 salespeople would be wonderful too if they would be themselves instead of trying to make themselves into clones of the founder. My advice for Mary Kay women is to pick out a single trait you admire about Mary Kay and improve *yourself* by becoming who you want to be, not another copy of Mary Kay.

Herb Kelleher and Mary Kay Ash exemplify *Fortune*'s inspiring leadership characteristic. They also make good poster children for corporate cults. According to the three-part definition, Southwest Airlines and Mary Kay are both corporate cults.

Knockout Facilities—or Separation From Community

"Knockout facilities may be the most persuasive way to tell employees they're valued," says *Fortune*. I would add that it's the most persuasive way to announce corporate cult status. I was explaining the three elements of a corporate cult to an audience in San Antonio recently. Halfway through the separation-from-community section, a seminar participant interrupted me to ask if I had been to USAA Insurance. "I'm going at 2:00 this afternoon," I replied.

The seminar participant was right; USAA's "knockout facilities" effectively separate its employees from the rest of the community. *Fortune* even called the campus a "compound." *Fortune* quoted a satisfied USAA employee as saying, "You become a part of this place, and it becomes everything you're about."

USAA's separation begins with one of the best day-care centers in the city. The company sponsors a van pool for commuters. The ground floor of the main building has a cavernous hall featuring a convenience store that specializes in personal goods like gifts and flowers for anniversaries and birthdays. It's just down the hall from the credit union, which is next to the post office and across from the medical clinic. The nurse's station was upgraded recently from a "cough and cold clinic" to a full-blown medical center right on the campus—excuse me, compound.

"Compound" is an accurate description. The entire facility is surrounded by a high fence and has entrance gates with uniformed guards. USAA provides insurance for military retirees. The nature of its business doesn't demand such a high level of security, it's there as a reflection of the military culture from which most of the employees came. The USAA cafeteria provides Thanksgiving dinners for employees at a discounted price. Many of them take advantage of it. It baked over 5,000 pies for USAA families last year.

The three gyms in the compound rate with the best a health club can offer. One is open twenty-four hours a day. There is a myriad of intramural basketball, softball, and tennis leagues that compete in the premier athletic facilities in the compound. There are also soccer fields and a golf driving range. Many employees bring their families to the compound for a weekend of picnicking, sports, and relaxing.

USAA is the best example *Fortune* could find of knockout facilities, and it's the best example of the third characteristic of a corporate cult: separation from community.

How Much Is Too Much?

Day-care facilities, laundry, banking, and athletic facilities. When considered alone, these are not bad things. They are all provided with the employee in mind. The purpose is to make the employees' life easier. They no longer need to stop by the day-care center, laundry, bank, or athletic club. With the convenience store on the USAA compound, employees don't even have to stop at the grocery store.

These are all good things for the employee, but they are also good for the corporate cult because they effectively separate the employee from the community. When the employee's work becomes her community, she can't leave the organization, because she would lose her community. USAA employees are like the cult members who can go home (check out), but they can't leave.

Corporate cults brag about their low turnover. That's not surprising. Turnover from all types of cults is low. The few cult members who escape typically must endure many hours of deprogramming to readjust back to society. That's because they are leaving an entity in which work, family, and community are one and are entering in a society in which work, family, and community are separate.

Sleeping

Sleeping seems to be a rather personal activity that most people would choose to do at home in their beds—except for those people who are members of a corporate cult. The practice of napping at work has become so acceptable that a book has been written on the subject,[18] and its author, William Larson, is making a living giving seminars on the topic.

Only a corporate cult would hire someone to tell its members how to sleep—at work, no less. If an organization *really* cared about its employees, wouldn't it discourage napping and encourage employees to go home and sleep instead?

Again, the corporate cult offers the seminar using the same excuse that it uses for most activities of this kind: the lie that goes, "We're doing this only as a service to our employees, who will be better people because of it." The corporation needs to ask the more serious question underlying this and many other personal-intrusion activities: "Wouldn't your employees be better people if they didn't *need* these programs in the first place?"

Army Colonel John Smith is an Army spokesman at the Pentagon who regularly catches a ten-minute nap after lunch. He does this because he rises every morning at 4:45 A.M. and doesn't return home until 8:00 P.M.[19] We've already established quite convincingly that the military is a cult, but it's still surprising to find characteristics such as these in seemingly empowered jobs like those at the Pentagon. If you're purposely napping at work, consider the possibility that you're working too much. Also consider the possibility that you're a member of a corporate cult.

Work Teaches Home Behavior

Employees of unculted organizations are taught at home how to function at work. In corporate cults, employees are taught at work how to function at home.

Total Quality Management (TQM) called for reskilling workers in an enriched job environment, whereas technological developments have deskilled them for an unenriched home environment. Through TQM initiatives, employees are learning more of the intricate details of the business in which they operate. At the same time, technological developments are causing them to learn less about the home in which they operate. Over time, store-bought goods have replaced homespun cloth, homemade soap and candles, home-cured meats, and home-baked foods. The main skill that is still required of family members is the hardest one of all—the ability to build family relationships.[20] People are getting worse at this at home.

Surprisingly, they are getting better at this at work. That's why *The Time Bind* reaches the intriguing conclusion that people are more secure, comfortable, and stress-free at work. Particularly for women, work has become a place where relationships are forged, friends are met, and landmarks are celebrated. That's because those things happen under the weight of the organization's thumb. The unwritten rule is, "Make relationships with friends at work or you will lose your job." "What I do" at work incrementally defines "who I am," i.e., who my friends are.

A husband and father, frustrated by work-family conflict, ruminated on a cure: "Family teamwork is crucial. We need to transfer the idea of teams we have in sports and production to the family." Isn't that where the idea came from originally?[21] It seems obvious that corporate cults have co-opted the best of family life and used it to advance corporate goals at the expense of their employees.

Self-improvement classes at work help employees learn how to function at home. But nothing at home teaches employees how to function at work. Thus, the corporate cult is the sacrosanct body, from which not only are physiological, security, belonging, and esteem needs met, but rules for family governance are also set. This seems awkwardly backward.

Madison Avenue has capitalized on corporate cults taking over home life. AT&T plays on work-family tension in a TV ad for cellular service that features a mother headed out the door for a client meeting. Her sad-faced daughters beg for a trip to the beach. "Mommy, when can I be a client?" the six-year-old pleads. The day is saved by AT&T's cellular service, which allows the mother to do both. The ad ends joyously for all when the mother's cellular phone rings on the beach. Since when is a day at the beach a *success* because it's interrupted by a business phone call? Seems like that would ruin a day at the beach.

You Will Be Funny!

A sense of humor is a very serious requirement at Southwest Airlines.[22] In one of six preemployment interviews, the prospective employee is often required to tell a joke. Even candidates applying for non-customer-contact jobs in disciplines such as finance and infotech are required to meet the company's requirement to be funny.

A finance project director commented about the process, "We are allowed to let our personalities show." Really? It sounds as if you are *required* to let your personality show! And you are required to have the right kind of personality. As one employee commented, "If you don't fit into the culture, you'll be rejected like a bad organ transplant." Southwest Airlines aims for a very narrow slice of the cohort horn when selecting employees.

It's a paradox that Southwest Airlines screens so carefully for "spirited" employees, then claims to allow people to be themselves. In corporate cult terms, the rules are, "You *will* be funny, and you *will* conform to the culture of this organization. You are allowed to 'be yourself' as long as yourself fits with the narrowly defined culture of the organization."

Corporate cults control their employees by selecting only those who will bare their souls. Following is an example of what happened to an employee who didn't want to bare his.

Slam the Boss—Drink a Beer

Dale Holtorf had invested ten years of his life with Millstone Coffee when the company tried to invade his personal space. Hard working and dedicated, he started in the warehouse and was soon recognized for his work ethic and positive attitude. He was promoted to a sales route, then to district manager before Millstone was sold to Procter & Gamble. P&G intended to expand the brand, so it gave him a promotion to operations manager in charge of opening a new territory in Colorado. He and his family were moved from Phoenix to Denver.

Distribution was increasing when his direct subordinate, a district manager, quit. Holtorf sacrificed family time in order to perform both jobs because he was so dedicated to getting the business launched in Colorado. He wanted to make the numbers look good for the upcoming national sales meeting at the Hilton in La Jolla, California. But they looked at more than numbers in La Jolla.

Upper management decided that inviting support staff to the meeting would increase team building for the organization. They had arranged a team-building event well in advance of the meeting. Upper management had secretly received embarrassing photos of middle managers from their spouses. As the photo was flashed on the screen, support staff would tell a fictional tale about the red-faced middle manager, of which Dale was one.

Most spouses sent high school graduation photos. Dale's wife sent a picture of him doing a Steve Erckel imitation at a family reunion. Dale was horrified to see the embarrassing photo displayed in front of his fellow workers, but that wasn't the worst part. The staff member—one of Dale's subordinates—created a mythical date between the two of them and went into explicit (although fictional) detail.

The event was titled, "Slam the Boss—Drink a Beer." It seems the company adapted the rules from the old beer softball routine where the objective is to drink a beer for each base gained. In this version, the idea was to drink a beer each time a boss was slammed by his or her subordinates. Upper management had even ordered the production of beer mugs with the acronym STB-DAB for "Slam the Boss—Drink a Beer."

Everyone thought the STB-DAB was a great success—except Dale. Hurt and embarrassed, he swallowed his pride and acted as if he enjoyed the event. When the vice president for human resources asked if the subordinate "slammer" would feel any repercussions in her next annual evaluation, he jokingly said yes, and everyone laughed.

He was fired the next day for sexual harassment. Apparently, his anger and resentment showed, and management decided he couldn't take a joke.

Millstone had invaded Holtorf's personal space. The resentment and anger that he felt were justified. He didn't deserve a pink slip from the company, he deserved an apology.

Corporations have no business digging into people's private lives. I tell my seventeen-year-old daughter, "If someone reaches into your blouse, run." The corollary for corporate cults is this: "If a corporation reaches into the 'bosom' of private feelings and emotions, run."

There's No Privacy in Corporate Cults

In the Victorian era, people were very private about their personal feelings and emotions. Opening up a *little* is a good thing. Going

on an afternoon TV talk show and spouting about your oddities
is insane. Acceptance of self is valuable, but the assumption that
acceptance is gained only by baring one's soul at any given moment is absurd. But that's how cults—and corporate cults—work.

There has been an open, even personal culture at Chicago-
based building products maker USG since CEO Bill Foote shared
with the company the painful eighteen-month agony of his wife's
struggle with and eventual death from cancer. Foote cut his travel
in half and reduced office time to have more for his children.[23]
While I admire Foote's actions, I have two questions: One, did it
take this life-altering event to get his priorities in order? And two,
didn't he have a family or community group to share with that
could have cared more effectively than a work group? There are
some things that it is better not to share. But in an era of secret-
telling and openness, everything and everyone is fair game. President Clinton set a bad example when he announced his preference
for briefs during a campaign appearance on MTV.[24] Did we really
want to know? Did we *need* to know? "The need to know is not the
point," writes Evan Imber-Black, a family therapist and author of
The Secret Lives of Families. "It used to be that people regarded their
private lives as treasures. Today, many have publicists putting the
information out, feeding the frenzy."

A person's private life used to be a *protected end in itself* that
was maintained in a private manner. The current environment has
changed private life into a purposely *exposed means to gain something else:* popularity and attention. "Many people mistakenly view
the workplace as a good place for baring the soul, but it's not," Dr.
Imber-Black says.[25]

"The more women and men do what they do in exchange for
money and the more their work in the public realm is valued or
honored, the more, almost by definition, private life is devalued
and its boundaries shrink," says Hochschild.[26] For unculted employees, work life supports private life. For corporate cult members, private life supports work life.

One Layer at a Time

One of my favorite people in the world is a former Xerox manager
named Rick Weintraub. It was while delivering a leadership semi-

nar with Rick that I encountered his favorite ice-breaker. "Tell the group something that no one in the room knows about you," he encouraged the attendees. Rick is well-meaning and sincere, and the question produced interesting stories and camaraderie. It's also a very common and effective cult technique.

The cult overtakes a member's "personhood" by getting the recruit to fully disclose secret sins, thoughts, and temptations to the group. This becomes a powerful tool that the cult can use to manipulate, blackmail, and emotionally bond members to the group. It is a means of depersonalizing the member or stripping him or her of the inner self and producing a forced submission to the group.[27]

Cult leaders delve into a person's psyche much like peeling an onion, one thin layer at a time. As the cult member incrementally discloses more intimate details of his or her personal life, control moves from the follower to the leader. Corporate cults are no different. The more they get the employee to disclose about his or her personal life, the most "stripped" and vulnerable to the corporation that employee becomes. When all the intimate details of "who I am" are exposed, the employee is left with only "what I do" as personal identity. That's when the individual becomes a committed member of a corporate cult.

If you're in Dale Holtorf's situation, it is painful and embarrassing, but it's better to be thrown from a careening vehicle than to crash with it. Some people *escape* corporate cults. Others, like Dale, are ejected. Get out any way you can! It's your choice to expose or conceal your personal life whenever you want. It's your identity; it's who you are. Don't give it up—to a cult or a corporate cult. People often expose themselves to a corporate cult because they are seeking love and meaning.

Looking for Love in All the Wrong Places

"People are constantly searching for meaning and purpose, trying to find their passion," says John Goldhammer, cult escapee and author of *Under the Influence*.[28] "Yet they continue to lose themselves in one group after another." He set out to discover how the "collective beast" operated. He found that organizations can't *give* to people without first *taking*. He's right. An organization exists only as a collection of members, and there are no magical, mystical resources that the organization can create separate from those already owned by its members.

New members of a cult are drawn in by "love-bombing,"[29] the practice of smothering an emotionally starved person with attention and affection. They are made to feel that everyone in the cult loves them and that nothing could be wrong with such a loving group of people. In corporate cults, this goes by the name of indoctrination training, culture class, and many other euphemisms. Love-starved people are hypnotized by the attention they receive as new members in corporate cults.

Kim Ode was a very popular feature writer for the *Minneapolis Star-Tribune*. She "Peter principled" her way into a feature editor's position. Since she was good at *writing* features, her editors made the absurd assumption that she would be good at *managing* writers of features. Actually, Kim was pretty good at the job. But she went back to writing after less than two years. "Managing the Generation X writers was a constant emotional struggle," she lamented. They don't accept themselves, so they seek acceptance from their coworkers in the organizational setting. They are prime candidates for corporate cults.

Middle management positions, like Kim's, are being washed out of company hierarchies for three reasons:

1. People are tougher to manage, so no one wants to do it.
2. Technology, particularly communications technology, is replacing the job middle managers used to do.
3. Pay is higher for doing high-value, very narrowly specific technical work than for managing work.

As mentioned previously, this downsizing contributes to the formation of corporate cults, because it removes old organizational structures from the middle of the competitive advantage selection model and moves employees to either end.

A Week in the Woods

New recruits are "love-bombed" at Sprint Paranet in Houston, Texas. The company first carefully selects employees for teamwork worthiness. Then new recruits are shipped off for a week in the woods, an intensive ropes course training and soul-sharing called "The New Hire Experience." "We're serious about culture around here," says Lisa Castillo, Sprint Paranet's employee development coordinator. "They (new hires) are immersed in the culture for enough time to be 'inoculated' with Sprint Paranet fever," says a coordinator. "The main goal is to pass along the Sprint Paranet Culture."[30]

At Sprint Paranet and many other organizations, employees' personal lives are being regularly invaded by corporations under the guise of "team building." In a fairly typical outing, thirty Ernst & Young executives spent five days of "enforced bonding" at Miravel spa near Tucson, Arizona. The consultants were forced to eat a vegetarian diet that centered on bean sprouts. The retreat's purpose was to "encourage more togetherness in the workplace and better health habits at home." Organizers encouraged meditation in a Zen garden.[31] This kind of personal invasion is clearly cultish. I predict a growing backlash against corporate cults that take over the personal lives of their employees via these pernicious techniques.

Creeping Socialism

The Ernst & Young anecdote uncovers an increasing reliance on groups. As I wrote this, Dallas was suffering through the second hottest summer in history. The ABC television network committed a *Nightline* segment to finding out how more than 100 people could die from heat exhaustion in an era of air conditioning.

"Alone" turned out to be the operative concept. The most recent victim had been a woman who was not known to her neighbors. She had cut herself off from the rest of the community, and numerous neighbors lamented that they had not stopped by to check on her. But they didn't even *know* her! None of them! Even the neighbor who had deposited many personal checks from the woman for cutting her grass couldn't recall her name.

The *Nightline* segment concluded that people were dying from the heat in un-air-conditioned homes because no one checked on them. In response, Dallas TV stations started running public service announcements encouraging people to check on their neighbors.

In a previous generation, family and neighbors would have checked on the woman. In this generation, the only community many people have is the one at work. The elderly woman in the *Nightline* story was retired. Without work, she was without family or community. One of the major reasons employees feel more at home at work is that they feel more appreciated and more competent there. Work is an emotional insurance policy against the uncertainties of home life, like being alone at the end of life.[32]

On a cold, wind-swept March day in St. Petersburg, Russia, I saw a baby carried by its mother. It was swaddled. Swaddling is the act of wrapping a baby so tight that it can't move its arms and legs. It's somewhat necessary in cold climates, but the Russians swaddle energetically, and continue to do so even after age and weather conditions no longer mandate it.

Swaddling was explained to me as a metaphor for life in the old Communist Soviet Union. A swaddled baby has no ability to do anything for itself. It is totally reliant on its adult attendant to take care of its every need. The metaphor says that swaddling is a way of discouraging independence and fostering state dependence among Soviet citizens. Creeping socialism does the same to American workers.

School used to be only from 9:00 to 3:00 on weekdays. In the 1960s, Head Start brought deprived children to school early for a healthy breakfast. It has been heralded as a successful and necessary program. There is currently a move to extend the school day beyond the dismissal bell in light of statistics showing that half of juvenile crime occurs between the hours of 3:00 and 8:00 P.M.

The after-school program is probably as necessary as Head Start. I'm not arguing the merits; I'm just observing that those types of group-care programs condition young people for a life in which many personal needs are met by a large corporate organization, as they are in corporate cults. Increasingly, organizations—whether corporate or governmental—are replacing the family as the source of nurturing in society.

Colin Powell Was Wrong

In a speech given before the Southwest Human Resources Meeting, General Colin Powell told of an interview that a network TV correspondent conducted with military personnel headed into the Gulf War conflict. The TV crew sought out a tank platoon that consisted of the typical Army cultural mix of whites, African-Americans, and Hispanics, all from different regions of the country and from different cultural backgrounds.

The reporter thrust the microphone into the face of a nineteen-year-old about to go into combat and demanded, "Are you ready, are you scared?" The cocky private responded casually, "We're ready, because we have trained for this. And I'm not scared," added the soldier, with a sweeping gesture to his platoon, "Because I am going into battle with my family."

Powell's emotional and challenging conclusion was, "If we can forge this group of culturally diverse individuals into a committed, unified fighting corps that would willingly die for each other, then there is hope for re-uniting a culturally divided America." He finished his stirring story to resounding applause.[33]

My unspoken response was a resounding *no!* There may be hope for reuniting a culturally divided America, but the example of the tank platoon is not how it will be done. The military is a cult. It is a societally sanctioned cult, which we allow to exist only because the mission of guaranteeing the freedom and sovereignty of the country is so important. As a society, we will not allow any other organization to use the techniques and tactics the military uses to instill commitment in a fighting unit.

The military's mission is important enough to justify the cultedness of military organizations. Selling copiers and making cars are not that important. People should always be an *end*, not a *means*. When they are used, as they are in the military, people are a means to an end. Granted, the end is important enough to justify the continuation of the best-known cult of our time, but we should not use it as a model for other organizations.

Us vs. Them

The military has long understood that *external* pressure on a unit increases *internal* cohesion. The stereotypical tough drill sergeant is the manifestation of the enemy to come for new recruits. The unit develops cohesion and commitment in order to survive the sergeant's persecution. The recruits coalesce into a tightly knit group because of the outside pressure supplied by the drill sergeant. They learn to cover for one another's mistakes and weaknesses, so that when they are in a real battle, they will fight as a team. It's a simple us-vs.-them concept.

The worst job I ever had was made miserable by the manager, who continually belittled all the employees. The only saving grace was that he was an equal-opportunity harasser. He made everyone's life miserable, so I had plenty of friends to commiserate with. He was the consummate micromanager who second-guessed every move and made a habit of degrading everyone's work. He once interrupted the review of my sales proposal to tell me I was stupid for leaving out a certain section.

Since he treated everyone in the company the same way, we all became great friends; we supported and comforted one another in the face of the negativity continually poured on us from our leader. We remain friends, six years after all of us left to escape this tyrant. The talented, independent people left. The weaker employees stayed because they were emotionally attached to the negativity and couldn't break free. He was the "drill sergeant" who provided the outside pressure that drove us together, increasing our cohesion inside the organization.

Sorry, General Powell, outside of the military, we should not allow cults like the tank platoon to exist. Only demoralized, emotionally weak people will stay in that kind of cult, where they are controlled by the leader. Eventually, the organization will die for lack of talent and diversity of input. The company in my example has died. I escaped after less than a year in that corporate cult.

I have stated clearly that the military cult is worth maintaining, but I wish General Powell would recognize it for what it is. Committing to forfeit your life for the organization seems to be the most convincing way of saying that the organization is more important than your family. Work also overtakes family in more subtle ways.

Work, the Best Excuse

Norman Kasal is a real estate specialist for the Motel 6 lodging chain. He tells of a family member who regards work as righteous.

"Work became the perfect excuse for not doing other things. Who could argue with work? And it made him look like the industrious, hard working, haggard and slightly deprived head of the household. Work was his badge of courage. 'Work had worked' as his excuse for years. We never count on him to show up on time for family get-togethers," says Norman. "He always arrives in a separate car." Over time, he established a "family" at work. These were friends who also worked all the time and stayed at the office.

Work can replace family without the force of the military behind it. But the anecdotes aren't all bad. There are some organizationally successful employers who choose to put family first.

Putting Family First

John Adams's retirement as chairman of the Houston-based unit of Chase Bank was a surprise to everyone in the industry, but the reason was not a surprise. "I've been here 25 years, and the bank's like a member of my family," Adams said. "But at the same time, it had put a lot of strain on my family."[34]

While I admire Adams's decision to put family first, his analysis seems rather confused. Was the bank a *part* of his family, or was the bank his family? I'm afraid the latter is true. That's why he had to leave a prestigious position, in which he enjoyed the work and had great success.

John Johnston is a firefighter in Waco, Texas. His department, like most others, works twenty-four hours on and forty-eight hours off. A firefighter can't take time off the way most other workers can, because fires can't be scheduled. This causes problems in the homes of many firefighters. A common complaint from spouses is, "I might as well be a single mother, because you're always at work, and I have to do everything myself anyway." This leads to a high divorce rate in the fire service.

Seeing so many tragic problems in their line of work tends to cause firefighters to trivialize problems at home. The spouse doesn't understand and gets angry because the firefighter seems unsympathetic.

The spouse doesn't understand, but guess who does? Other firefighters. So the firefighter soon gives up sharing with the spouse, because he or she doesn't understand. This further exacerbates the problem, because the firefighter draws further away from his or her biological family and closer to the work family. While at home, the firefighter begins to long for the comfort and emotional satisfaction of the firehouse. Work has become home, a place of emotional support and nourishment.

Firefighters are already a "family" by many aspects of the definition. Living together for twenty-four-hour periods means sleeping, eating, exercising, showering, even doing laundry together. Those are all family activities that are shared with their corporate family at the firehouse. People who work in those situations need to be especially wary of corporate cult behaviors.

The Police Family

A member of the cross-trained police, fire, and emergency medical personnel team at Dallas/Fort Worth airport tells of a fellow officer who had terminal brain cancer. He's proud that he and his fellow officers set up a schedule of continual care for their sick colleague. They took his two sons to baseball games, established a catastrophe fund, and prepared meals for the family. "It was amazing the amount of love and support that was offered to a member of our work family." During his last week of life, officers were stationed outside his hospital room day and night, to offer any assistance the family might need. When I asked if that seemed cultish to him, he responded, "I believe our department's culture is a cult, and should be looked on in a positive manner."

The work group truly became a family to this officer's biological family. It's difficult to condemn the department members for all the wonderful and caring things they did for the family of their colleague. However, I still think it points up the movement of the corporation into areas that traditionally were performed by the family. There is a dangerous blurring of the line between work and family. This is a conflict the family eventually will lose because it doesn't have the resources the corporation owns.

When Your Family Works With You

Auto parts manufacturer FelPro has turned families into a human resources competitive advantage. As a result of encouraging employees to recruit family members, fully two-thirds of the employees work alongside relatives. FelPro claims that this makes carpooling, daycare, and discipline problems easier to handle. The concept sounds decidedly Japanese, where employees conform to very strict organizational norms to avoid defaming the family's honor. In this technique, the corporate cult reaches into the family relationship system to control employees more effectively.

Corning is quite proud of its competitive advantage through research and development. Part of its plan for sustaining the advantage is to hire good people. It does so by hiring many husband-wife teams. One member of a husband-wife team commented, "I think Corning realizes that happy people tend to be more productive." I would agree; cult members are a very happy lot. So are corporate cult members.

Some corporate cult members have gone so far toward making work their family that they have even adopted "children" at work. Microsoft product manager Pamela Goldschmidt explained how her attention could be so consumed that she didn't know the details of her company's high-profile antitrust case. "These [new products] are my children," she explained.[35]

When work becomes a family, the workplace is a corporate cult. Specifically how the culture of corporate cults varies from that of unculted organizations is the subject of Chapter 5.

Notes

1. Thierry Pauchant, *In Search of Meaning: Managing for the Health of Organizations, Our Communities and the Natural World* (San Francisco: Jossey-Bass, 1998).
2. Evan Imber-Black, *The Secret Lives of Families* (New York: Bantam Books, 1997).
3. Scripps-McClatchy, "Extended Stay: Percentage of Moving Americans Has Fallen," *Dallas Morning News*, July 23, 1998.
4. Dana E. Friedman, *Linking Work-Family Issues to the Bottom Line* (New York: Conference Board, 1991).
5. Palmer Morrel-Samuels, "Employee Motivation & Performance Assessment of Chelsea, MI," in Sue Shellenbarger, *The Wall Street Journal*, July 22, 1998.

6. Cynthia Crossen, "How Can Families, Pets, Bosses, All Be Dysfunctional?" *The Wall Street Journal*, November 19, 1997.

7. Carolyn Corbin, *Conquering Corporate Codependence* (Englewood Cliffs, N.J.: Prentice-Hall, 1993).

8. Peter Block, *The Empowered Manager* (San Francisco: Jossey Bass, 1987).

9. Associated Press, "Ohio Firm Embraces Hug Policy," *Dallas Morning News*, January 28, 1998.

10. Andrea Petersen, "Metaphor of a Corporate Display: You Work and Then You Die," *The Wall Street Journal*, February 12, 1998.

11. Thomas Socha, *Managing Group Life*, ed. Lawrence Frey & Kevin Barge (Boston: Houghton Mifflin, 1997).

12. D. Conquergood, "Homeboys and Hoods: Gang Communication and Cultural Space," in *Communication in Context: Studies of Natural Groups* (Hillsdale, N.J.: Lawrence Erlbaum, 1994), pp. 23–55.

13. K. Lindsay, *Friends as Family* (Boston: Beacon Press, 1981).

14. Cynthia Crossen, "How Can Families, Pets, Bosses All Become Dysfunctional?" *The Wall Street Journal*, November 18, 1997.

15. Ibid.

16. Andrew Scharlach and Esme Fuller-Thomson, "Coping Strategies Following the Death of an Elderly Parent," *Journal of Gerentological Social Work* 21 (1994): 90.

17. Anne Fisher, "The 100 Best Companies to Work For," *Fortune*, January 12, 1998.

18. William A. Anthony, *The Art of Napping* (Burdett, N.Y.: Larson Publishing, 1997).

19. Ellen Gamerman, "Professionals Give Nod to Napping," *Dallas Morning News*, August 16, 1998.

20. Arlie Russell Hochschild, *The Time Bind* (New York: Metropolitan Books, 1997).

21. Ibid.

22. Fisher, "100 Best Companies to Work For," *Fortune*, January 12, 1998.

23. Sue Shellenbarger, "A CEO Opens Up About Loss and Finds He's a Stronger Boss," *The Wall Street Journal*, September 10, 1987.

24. Jean Nash Johnson, "Dirty Laundry," *Dallas Morning News*, August 15, 1998.

25. Imber-Black, *The Secret Lives of Families* (New York: Bantam Books, 1997).

26. Arlie Russell Hochschild, *The Time Bind* (New York: Metropolitan Books, 1997).

27. John Edminston, www.ultra.net, December 1996.

28. John Goldhammer, *Under the Influence* (Amherst, N.Y.: Prometheus Books, 1996).

29. Edminston, www.ultra.net.
30. Sprint Paranet New Hire Experience Brochure, Houston.
31. Tatiana Boncompagni, "Doing Hard Time at Corporate Retreat," *The Wall Street Journal*, 1997.
32. Arlie Russell Hochschild, *The Time Bind* (New York: Metropolitan Books, 1997).
33. Speech by Colin Powell, Southwest Human Resources Meeting, Fort Worth, Tex., October 10, 1996.
34. Andy Dworkin, "Adams Resigns Chase Texas Positions," *Dallas Morning News*, July 16, 1998.
35. Amy Harmon, "Microsofties Say They're Right as Rain," *The New York Times*, May 26, 1998.

Chapter 5

Organizational Culture: The Way We Do Things Around Here

*Y*ou may have noticed by now the similarity between the words *cult* and *culture*. Both have the same genesis; the word came from the concept of cultivating crops. In farming, the root word means preparing the soil for development of a prescribed kind of growth. In organizations, culture means preparing the organizational environment for development of a prescribed way of thinking and acting.

The thumbnail definition of corporate culture is "the way we do things around here." It varies a good deal among organizations, and managers are increasingly concerned about it, because it has a big effect on the bottom line. Even members of the Wall Street community are taking notice because there's a growing belief that nonfinancial factors like employee motivation have a direct effect on customer satisfaction and ultimately stock prices.[1]

"As little as one-third to one-half of most companies' stock market value is accounted for these days by hard assets such as property, plant and equipment," a Brookings Institution report says. "The growing share lies in soft attributes not traditionally viewed as assets at all, such as patents, processes and customer or employee satisfaction."[2] Through an elaborate 800-store study, Sears found that employees' attitudes about their workload, treatment by bosses, and eight other such matters have a measurable effect on customer satisfaction and revenue. When employee attitudes on ten measures improved by 5 percent, customer satisfaction jumped 1.3 percent and revenue 0.5 percent.[3]

As the U.S. economy moves from a production to a service economy, competitive advantage will move from production efficiency to customer satisfaction, as shown in Figure 5-1. Satisfying customers is much more reliant on culture than is production efficiency. It's relatively easy to replicate competitive advantage in a product or process, but it's very difficult to replicate culture. Corporate cults are trying to replicate culture just as Henry Ford replicated the assembly line process and McDonald's replicated the fast food service process. To do so, they first select members carefully, as explained in Chapter 3. Next, they replicate the culture by carefully and distinctly defining acceptable behavior in the organization.

Hofstede's indices provides an effective framework for analyzing how organizational culture is replicated in corporate cults.

Hofstede's Indices of Organizational Culture

Geerte Hofstede first gained fame when he surveyed more than 100,000 worldwide employees of IBM about their relationship with their organization. He factor-analyzed the results and determined four factors that distinguish national cultures. We have always known that national cultures differ, but we weren't exactly sure *how* they were different. Hofstede's resultant 1980 book *Culture's Consequences* answered that question.[4]

Hofstede then used the same methodology to differentiate among *organizational* cultures. You've been in many different organizations and noticed that their cultures differed, but you probably couldn't categorize the differences. Hofstede performed this task

Figure 5-1. Basis of Competitive Advantage

Product	**Service**
Process	Culture
Efficiency	Behavior

for us in his 1997 book *Cultures and Organization: Software of the Mind*.[5] Three metaphors are expressed in the complex, but meaningful title.

First, the computer has hardware that can be seen, but it's run by software that can't be seen. Second, you have a body that can be seen, but it's run by a mind that is unseen. Similarly, organizations have visible elements like people and buildings and output that can be seen, but they are run by culture, which can't be seen.

Hofstede says that the culture that runs organizations is like the software that runs computers and the mind that runs bodies. It invisibly performs the management function. Like the wind, we can see its *result*, but we can't see *it*. Hofstede helps us "see" the organizational culture by categorizing it according to six measures.

The measures are indices, so organizations are not either/or, they are along a spectrum from one end of the index to the other. If we could compare every organization by placing it appropriately along the index, we could see the variance among organizations on any of these indices. The measures are relative to other organizations.

The six elements for measuring organizational culture enable us to determine the level of cultedness in any particular organization. The six elements are shown in Figure 5-2.

Process vs. Results

Most sales organizations honor results. The general attitude is, "We don't care how you get orders, just get 'em." These organizations are unculted, because individuals are free to pursue their own method of business transaction.

Choice is the major differentiator between culted and unculted organizations. Individuals have choices in unculted organizations

Figure 5-2. Hofstede's Indices of Organizational Culture

Process...	vs.	....Results
Organization..................................	vs.	....Individual
Worker..	vs.	....Job
Open..	vs.	....Closed
Tight Control................................	vs.	....Loose Control
Practical..	vs.	....Pragmatic

and don't have choices in culted organizations. Members of culted organizations may *have* choices, but organizational coercion keeps them from being exercised. Culted employees have turned over the right to make those decisions to the organization.

Organizations on the process end of the index are culted, because the manner of acting and reacting in the organization is distinctly prescribed. As in the specialist collection, employees were selected for membership in the organization because of their behavioral patterns, so maintaining these patterns is extremely important. Members self-select to corporate cults because they *like* the process of the organization. It is the continuity of behavior that provides predictability and stability for the corporate cult member.

This may seem counterproductive for the organization—i.e., if only the process is honored, where is the efficiency of performance that is claimed for the specialist collection? It's found in the commitment to the organization, as shown in Figure 5-3. The process defines "what I do," which is measured in quantitative terms, which defines "who I am." Thus, the genesis of ego support in a corporate cult is the process. Success is defined by process performance. The important question is not "Did you get the job done?" but "Did you do it in the prescribed manner, based on corporate cult rules?"

I once worked for Penn, the tennis ball company, a subsidiary of General Tire & Rubber. At Penn headquarters in suburban Pittsburgh, four product managers' offices lined the hall next to the president's office. A humorous game of "face time" developed along the hall. The first to go home was shamed and the last was somehow honored. Who was there to honor him was another question, but you see my example. The process for success in the organization was based on the number of hours spent at the office, not on performance in the marketplace.

Organization vs. Individual

This index is perhaps the most important measure of corporate cults. Corporate cults honor the organization over the individual.

Figure 5-3. Causality of Ego Maintenance in a Culted Organization

Process	→	What I Do	→	Quantitative Measures	→	Who I Am

Chapter 1 makes the case that the tension between wanting to be an individual and wanting to be a member of an organization is at the heart of management theory. Virtually all theories and practical applications, from TQM to empowerment, from reengineering to teams, attempt to achieve the proper balance between the power of the organization and the power of the individual.

This is the key to life in a corporate cult: The member feels like an individual, but in reality, she has simply found a corporate cult that is highly aligned with her individual values—or she has aligned her values with those of the organization. The member is *willingly* subservient to the organization, so she describes herself as being at the individual end of this spectrum. But by any reasonable measure, she is at the organizational power end of the continuum.

"Softies" from Microsoft are proud of the individualism that allows them to work all hours of the night. Employees are trying to replicate the formula they have seen applied to their recent predecessors: A few years of hard work lead to riches. Their sense is, "If I subvert my own interests to the organization for an intense, short period, that will serve my own interests, which are to be rich."

The sad part of the story is that for a charmed few, the formula works, as it does for a charmed few early entrants in multilevel schemes. The latecomers end up stuck in the corporate cult as long-term servants to the organization. But again, here's the surprising part: They still *feel* as if they are being honored as individuals.

The military, the archetypal corporate cult, is at the extreme organizational end of this index. The military trains its members to be very standardized, producing a group that thinks and acts alike. The purpose of mimicry in the military is to produce a group of individuals who subvert their own needs to those of the organization.

Members of the military often enjoy this "higher calling" because it's their first discovery of a cause greater than themselves. Subservience is important to the functioning of the military, because command is essential to success in battle. The officer must be able to command the soldier to subordinate his personal interests to those of the group.

Similarity also allows for quick replacement in times of crises, like battle. In peacetime it allows for ease of replacement in duty assignments. The ability to predict a group member's actions allows for easy change of duty. So, "what I do" can easily be changed, because "who I am" is the same throughout all the troops. "Who they are" are soldiers who have subordinated their individual interests to the interest of the whole.

On the other end of the spectrum, we find organizations that honor the individual. An organization that honors the individual is something of an oxymoron, because the purpose of all social organizations is the perpetuation of the organization, which is gained through subjugation of individuals. But remember, the indices of organizational culture compare organizations *against other organizations*, not against an absolute standard or definition. So there *are* organizations that honor the individual more than others do.

An example is Trammel Crow, the highly successful national real estate company, which encourages employees to essentially start and run their own businesses under the umbrella of the parent corporation. The process has produced numerous millionaires and lots of satisfied employees.

Worker vs. Job

Corporate cults honor the worker, not the job the worker is doing. Corporate cult members are hired for who they are, not what they do. This is the most noticeable difference between the old-style economic cults known as company towns and the new emotional corporate cults. Corporate cults at the turn of the twentieth century culted workers by economic means. Corporate cults at the turn of the twenty-first century cult workers by emotional means. The burgeoning factory system in the early 1900s brought about a wrenching change in society as the economic environment changed from agriculture to industry. Through this change, workers were reduced to chattels who existed only to perform work in the growing factories of the booming Industrial Age. In those sweatshops, the job being performed was honored over the needs of the individual worker.

Emotional corporate cults of the twenty-first century are the opposite. People join not for economic survival, but for emotional survival. In corporate cults, they find the attention they have not received from the other circles of their lives: family and community. The corporate cult becomes their family and community, to the exclusion of their biological family. So, it is through honoring the worker over the job that corporate cults find and retain members

Open vs. Closed

Corporate cults are closed; unculted organizations are open. There are two ways to operationalize this measure. The first is to consider how difficult it is to gain entry into the organization, and the second is to consider how tightly the organization guards information.

Entry Into the Organization

Most churches are relatively open. You can show up Sunday morning and be a member by noon.

Students tell me that the university where I teach is more difficult to get into. They have to pay an application fee, submit transcripts, sign numerous papers, and survive at least one interview.

Jobs have varying entry requirements as well. It's pretty easy to get a job at McDonald's: You complete a short application and one interview. To get hired at Southwest Airlines, candidates for employment must go through six different interviews to determine if they have "spirit."

Corporate cults are careful about selecting people for the organization, because only a certain type will fit. Corporate cults are specialist collections in which only narrowly prescribed personality types are allowed. If you aren't the type the organization is looking for, you don't get in.

Running Candidates Through a Narrow Screen

Norman Brinker created the casual dining segment of the restaurant industry when he started Steak & Ale. Before he did this, restaurants between expensive steak houses and fast-food places didn't exist. He sold Steak & Ale and started Chili's under the umbrella of Brinker International. He had a wonderfully successful run of new restaurant ventures through the late 1980s and early 1990s, including Romano's Macaroni Grill, Grady's, Cozymel's, and Baker's Corner restaurants.

Brinker International believes the greatest determinant of individual restaurant success is not location, the food, or the atmosphere. It's the manager. That's why, early in Brinker's career, he committed resources to determine what makes a successful restaurant manager. He called in a group of industrial psychologists and asked them to test his most successful managers to see what made them tick. The battery of tests determined that these successful managers had three dominant characteristics: (1) they were very high Type A people who never hesitated to take charge, (2) they worked well with people, and (3) they were highly intelligent. You can probably guess Brinker's orders to his recruiters: "Get me some more of these!" And they did. Through a long-term relationship with the same consultants, Briker has continued to refine the equation. In doing so, it has perpetuated the narrow stereotype of its restaurant managers.

That's good because it produces successful restaurants. It's bad because it produces corporate cults, or what authors Greg Dess and Joe Picken call the "dominant logic."[6] This means that employees all think alike. When restaurant managers in the Brinker organization do well, they are promoted to regional managers, and eventually into the corporate office. They are replaced by new restaurant managers who have the same personality type. There is a very clearly defined dominant logic in the organization. The route up the corporate ladder is well defined as "who you are," not "what you do."

Homogeneous vs. Heterogeneous Advantages

Studies have shown that heterogeneous groups make more effective decisions than homogeneous groups, because they have more diversity of input. One particular study goes further: It says that groups that have higher levels of conflict make better decisions than those in which everyone agrees.[7] So, what's going on here? How can these organizations be successful when they select from a narrow personality band? Won't the homogeneity of the group limit the organization's effectiveness? Yes—and no.

Yes, because the narrow personality band will produce a dominant logic. No, because the narrow personality band that is used to populate corporate cults tends to cut across other, more typically

defined measures of diversity. So corporate cults have a homogeneity of personalities, but a rainbow of race, ethnicity, gender, and
religious differences. Microsoft has found that "Softies" come in
all colors, and Southwest Airlines has found "spirit" in people
from many different racial backgrounds.

Sharing or Guarding Information

The second way of looking at open versus closed is to measure
how openly the organization shares information with the public.
Suppose the phone rang and the caller announced, "It's CBS; our
60 Minutes film crew will be there in ten minutes." In an open
organization, the receptionist would reply, "Great, come on over!"
In a closed organization, the receptionist would drop the phone
and lock the door.

I taught an organizational behavior class to engineers at Lockheed Martin Corporation recently. Lockheed is a defense contractor, and this particular division makes missiles. I had to complete
a form and have a picture taken for a pass that I was required to
wear while I was on the Lockheed campus. There are metered
gates at all employee passages that monitor a special mircochip in
the badge. The device tracks and logs every employee's arrival and
departure times throughout the day. The company periodically
performs audits to verify that the electronically recorded times are
accurate and in line with the work performed by that individual.

The organizational culture at Lockheed is understandably
closed, because it is a defense contractor. As a matter of fact, there
is some indication that Lockheed is pretty open with information,
as evidenced by the release of the book *Augustine's Travels* by former CEO Norman Augustine.[8]

The next semester I called to ask if students in a team-building
class could observe a team meeting at Lockheed. The immediate
answer was no. When I phoned two different divisions of GTE
with the same request, the unqualified answer was, "Sure, send
'em over!"

Corporate cults are closed; unculted organizations are open.

Tight Control vs. Loose Control

Corporate cults are tightly controlled; unculted organizations have
loose control.

A proverb distributed over the Internet states, "The early bird gets the worm, but the second mouse gets the cheese." Unculted organizations honor innovation and new ways of solving problems that continually renew the organization through intrapreneurship. They reward the early bird by allowing her to get the worm. Culted organizations "cut off the head" of the innovator in an attempt to keep the organization under strict control. It's the second, third, or fourth person to try a new method that finally "gets the cheese."

Reach Out and Touch Your Employees

One way of maintaining control over employees is for the corporate cult to "reach out and touch" the employee. Technological improvements in communication make this easier. A small study in the gas and oil industry measured the number of instantaneous communications devices used by managers to stay in touch with their subordinates. All the supervisory-level managers had at least one of the following: pager, E-mail, and cellular phone. Among middle managers, all of them had at least one such device and more than two-thirds had more than one.[9]

Of course, the claim is that this makes the employee more productive and more responsive to customers, and ultimately produces more rewards for the employee. It also allows the organization to maintain closer control over employees and prevents them from separating from the organization.

UPS is known as a bastion of scientific management, in which delivery people are measured on even the slightest detail. Drivers are taught to walk four to six feet per second, carry packages under the left arm, and enter the truck with the right foot. This high level of control has made UPS a very successful company. The only freedom experienced by the drivers was when they were on their route alone, delivering packages. Until now. The delivery staff is upset about the new electronic signature pad that automatically records when and where the driver makes each delivery. This "electronic umbilical cord" enables supervisors to analyze each stop made by the driver and to literally question his or her every move.

Like many other elements of corporate cults, instantaneous electronic communications devices are presented under the guise of freeing the worker, when in actuality they are enslaving the worker, putting him or her under the control of the organization.

This index of control is most easily measured by comparing employees at the same level in two different corporations. The corporate cult will force the employee to get a lot of approvals before taking action, whereas the unculted organization will require few or no approvals. The interesting thing about corporate cults is their public accentuation of the *freedom* employees have, so that employees *feel* that they have a great degree of control. It's only when they are compared with employees at the same level in other corporations that differences in control levels are discovered.

A second way of measuring control is to compare the expenditure freedom of employees at the same level in different corporations. Corporate cults allow the employee only small expenditures without managerial approval, whereas unculted organizations allow the employee a great deal of latitude.

Total Quality Management overused the example of Japanese auto manufacturing plants, where each employee was empowered to "pull the rope" and stop the assembly line when product quality was threatened. Upon further research, you would find a huge corporate culture stigma *against* "pulling the rope." Yes, you can pull it whenever you want, but you'd better be ready to face the consequences of your action. Pulling the rope means that you are accusing a teammate of inferior work. The inquisition that follows the rope pulling isn't worth the hassle. Thus, even though the written rules approve rope pulling, the culture disallows it through severe punishments.

This is how corporate cults function: They state great freedoms and accentuate them with "brightly colored ropes" and statements of empowerment and liberation. But their unwritten mores and culture produce exactly the opposite. Sure, you have the power to pull the rope. But before doing so, you should check to see if it activates a trap door under your feet. When you pull the rope in a corporate cult, you are accusing a fellow member of not living up to "who I am." Complainers and rope pullers don't fit into corporate cults.

Practical vs. Pragmatic

In this usage, practical is the means of action and pragmatic is the consequence. Corporate cults focus on the practical, or means for accomplishing goals, rather than on the ends, or results of actions.

Life in corporate cults is highly driven by controlled behaviors. There is a belief that something greater than the individual exists: the corporation and its rules. The codes of behavior become sacrosanct.

"Theirs not to reason why, theirs but to do and die."[10] The Light Brigade charged into the valley knowing that the result would be death. But they lived and died by the commitment to a higher calling, the ideal that following orders was greater than life itself. Corporate cult members don't chafe under this set of strict rules. On the contrary, they *thrive* under strict rules. Corporate cult members gain identity from affiliation with the corporation, and thus rule-following enriches their lives and their identity. Without group identity, they would have no identity at all. They faithfully labor under the rules because that's where they find direction and meaning for their lives.

Unculted organizations are more practical in their operations. They allow individuals to figure out which means are best for achieving the end, for both the group and the individual. These organizations set off with a goal in mind and assign projects to thinking people with good judgment to complete them. Leadership states the goal clearly and often, then allows members the freedom to figure out how to reach the goal.

This index of practical vs. pragmatic is based on two major ethical concepts. Pragmatic thinking is nonconsequential, and practical thinking is consequential.

Unculted organizations apply consequentialist thinking, which is behavior that focuses on the outcome. It can be summed up in the statement, "The ends justify the means." It is a godless way of thinking, because it assumes that humans are the highest form of being and that their "big brains" enable them to make the right choice that produces the greatest benefits.

Consequentialists in business will rape the environment, exploit workers, cheat government regulators, shortchange customers, and steal from competitors, as long as the outcome is a profit for their corporation. The only reason for a consequentialist to follow rules is to avoid getting caught. Companies run by consequentialists don't sound like very good organizations to work for, a fact that corporate cult leaders like to use in recruiting and retaining members.

Corporate cult leaders like to use consequentialists as whipping boys in their crusade to convince prospective members of the righteousness of their group. A corporate cult leader will argue that there is a proper form of conduct, and that he has found it.

Corporate cults apply nonconsequentialist thinking. They believe that there is a correct way to do things, no matter what the outcome might be. They don't believe that the ends justify the means. They concentrate on the means. Corporate cults take this point of view, and that's what makes them attractive to people with metaphysical or mystical belief patterns.

Nonconsequentialists are found in corporate cults because they believe that there is a proper, correct, or righteous way of acting. This aspect is critical to commitment in religious cults. Members join them and remain committed to them because of their higher calling. They believe that there is "proper" and "improper" conduct and that their cult has discovered the rules for proper conduct. Their beliefs are so strong that they are willing to die to defend them. This is the extreme form of nonconsequentialism: a belief that behavior is so right that no matter what the cost, the member will act this way. While this is admirable in many settings, cults have subscribed to a wayward form of conduct, and corporate cults have done the same. Corporate cult members have determined the proper form of conduct and continue to do it, even though the consequences may be dire. The only difference between religious cults and corporate cults is the direction of devotion. Religious cult leaders claim to direct followers' devotion to God, when they actually direct it to themselves. Corporate cult leaders claim to direct devotion to conduct, when they actually direct it to the organization.

Ashby's Requisite Variety

Organizations thrive on standard rules. Concise rules make running the organization easier, but they make things tougher for people in the organization. The concept of simple rules is exemplified by speed limits. When state speed limits were federally regulated, there was a national code stating that only interstate highways outside of city limits could have a 65 mph speed limit; all other highways had a maximum of 55. That meant that on Texas state highway 287, the speed limit on the 420 miles from Fort Worth to Amarillo was 55 mph, even though it is a four-lane divided highway.

Ashby's requisite variety states that only variety can regulate variety.[11] As the environment becomes more complex, a more complex rule structure is needed to deal with it. If Ashby's requisite variety were applied, there would be numerous different speed limits on highway 287, perhaps ranging from 20 in school zones to 90 on open stretches of highway. Ashby's law would call for a variety of speed limits to reflect the varied conditions along the route.

However, the rules were made to satisfy the rule enforcers, not the rule followers. It's easier for the enforcers to have only one speed limit, and to bend the desires of all the drivers to one set standard. They enforce one speed despite the displeasure of the highway users. A complex environment demands a complex set of rules.

But not in corporate cults. They claim that they favor "people doing their own thing" and "empowerment" by having only a few rules. This is supposed to free employees to structure their jobs as they wish, but in actuality it has the opposite effect. A small number of rules averages out the effects on the workforce, thus satisfying only the "average" employee, who doesn't exist, and dissatisfying everyone else. The intent is to satisfy everyone an "average" amount, but the effect is to dissatisfy everyone—except the corporate cult, whose life is made easier by having fewer rules to enforce.

Corporate cults are often the worst violators of Ashby's requisite variety. By grouping everyone under the same codes, they force conformance to a standard set of rules for everyone to follow.

Rising Above a Slimy Culture

Toni Trueblood had covered the White House for Metromedia radio network and was at the top of her industry as the cohost of a popular Dallas morning drive-time radio show when she got sick and tired of the culture of the organization she worked for. Her cohost was having a public affair with his producer. The fact that they were both married didn't keep them from appearing at public events together to promote the radio station.

When Toni appealed to management to do something about this, they said that they had no evidence, and that it was a personal problem that didn't affect business.

Perhaps it didn't reflect badly on the radio station, but Toni felt it reflected badly on her. She described the environment at the radio station as "just slimy." She quit and moved her talent to another radio station where she felt more comfortable with the environment.

Toni's story serves as an example that often "what we do" becomes a part of "who we are." Humans don't have an impenetrable shell around them. Toni could not stand the sliminess anymore. She could not maintain her own integrity and self-respect while working in a narcissistic organizational culture. She could metaphorically wade through the slime for some time period, but eventually it began to creep up over her boots.

She quit—not because she could not separate what she did from who she was, but so that she could separate who she was from what she did. The organizational culture was so oppressive that her shell was not tough enough to withstand it. Her hip boots were not high enough, and they could not be stretched to be high enough. I am proud of Toni. She maintained her self-worth by separating who she is from what she does. Who she is is more important, and she preserved that by quitting.

Changing Culture

My Ph.D. dissertation studied U.S.-Russian joint ventures as a means of risk reduction for internationalizing companies. One of the first Russians I met was a Russian theatrical director. I met him at a friend's house, where he was a dinner guest. I was interested in business education, so before dinner, I explained my off-the-cuff plan for the future of Russian business. "It seems to me," I stated pontifically, "that students who reach the college level in Russia are well screened, so they are good students. They have a good grounding in math, science, the arts, and literature."

"Yes," he proudly confirmed.

"So, it seems to me," I continued, "that if those well-educated young people are just given a patina layer of free-market indoctrination, you could turn the country from socialist to capitalist pretty quickly."

The director thoughtfully gazed at the ceiling, as though he were trying to think of the correct English word. He wasn't. He was recalling a story. "Have you heard about the building of grass tennis courts in Russia?" he queried. I had worked in pro tennis in the 1970s, and I was quite sure there were no grass tennis courts in Russia. "No," I played along.

He launched into his story with great zeal and interest, reflecting his experience as an actor and a director. "Well," he said, "Russians decided they want to build grass tennis courts, best in world." He spoke with a heavy accent, leaving out many of the articles: "They go to best in world, Wimbledon. Managers at Wimbledon take them to courts, they give specific instructions. You know, the British love precision." He beamed at me. "Kneeling on court, they say to Russians, this is how to build grass tennis courts:

1. Remove two meters of dirt.
2. In hole, put exactly 50 centimeters of #5 brick sand from Meriweather.
3. Then add 15 centimeters of gray clay from the North Sea
4. Then add 15 centimeters of sheep dung from Scotland.
5. Then add 10 centimeters of washed #10 brick sand from Gloucester.
6. Then add 10 centimeters of diatomaceous earth from Whitestall.
7. Pack well.
8. Spread tuff grass seed at exactly 50 seeds per square centimeter.
9. Water, and cut, each day . . . for 200 years."

His right hand was still making a scissors motion in the air when we were called to dinner. The story was over. When I visited Russia a few months later, I discovered that he was right; changing culture takes a long time.

I've lectured in universities in St. Petersburg and Moscow. At a lecture to graduate students at Bauman University in Moscow, I felt that the lesson was going very well. The graduate students were attentive and nodded their heads in agreement as I spoke. When I asked for questions, a student eagerly asked about a business strategy model: "Dr. Arnott, in this model, who sets the price?" The simple statement that the price was set by the convergence of multiple suppliers and buyers would not be understood by this class who had grown up in a socialist system. After seventy years of socialism, the country was not going to change quickly. People's programmed way of thinking would not allow them to consider a system in which prices were not set by some overarching power.

"Water and cut, for 200 years." That's how long it takes to change culture. And it's an indication of how firmly culture is embedded in corporate cults. Chapter 12 offers advice for avoiding corporate cult membership. Here's a preview: Don't try to change your organization. Remember the dicta, "Water and cut every day, for 200 years."

A Case Study

Eaton Corporation created a corporate cult under the guise of empowerment at its forge plant in South Bend, Indiana.

- Empowerment was considered a near-religion.
- A team that produced a batch of defective goods was brought before the entire staff to explain its misstep.
- Employees were subject to daily locker searches, conducted under the banner of empowerment, by fellow employees.
- An underperforming team was hauled up before the workforce for a vote of excommunication.
- A worker who clashed with others was ordered to visit a shrink.
- A team's questioning of a fellow member explored fights with his girlfriend and other personal matters.
- Managers were replaced by "vision supporters."
- New hires were indoctrinated with company lingo in standardized training sessions. *We* is acceptable; *I* and *you* aren't.[12]

Corporate culture, "how we do things around here," varies a great deal among organizations. Corporate cults tend to honor the process over results, the organization over individuals, worker over job. They are more closed than open, have tight control, and are more practical than pragmatic. Hofstede's indices give us a feeling for the overall organizational culture at corporate cults. But by definition, cults have three characteristics: devotion, charismatic leadership, and separation from community. The following three chapters focus on those traits.

Notes

1. Sue Shellenbarger, "Businesses Compete to Make the Grade as Good Workplaces," *The Wall Street Journal*, August 27, 1997.
2. Sue Shellenbarger, "Companies Are Finding It Really Pays to Be Nice to Employees, *The Wall Street Journal*, July 22, 1998.
3. Anthony J. Rucci, Steven P. Kirn, and Richard T. Quinn, "The Employee-Customer Profit Chain at Sears," *Harvard Business Review*, January 1998.
4. Geert Hofstede, *Culture's Consequences: International Differences in Work-Related Values* (Berkeley, Calif.: Sage Publications Inc., 1980).
5. Geert Hofstede, *Cultures and Organizations: Software of the Mind Intercultural Cooperation and its Importance for Survival* (New York: McGraw-Hill, 1997).
6. Joseph Picken and Gregory Dess, *Mission Critical* (New York: Irwin, 1997).
7. S. W. Litterer, "Conflict in Organizations: A Reexamination," *Academy of Management Journal* 9 (1966): pp. 178–186.
8. Norman Augustine, *Augustine's Travels* (New York: AMACOM, 1997).
9. Hussein Barzin, "Instantaneous Communications in the Oil & Gas Industry," unpublished paper, 1997.
10. Alfred, Lord Tennyson, "The Charge of the Light Brigade," *The London Examiner*, December 9, 1853.
11. W. R. Ashby, "Variety, Constraint, and the Law of Requisite Variety," in W. Buckley (ed.), *Modern Systems Research for the Behavioral Scientist* (Durham, N.C.: Duke University Press, 1968), pp. 129–136.
12. Timothy Aeppel, "Not All Workers Find Idea of Empowerment as Neat as It Sounds," *The Wall Street Journal*, September 8, 1997.

Chapter 6
Devotion to a Corporate Cult

*C*orporate cult members have three characteristics: They are devoted to their organization, they have a charismatic leader, and they are separated from their community. This chapter describes the first characteristic, devotion.

Devoted to the Wrong Thing

Employees often misplace devotion by committing those things to organizations that should be given to family and community. The following anecdotes exemplify how that's done.

Sherry watched as her husband became "a different man from the one I knew." He was director of human resources at an energy company. They had been married ten years when he took on a reengineering project at work. He spent all his energies on work. The new project was all he thought about. "When we had dinner out, even vacations, they were always with [fellow employees]," said Sherry. "When I asked for time together, he pulled out his Franklin Planner to see if he could fit me in."

Sherry got a divorce. Ironically, she now sees herself caught in the same trap, having taken on a project to install a new software system to control benefit costs in the human resources department she directs. Since taking on the project, she says, "Who I am is what I do. I arrive at work at 6:30 A.M. so that I can do my schoolwork [she takes college courses at night] before other people get to the office. I usually leave about 8:00 or 8:30 P.M., although many days I exercise at the company health club before leaving the building. It helps me relieve some of the stress of this project."

I asked whether, had she been living this workstyle (which mirrored her husband's) when she was married, *her* workstyle would have caused the divorce. "Oh no," she responded confidently. "He never would have noticed I wasn't there."

Sherry's husband started working at the energy company with the same attitude most workers had. Like Odysseus, he *loved* his wife, but he was *devoted* to work. As time wore on, he became more attached to the rewards at work than to the rewards at home, or he thought he could have both: the rewards of work and the satisfaction of a marriage. He thought he could take his marriage relationship for granted. This is an all-too-common story, which we have all heard at one time or another.

"I guess, basically, I am a people pleaser," Sherry admitted. "The company likes people like that. Who we are is what we do. I call the office for my messages at least twice a day . . . even when I am on vacation. I guess I like the recognition. I feel important because someone has called me," she admitted. "I take it too personally. Someone called to complain about the new software system, and I defended it. After hanging up the phone, I realized it's just a stupid system; why did I take that personally? The caller wasn't complaining about *me*, he was complaining about the *system*. I was defending a piece of machinery! I wish I could have separated my personal value from the project, but I couldn't."

The reason she couldn't separate her personal feelings from the project was that she had become devoted to the project. That happens a lot in corporate cults. There are a lot of cultic features in the language she used to describe her workplace. After the divorce, instead of broadening her own life to avoid a corporate cult, she followed her former husband's track directly into one.

Sherry showed me her business card. Along with the company name and her name and title, the card carried the company's priorities: "Shareholders, customers, employees." "It's on every business card," said Sherry. "It's not right; employees should come first."

"Some people are bailing out of this culture," Sherry said. "We've had three people quit in just the last month. The president of the company, who was in line to be the next CEO, decided he was good at project management, but didn't want to lead the company. He is a real nice family guy in his mid-fifties. I cried when he left. He decided he wanted to spend more time with his kids and volunteer at his church. I admire his decision," she said.

"A second person was a vice president of human resources who had been with the company for twenty-three years. He was 41 years old and went through a self-discovery period. He just decided work wasn't worth it. The third was a lady with kids ages 15, 12, and 10 who said she couldn't be called in the middle of the night anymore."

Sherry was clearly devoted to her workplace. But perhaps not as devoted as members of "the Firm."

"The Firm"

Long before Tom Cruise played the part of a hot-shot young lawyer in *The Firm,* there was the *real* "firm." It's McKinsey and Company, one of the most prestigious, successful, and envied consulting businesses in the world.[1] One of the reasons McKinsey has been able to maintain its success is its strong organizational culture. Employees are called "members" and are conditioned to think and behave according to carefully scripted rules; they are told how to dress (men must wear long socks under a suit), and professional language is used in place of business language. McKinsey is called the Firm, never the company; jobs are "engagements," and the Firm has a "practice," not a business. Younger members are expected to live their lives for the Firm and to follow the rules, procedures, and dictates of tenured members. Punishment for breaking the rules is often subtle: A member may get overlooked for a committee assignment. When it's more overt, a member is asked to leave. All members know that complying with the carefully scripted rules is the greatest predictor of success within the Firm.[2]

Coincidentally, Trilogy Software in Austin, Texas, has been called "the firm" by potential employees because the company's lavish recruiting tactics resemble those of the notorious law firm Bendini, Lambert & Locke in the John Grisham novel. New employee Dana Glazer said her family joked that she was going to work for Bendini, Lambert & Trilogy.

Trilogy University is a boot camp for new recruits in which classes run from 8:00 A.M. to midnight. Trilogy caters meals and maintains a stocked break room to keep members from leaving the premises. For recreation, group trips are planned to nightclubs and the beach.

Starting salaries range from $45,000 to $90,000, but employees aren't hired to do a specific job. They are hired for who they are, not what they do. Two recruits handing out material in the hot sun on the campus of the University of Texas discovered that they had no money with them to buy drinks. They explained, "Trilogy has been doing everything for us," so they didn't think to carry money.

On a company trip to Las Vegas, employees were encouraged to place $2,000 bets on a roulette wheel. Trilogy would supply the money up front and would deduct losses from the employee's upcoming paychecks. Those who took the plunge bought $2,000 worth of notice from the Trilogy CEO—and a large dose of devotion.[3]

Trilogy University seems to have it all: devotion, charismatic leadership, and separation from community. The indoctrination procedures are clearly cultic, as they are in another, more widely known software company.

Devoted to Code

Members of corporate cults are devoted to the set of rules often known as a code of conduct. At Microsoft, "devoted to code" has a double meaning. Devotion is abnormally high at Microsoft because employees believe that they are doing something more than just writing code, they are changing the world. "Softies believe in the liberating nature of software and in their mission to deliver it to the world."[4] It's this kind of higher-level righteous belief system that forms a devotional bond between employees and corporations. Workers who believe they are providing a greater good for the world will readily sacrifice themselves to this higher calling. That's how devotion, the first dimension of corporate cults, gets established.

Chapter 8 explores the third dimension, separation from community, but the concepts naturally weave together, as shown in the following excerpt about Microsoft:

Insularity at Microsoft helps to reinforce a monolithic culture in which employees cultivate an almost fanatical devotion to their work and to Bill Gates, whose combative
cross-examinations on minute details are as legendary as
his accessibility by E-mail to the lowliest employee.[5]

This is reminiscent of the work as a dysfunctional family concept
portrayed in Chapter 4. Children who are beaten by their parents
remain devoted to them, just as employees who are mentally and
emotionally strafed by Gates remain loyal. "Even reasonably cyni-
cal people get starry-eyed over Bill," observed one of Microsoft's
newer managers.[5] Devotion goes beyond reason in corporate cults.
    America's largest software company has cultish traits, but so
does America's largest employer.

The Nation's Largest Employer

In mid-1997, retail giant Wal-Mart passed General Motors as the
nation's largest employer. While this major change exemplifies the
movement from a production to a service economy, it also presages
significant changes in how workers are connected to their workplace.
    By pushing more responsibility down through the organiza-
tion, Wal-Mart consistently ratchets up the stress level of employees. Its 687,000 employees are constantly pushed to improve
performance. Employees are tied to the organization through
profit sharing in Wal-Mart stock. Thus, employees' retirement
funds are determined by the organization's success.
    Wal-Mart is proud of its promote-from-within policy. About
60 percent of management-level employees started out as hourly
workers. However, the promotion to management is not as glori-
ous as it may seem: Most promoted people must move, and their
weekly hours increase from forty-five to fifty-one, with some weekend work thrown in.
    Employees' work is meticulously time-managed. They must
clock out for an unpaid one-hour lunch and two fifteen-minute
breaks each day. Nancy Handley is an hourly employee who manages a men's-wear department at a Wal-Mart in Missouri. When

her forty-five-minute commute is figured in, she spends eleven hours away from home and gets paid for seven and a half.[6]

Wal-Mart exemplifies how retail sector employees are easily culted. By investing retirement funds in company stocks, promising to promote from within, and not paying for lunch or rest breaks, service firms like Wal-Mart are buying the devotion of their workers. When employees use their 10 percent employee discount to buy everything from canned foods to clothes, they could be heard humming, "I owe my soul to the company store."

Long hours are expected of Wal-Mart managers. Every week, fifty to sixty regional managers board Wal-Mart's fleet of fifteen corporate aircraft to travel from store to store to reinforce the Wal-Mart culture and solve practical business problems. The typical manager in the group will spend 200 days a year doing this, in a job that has a life expectancy of only about eight years before burnout occurs. After solving problems all week, the regional managers attend a 7:00 A.M. Saturday meeting to go over their week's work and decide what needs to be done to keep operations improving.

"Neither Rain nor Sleet nor Dark of Night"

GEICO insurance relies heavily on advertising to produce phone call leads, which are processed at five call centers spread around the country. The devotion level of new recruits is tested by giving them working schedules that constantly change to accommodate the flow of incoming calls.

The calls can be instantly switched between the centers to manage workloads. This technology creates the possibility for worker flexibility, yet the company has a zealous attitude about worker attendance.

When an ice storm virtually shut down automobile traffic in the home city of one of the centers, GEICO refused to use the switching technology to accommodate its employees. It demanded that workers show up on time. It seems ironic that an insurance company would risk the health and lives of its workers simply to maintain company rules. The managers were given a technology tool that was designed to provide flexibility for the workforce. However, when implemented, it was used to produce exactly the opposite. The call center technology is used to *control* employees instead of to *empower* them. Devotion is a condition of employment in the call center. The corporate culture clearly says that phone calls are more important than employees.

The Ultimate Company Man

Shotze Loggins (not his real name) is devoted to his organization. He is in his fortieth year as a project manager at Lockheed Martin. Shotze could retire and earn almost as much as he now does by working. He's at the top end of the salary scale for his grade, so he doesn't get paid for overtime. But he is so devoted to the organization that he has typically worked ten-hour days and shown up when he is not scheduled to work.

He says that he enjoys work more than he enjoyed his last vacation. His office is adorned with photos of him shaking hands with current and previous company officials. After a recent heart attack, his doctor ordered him to work only half days. He's not the same old Shotze, according to his workmates.[7] Without work, Shotze has lost his zest for life. He was devoted to his organization. That's not a good thing to be devoted to.

How does this happen? Devotion does not occur overnight, it grows. The growing process is called "escalating commitment to a cause."

Escalation of Commitment

People like to think they make correct decisions in life. That's why, after making a decision, they sometimes go to extraordinary lengths to prove that the choice they made was the right one. The desire to avoid making bad decisions gets people caught in a trap called "escalation of commitment." A classic example is U.S. involvement in the Vietnam War. President Kennedy sent only advisers to Southeast Asia. Johnson escalated the war by first sending just a few defensive troops, then large-scale movement of troops took place.

Recently released presidential papers indicate that Johnson didn't end the war earlier because the Democrats had taken a public relations shellacking when they were seen as "soft" on Communism in the 1950s. They weren't about to let that happen again. By ending the war in Vietnam—which by all normative reasoning was the right thing to do—Johnson and the Democratic Party would have been seen as caving in to Communism. He wouldn't allow his party to take a defeat, so he continually escalated his country's commitment to a losing cause. Johnson and his advisers knew that it was a lost cause, so they kept much of the troop commitment secret.

Employee devotion comes from this same type of escalation of commitment to the workplace. In the chapter-opening example, Sherry's devotion was so great that she found herself defending an inanimate software system!

Here's how escalation of commitment affected my life. I was working for a Swedish beverage company called Pripps when it closed its U.S. operation after six years of trying to introduce a new sports drink. I had an adequate severance package, so I didn't have to rush into a new job right away. But after a few months of unemployment, I was anxious to do something. I accepted a job that was recommended by a lifelong friend. I was aware that the owner-manager of this small business could be gruff and nasty, but I thought I had enough maturity and self-confidence to handle it. We shook hands on terms of employment and agreed that I would draft a contract in a few days, and I started to work. When I presented the draft as agreed, he made an impassioned speech about how contracts were only for those who don't trust one another. I heroically tore up the contract and tossed it in his trashcan.

It was heroic, but stupid. I should have left the contract on his desk and told him I could be reached at home when he was ready to talk. I didn't because I had escalated my commitment to the job. Quitting just a few days after accepting the new position would have been an admission on my part that I had made a mistake. The job came as a result of a recommendation from a lifelong friend, through whom I was tied to many other professional colleagues whose respect I craved. Leaving in the first week would have been tough on my personal ego and my professional reputation. The decision to stay escalated my commitment to the company and made me devoted, even though I didn't want to be.

Of course, the real mistake was *starting* to work without a contract in the first place. I was anxious to get to work and to show my commitment to my new company. I put the identity of the organization in front of my personal identity. A year later, when I quit the organization to enter a Ph.D. program, I asked for the $10,000 bonus that was in the contract—which was now in its eleventh month in the landfill. The guy who didn't like contracts didn't remember that part of the agreement.

I made two escalation of commitment errors: starting to work without a contract, and continuing to work when the contract was questioned. Why did I do that? How could I have been so stupid? It wasn't stupidity; it was my fear of embarrassment over admitting I had made a mistake. I had a clear choice of individual independence or organizational membership, and I chose wrong. My pride wouldn't let me admit that I had taken the wrong job. I had escalated my commitment and couldn't get out. Fortunately, there were no deaths recorded, as in the Vietnam War escalation of commitment example, but there was a lot of emotional turmoil and pain for me.

Embarrassment is painful. Embarrassed people feel as though they are in public with no clothes on. If I could have mustered enough self-confidence, I could have withstood the embarrassment and saved my family and myself a lot of misery. Instead, I let my escalating commitment draw me deeper into the organization—at the expense of my personal well-being.

What Is Gen X Devoted To?

There are startling differences in the devotional ties that are felt by Gen X and those felt by previous generations. "There's a complicated emotional roller coaster in the lives of generation X. Life is chameleon-like, but that doesn't mean that Xers never latch onto anything emotionally. They do, but they are forced by circumstances to be more cautious caretakers of their emotional commitments, hedging a bit and always prepared for change."[8] Compared to other generational cohorts, Xers are the most independent. "Xers have lived their whole lives believing no institution can be trusted. Self-help is their only resource and their only protection."

This would seem to predict that Xers are so independent that they can't be culted. That's my hope, but I'm afraid it's not going to happen. Remember, the key descriptor of this generation is that there isn't a key descriptor. Affiliation is a need, so it must be satisfied somehow. Gen Xers do this by forming what are called "enclaves."[9] These are small groups, perhaps with six to eight members, that form extremely tight bonds of lasting friendship. When this information is allied with the data showing Gen-Xers' commitment to work, it makes them seem like prime candidates for corporate cult membership. Many of them will form enclaves in corporations, and thus become members of corporate cults.

Xers are the most peer-focused generation ever. They place an overwhelming reliance upon friends for advice about what to buy and what to believe. From private families to public institutions, the traditional sources of emotional sustenance don't work for Xers.[10]

Gen Xers satisfy the need for affiliation through untraditional, smaller, more tightly knit groups that meet on their own schedule with their own set of rules and conduct. When such a set of rules and conduct includes devotion, a charismatic leader, and separation from community, the group is a cult. When the group is in a business organization, it's a corporate cult.

Organizations Don't Exist

It's unreasonable that employees should be so devoted to organizations, because *organizations don't exist*. An overview of social science research is necessary background to explain what I mean.

Much of our understanding can be divided into *concepts* and *constructs*. It's like an iceberg floating in the sea. If you and I took a boat to the iceberg, we could climb onto it. We could observe the top of the iceberg through scientific exploration. We could see, touch, feel, and measure it. In this analogy, the top of the iceberg is a *construct*. It makes itself amenable to easy scientific observation. We know that there is another part of the iceberg below the water, but we can't observe it. In this analogy, the underwater part of the iceberg contains the *concepts*. These are the thoughts, feelings, and images that make up the culture of societies and organizations. Concepts exist only in our minds and are not easily measured.

Social science research attempts to tie below-water concepts to above-water constructs. For my Ph.D. dissertation, I studied organizational risk. I theorized that risk—a below-the-water concept—in U.S.–Russian joint ventures could be measured by seven quantifiable variables of the business collaboration.

An organization, the milieu that people have so much devotion to, doesn't exist because it's a concept, not a construct. I often challenge my students to "show me an organization." They will cite a building. "That's a building, not an organization," I reply. "How about the bank account?" a student suggests. "That's money, that's not an organization," I reply. "What about the organization chart?" the student attempts. "That's lines on a piece of paper," I reply. "Organizations are made up of people," they claim. "Yes," I answer, "organizations are a *collection* of people, but people are not the organization. People are people."

Frustrated, but hopefully enlightened, the students agree with authors Jensen and Meckling, who state that "organizations are legal fiction," meaning that organizations exist only in conceptual legal form, not in construct form. "Organizations are a nexus for contracting parties," say Jensen and Meckling.[11]

A nexus is a meeting place, as shown in Figure 6-1. In Jensen and Meckling parlance, Dallas Baptist University is a nexus for contracting individuals. I have a contract to teach; students have contracts for courses; the cleaning service has a contract to clean buildings; a book retailer has a contract to sell books. The nexus, or meeting place, of all those contracts is a place that in "legal fiction" exists as an organization that we call Dallas Baptist University.

However, this organization exists only to satisfy the individual contractors who make up the nexus. If I cancel my contract to teach, and the students cancel their course contracts, and the cleaner cancels his contract, and the bookseller cancels her contract, the organization that we know as Dallas Baptist University will cease to exist, because it will cease to be a nexus for contracting parties.

I like this definition, because it empowers the individual. Organizational participants tend to blame organizations for forcing them to do something they would rather not do. If organizations don't really exist, how can they force a person to do anything?

Figure 6-1. The Organization as a Nexus for Contracting Parties

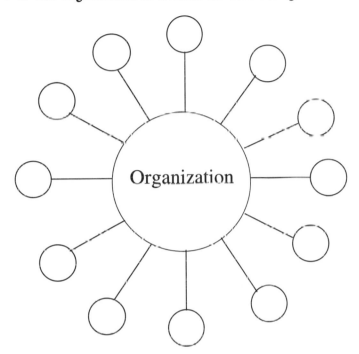

Only individuals, making individual decisions, give organizations movement and life. Organizations exist only as a *means* to accomplishing *ends.* They exist to meet people's needs.

If organizations don't exist, how can people be devoted to them? Good question. They shouldn't be. That's why corporate cultism is like worshiping a false god. Often, we confuse the organization with its cause. I am not devoted to Dallas Baptist University, but I *am* devoted to its cause, Christian higher education. And I can be devoted to the *people* in the organization, because people *do* exist. But devotion to an organization is foolish. Are you devoted to your organization? Figure 6-2 provides a list of devotion behaviors.

People have more value than the contracts they make. Organizations are a means to accomplishing ends. People are ends. Employees who join a corporate cult lower themselves from ends to means. When that happens, they replace individual identity with

Figure 6-2. Devotion Behaviors

Overdevoted Employees:

- Are always "fine".
- Don't take vacations.
- Work late often.
- Don't have friends outside the workplace.
- Get emotional about their work.
- Are overly serious about their work.
- Take work home on a regular basis.

organizational identity. That's tragic. Organizations are means that don't exist. People are ends that do. They exist in three parts: body, mind, and spirit.

Body, Mind, Spirit

The self can be viewed as having three elements: body, mind, and spirit. We should give our bodies and minds to the organization; we should reserve the spirit for more meaningful pursuits. The antagonist will ask me, "Dr. Arnott, are you saying that we should not care about our work?" No, I am not saying that. You should care about your work, and you should put your best effort into it: body and mind. But not your spirit.

You should put your spirit into the *cause* of the organization. For me, that is Christian higher education. You should put your spirit into the *people* of the organization. For me, they are the individual students, faculty, and staff. But employees who devote their spirit to an organization will be disappointed. They may have mistakenly given their devotion to the organization when they intended it for the cause and people the organization is allied with. Devotion to people and causes can produce long-term satisfaction, resulting in great fulfillment. Devotion to organizations provides very short-term satisfaction, resulting in severe disappointment.

When a Project Takes Over a Life

Joe, a successful engineer at a nationally known manufacturing company had never shown indications of becoming culted, and he had many interests outside the company. However, an unexpected fever of devotion overtook him, and it almost ruined his life. He was assigned to take on a project that had languished within the company for years. He devoted himself to the project and produced enough early success to convince management to proceed with development of the program.

Joe brought the demonstration phase to completion within the difficult time and resource budgets that had been set for it. When the program moved to the prototype phase, it was handed to a more senior engineer. He then spiraled into a cultish level of devotion, working extremely long hours every workday and weekends. He forfeited his outside activities, including a girlfriend.

Finally, deteriorating health forced him to take some time away from work. When he returned, he was transferred to another project. He felt betrayed and complained to his superiors that they didn't understand, he had "given birth" to the project and had a devotional attachment to it.[12]

Devotion to organizations and projects is improperly placed. Devotion should be reserved for family and community. It should not be wasted on corporate cults.

"I'm Fine"

How do you know if you have too much devotion for your workplace? The following story portrays a person whose response was perhaps not totally voluntary.

Farmer Jones was giving court testimony about an auto accident in which he had been injured. The fast-talking defense attorney was certain he could trip up the slow-talking farmer on the witness stand.

"Mr. Jones," he began, in rapid-fire style, "Is it true that soon after the accident, you uttered the phrase 'I'm fine'?"

Farmer Jones began his answer in a slow drawl. "Well . . . it was Tuesday," he droned.

"Mr. Jones, we know the accident happened on a Tuesday," interrupted the defense attorney. "Did you say, 'I'm fine'?"

Farmer Jones was unaffected by the interruption and continued his slow presentation of the facts. "I loaded my mule Betsy in the trailer to take her to town to see the vet."

"Mr. Jones, we know a mule was involved," interrupted the defense attorney again. "Did you say, 'I'm fine'?"

"I hooked the trailer to the truck, and we started into town," continued farmer Jones. "Where the county road crosses highway 11 a truck came out and hit us."

"Mr. Jones, we know where the accident happened," attacked the attorney. "Did you say, 'I'm fine'?"

Farmer Jones was still unaffected. "Betsy was throwed in the south ditch, I was throwed in the north ditch. Pretty soon a highway patrolman stopped. He went in the south ditch and I heard a shot. He comes over to me, with his gun still drawn and says, "Your mule was pretty bad off and I had to shoot her. *How're you?*"

And farmer Jones answered, "I'm fine!"

Wouldn't you?

Farmer Jones said "I'm fine" because he had seen what happens to people who *aren't* fine. The next time you are in the office, you might ask your fellow workers the same question, "How're you?" You are likely to get the same answer Mr. Jones gave the highway patrolman. Then you have to determine are they really fine, or are they artificially devoted to the organization because they have seen what happens to people who *aren't* fine?

Organizations need people who aren't "fine". They don't exist in corporate cults, at least not for very long. Members of corporate cults are always fine no matter what the circumstances. That's because they have learned to put the organization first and their personal lives second. They are always fine because they have seen what happens to people who aren't fine. Those who aren't fine leave the corporation, either by choice or by force. Corporate cults do not tolerate people who aren't fine. If people are "not fine," this indicates that there is something wrong with the corporation. Corporate cults cannot admit that things are wrong, because that would decrease the value of the corporation for those who are devoted to its existence for their emotional security.

The three traits of a corporate cult are devotion, charismatic leadership, and separation from community. This chapter explains individuals' devotion to the organization. Sometimes the devotion is directed to the charismatic leader, the topic of Chapter 7.

Notes

1. J. Huey, "How McKinsey Does It," *Fortune*, November 1, 1993.
2. Renee Meyers, "Managing Group Life," in *Communications in Organizations*, ed. Lawrence Frey and Kevin Barge (Boston: Houghton Mifflin, 1997).
3. Evan Ramstad, "How Trilogy Software Trains Its Raw Recruits to Be Risk Takers," *The Wall Street Journal*, September 21, 1998.
4. Amy Harmon, "Microsofties Say They're Right as Rain," *The New York Times*, May 26, 1998.
5. Ibid.
6. Louise Lee, "I'm Proud of What I've Made Myself Into—What I've Created," *The Wall Street Journal*, August 28, 1997.
7. Dam Nguyen, "Cultedness in the Defense Industry," unpublished paper, December 1997.
8. J. Walker Smith and Ann Clurman, *Rocking the Ages* (New York: Harper Business, 1997).
9. Ibid.
10. Ibid.
11. M. C. Jensen and W. H. Meckling, "Theory of the Firm: Managerial Behavior, Agency Costs, and Ownership Structure," *Journal of Financial Economics* 3, n. 5 (1976).
12. Author unknown, paper written for Organizational Behavior class at Dallas Baptist University, December 1997.

Chapter 7
Charismatic Leadership

*L*eaders of the economic corporate cults of the company town era unscrupulously strong-armed employees into submission. The workers didn't *enjoy* being in the company town, they were *financially enslaved* by it. The volunteer nature of the emotional corporate cults of the new century demands a very different leadership style, one that emphasizes employee empowerment. Members join the organization freely and are given a great deal of freedom within the broad confines of the corporation. They don't *feel* culted, but they are because they are following a charismatic leader who appeals to their emotions.

Corporate cult leaders often appeal to positive emotions, but not always: They may appeal to fear, uncertainty, and insecurity, to name just a few that are not positive.

Peter Arnell runs an advertising agency in Manhattan that has several high-profile fashion clients. His supporters say he is just a world-class taskmaster who relentlessly drives his employees to do their best.

But employees and clients also say they have heard and seen Arnell use foul and abusive language to reduce office workers to tears for the way they took a message, phrased a question, or cleaned the top of his desk. His behavior, many colleagues acknowledge, can often be miserable, even unbearable. Four former employees filed a lawsuit in U.S. District Court in Manhattan, seeking damages as a result of months of abusive tirades by Arnell.[1]

How Cult Leaders Manipulate People

Leaders of traditional cults use a standard group of mind-control techniques to ensure group conformity and control.[2] Many of the following ten cultic techniques are probably used by the leader of your corporation.

1. *Submission to leadership.* Cult leaders are strong, controlling, manipulative people who demand submission from members. This style was more prevalent in the old-style economic cults of the Industrial Age, when corporate cults were contained in company towns. In the emotional corporate cults of the Information Age, membership is voluntary, so it is maintained via the satisfaction of affiliation and affection needs.

2. *Polarized world-view.* The group is good, everything else is bad. This is called "either-or" thinking, and it is prevalent in children. By early adulthood, most people gain a better understanding of the "shades of gray" of life and adopt a dialectic style that allows good and bad elements to be considered at the same time. Some people who are raised in strict environments—religious or otherwise—fail to make this important change and thus are good candidates for corporate cults. Often, they are very competitive people whose only means of seeing relationships between organizations is to visualize their own company as good and the competition as bad.

A seatmate on a recent airline flight told me that she had been approached by a competitor about the possibility of changing jobs. She felt guilty for simply having had the conversation, even though she did nothing to initiate it. She has a very polarized view of the world. Microsoft president Steve Ballmer is famous for motivational presentations to the faithful that are virtually cheerleading sessions challenging employees to "smash our competitors."

3. *Feeling over thought.* Emotions, intuitions, and mystical insights are promoted as more important than rational conclusions. People join specialist collections because they want deeper involvement in the organization. That's what produces the emotional characteristics of corporate cults. Rational people join a collection of specialists because they want to concentrate on the task. By self-selecting to specialist collections that produce corporate cults, employees are primed to concentrate on the emotional, feeling side of the organization. Devotion to the organization and the leader is

developed by the use of metaphysical terms like visioning, clair-voyance, foresight, and prophecy. Goals are stated in qualitative rather than quantitative terms because this fits better with the affective entrapments used in corporate cults.

4. *Manipulation of feelings.* Techniques are designed to stimulate emotions, usually employing group dynamics to influence responses. A Mary Kay convention is a cheerleading love-fest that is designed to stimulate emotions. It's an important annual event that is used to transmit the culture to new recruits. The convention is held only once a year, but cultic methods continue year-round at Mary Kay and other corporate cults. A Mary Kay employee shared with my university class an incident in which a fellow worker needed money for a personal problem. A voluntary fund was started for the cause. Initially, she didn't contribute, because she really couldn't afford to. When it became publicly known that she had not contributed, she was shunned until she did so. The group technique of peer pressure had been used to stimulate feelings of guilt.

5. *Denigration of critical thinking.* This can go as far as characterizing any independent thought as selfish, and rational use of intellect as evil. This is the modus operandi in the kibbutzim of Israel, the last bastion of almost pure socialism. Kibbutz members are continually encouraged to subordinate individual interests to the interests of the whole. This happens in corporate cults as well. It can take the form of a transfer to another city, working late, multiple grueling trips overseas, or massive overtime. All these are techniques used to make the employee's personal interests subordinate to the group.

6. *Fulfillment can be realized only in the group.* This is reinforced in corporate cults by anecdotes of people who left the organization and failed. The obvious implication is, "The grass is *not* greener on the other side of the fence. As a matter of fact, it's brown and poisonous over there." Corporate cult members are encouraged to stay at "home," with the corporate "family."

7. *The ends justify the means.* Any action or behavior is justifiable as long as it furthers the group's goals. In the movie *Primary*

Colors, a fictionalized Bill Clinton is played by John Travolta. In the capstone scene of the closing act, he justifies to a staffer his campaign's multiple gross breaches of ethics by explaining that if he didn't break the rules, the other party would win, and that would be a catastrophe! The staffer changes his mind about leaving the campaign. He stays with the corporate cult, which believes it can make its own rules because winning the campaign (the end) is a greater good than the rules being broken (the means) to accomplish the good. The campaign has to be unethical to build the kind of America it *knows* will be right for other Americans. It is willing to do wrong for a right cause.

This is a totally unsupportable ethical position that is based only on relativism and denies that any absolute truth exists. The corporate cult creates whatever version of truth will produce the end it wants to achieve. The ends justify the means in corporate cults. In noncults, the means *are* the ends, because there is a belief that a higher power has established an absolute truth that is unchangeable. Humans are seen as continually and always subordinate to this greater truth. In corporate cults, members are continually and always subordinate to the leader.

8. *Group over individual.* The group's concerns supersede an individual's goals, needs, aspirations, and concerns. Conformity is the key. An adult student in a graduate class didn't like my insinuation that the U.S. military was a cult. She was proud of her husband's long service as a helicopter pilot and instructor. I asked, "Did he pledge to give his life for the organization if necessary?" Her answer was obviously yes. That's a cult.

Most group-over-individual anecdotes are more subtle than a pledge to give one's life. However, there is always some level of subordination of individual interests to group interests. It's absolutely necessary for maintenance of a corporate cult.

9. *Severe sanctions for defection or criticism of the cult.* This can even apply to negative or critical thoughts about the group or its leaders. When people leave your organization, do they stay in touch with colleagues from your company? If they do, your corporation is probably not very cultish. If they don't, you may be in a corporate cult. Leaders of corporate cults make sure that all ties

with defectors are cut. If leaving the organization can ever be portrayed as a path to success or happiness, the leader's hold on the cult is in danger. A strong wall of protection is maintained around the cult, first by quickly eliminating critics, and second by cutting communication with them.

10. *Severing ties with family, friends, goals, and interests.* This is done more overtly in religious and traditional cults. It is accomplished more covertly in corporate cults. Members are separated from their community by the many corporate-sponsored functions described in the next chapter.

These are ten techniques for manipulating members in traditional cults, most of which are religious in nature. Compare these ten to the norms—written or unwritten—that govern a work team, department, project team, or perhaps your entire organization. If the similarity is frightening, your leadership has built a corporate cult.

The Cult I Worked For

While working for a small company in the car promotions business, I had a boss much like Peter Arnell. He was a rager. He would blow his top about once a month, ranting and raving, yelling at anyone in his way, up and down the hall of our small office suite. He maintained very strict control of the organization. To avoid sending him into a frenzy, everyone tiptoed around him. What a kook! I worked there less than a year and barely escaped with my sanity.

This organization had many of the elements of a cult. The nature of the work meant that we had to work very hard during a two-week promotional event, which took place away from home. During these two weeks, the tyrannical leader demanded a high level of devotion. We were away from home, cut off from family and community distractions, so we were separated from community for that time period. The leader enjoyed the event because during it, the organization became more cultish. We were devoted to the organization and separated from community, and he was charismatic.

It was highly unusual to have a promotion near home, so when we did, I arranged for my in-laws to bring my nine- and seven-year-old children to the event. When the leader found that they were there, he made a point of seeing that I had plenty of work to keep me busy, so that I couldn't have time with my family. He commented that my family interest detracted from my work effectiveness.

This man was clearly a charismatic leader, but he played on the emotions of fear and intimidation, not the positive emotions we usually associate with the term *charisma*.

Appealing to the Need for Family

Cult leaders, corporate and otherwise, appeal to emotions to gain members, because they know that the emotional ties of familial relationships are missing from the lives of so many people. Josh tells the heartwarming story of paying a surprise visit to his college-age son at a basketball game. Spectators saw him run across the gym floor and his son hurtle down the bleachers, and a cheer erupted as the two of them hugged at courtside. Josh said he was totally surprised and confused by the response of the college students until he realized that few of his son's classmates had that kind of relationship with their fathers.[3]

Family is a need that doesn't go away. In the early part of this century, the economic situation led people to move across the country, away from their families, but the need for familial affection didn't go away. It is this need that leaders speak to so well. Many of them do it overtly, but they don't force it, it comes naturally.

Scare Me—Please

I finally figured out why teenagers like horror films. It's because the fright gives them an adrenaline rush. That part's not too difficult to figure out. But why do they want the adrenaline rush? Because it's the only thing that appeals to their emotions. Teenagers, like many Americans, are starved for emotional stimulation. This is what cult leaders give them: the emotional rush they have been missing in life.

Corporate cult leaders have an intuitive sense about how to use emotional appeals to recruit and retain members. The same intuition beckons members to follow the emotional inducement offered by the leader.

In-Groups and Out-Groups

I asked Lydia, a vice president at a major airline, how the organization had maintained a small-company culture as it grew to one of the largest airlines in the country. She didn't hesitate a second. "When there isn't a fight," she answered, "we start one." I thought that seemed counterintuitive. Hadn't I taught my students and seminar attendees to "put out fires," to "make peace," to "eliminate conflict?"

Lydia was using an assumption that I have come to understand and agree with. It's the assumption that *there will always be conflict*. She's right; there always will be conflict. Economics is the study of the distribution of scarce resources. The money that is now in your pocket was someplace else yesterday and will be somewhere else tomorrow. You don't create money; you simply move it around. The same is true of conflict: There always *has been* and always *will be* conflict. If you accept that assumption, then the objective of the leader is not to eliminate conflict, but to move it around.

This concept of conflict as an economic good has a corollary in physics: Matter cannot be created or destroyed; only the form can be changed. The same is true for conflict: Leaders can't destroy it, they can only move it around. Corporate cult leaders use this concept to their advantage. They continually "start fights" with real or perceived enemies to rally the troops.

Lydia's comment made sense in the context of the video I had just seen about the history of her company. The subject of the video depicted how the airline had won fights against state legislature to obtain licensure to make its first flight. Then came various competitive battles with other companies and a fight against restricted flights out of the company's home base. The transparent theme was that of a struggling, underdog scrapper of a competitor who continually beat the odds to win battle after battle.

There were many fights, and the company had won them all. They were all *outside* the organization. The airline had very carefully followed the strategy of creating well-defined in-groups and out-groups. It was always the in-group battling against a sinister out-group. This works in organizations, and particularly in corporate cults, because the group needs some external foe against which it can concentrate its energies. If conflict is an economic good and will always exist, the objective is to keep fights going—with external enemies. Fanning the fires of conflict *outside* the organization keeps conflict *within* the organization to a minimum.

External Pressure = Internal Cohesion

People who survive a tragedy such as a shipwreck or a plane crash often form enduring, close friendships. Leaders of corporate cults are aware of this and use it to their advantage. They must maintain the specter of an external threat, some bogeyman who is going to harm the individuals or the organization if they don't conduct themselves the way the leader directs. "When there isn't an enemy, find one," is the dogma by which corporate cults are maintained.

Wal-Mart does this very effectively. "Associates" are considered part of the "Wal-Mart family." Stock ownership by employees is promoted at every opportunity. Cindy Brown is so proud of her role as an associate and as an employee stock owner that she will drive past the closer K-Mart—"Who only sells junk, and people who shop there should be skinned alive"—to support *her* store.[4]

Wal-Mart also plays prerecorded messages to stockers in its stores in the middle of the night—a strange medley of encouraging messages that affirm the organization, its goals, and mandates. They eerily remind me of George Orwell's *1984.*

Coaches of athletic teams use the external pressure technique effectively. They love it when a newspaper columnist calls their team inferior in any way. The coach clips the article and pins it to the locker room bulletin board. External pressure—contrived or real—creates internal cohesion.

The U.S. Department of Justice antitrust suit brought against Microsoft in 1998 was seen as a threat by insiders. Defense of the company went beyond the expected rallying of workers around a besieged employer. In fighting the case, Softies believed they were defending both the best form of capitalism for the future and their own way of life.[5]

One of the best analyses ever done by a graduate student in my strategy class was a paper attributing the tough financial straits at Greyhound Bus Lines to the lack of a competitor. When the external pressure of a competitor goes away, internal cohesion is decreased. A competitor motivates the troops and gives them a reason for fighting. It stimulates the adrenaline spurt that makes work emotional. Without a threat, the group's performance falls off.

Retired General Colin Powell tells the story of meeting with then Russian President Mikhail Gorbachev in March 1988. Gorbachev was trying to convince the elite American delegation that perestroika and glasnost were not just another in a long succession of Soviet tricks; they were real and he was committed to them. Not being successful with other members of the delegation, he turned to Powell. "Ah, soldier, you will have to find a new enemy!" he exulted. Powell was too shocked to respond, but his unspoken answer was, "No, I like this one, because I know it and I have been very successful against it."[6] General Powell became a successful military leader largely because he was able to maintain morale when the enemy went away. That's a difficult thing to do in organizations. It's easier to use the corporate cult method, "When there isn't a fight, start one!"

Anyone who has a sibling has a good understanding of this concept, because they lived it in their childhood. Siblings will fight like cats and dogs until the neighbor kid picks on one of them. Then they close ranks to defend the one picked on from the outside threat. If the mother wanted to perpetuate peace around the house, she would stop trying to eliminate conflict and create some—with the neighbors. Like corporate cult leaders, she would be practicing the economic concept of conflict. She would be creating family peace by moving the conflict outside the house. Many organizations use the economic concept of conflict to sustain membership.

The Internal Revenue Service

The IRS is a multifaceted organization with many confusing overlying levels of management and bureaucracy. Historically, the organization has been rife with conflicts. That may be ending. It has found some identifiable threats—or perhaps the threats found it. These threats are the Fair Tax movement, which wants to replace the IRS with a national sales tax, Congressman Dick Armey's campaign to enact a flat tax, and a campaign to eliminate the IRS all together.

IRS Commissioner Charles Rosetti may be able to parlay these multiple threats into the external pressure needed to create internal cohesion. Over so many years without a threat, the agency grew complacent and conflicts brewed. Turf wars were a regular occurrence. Rossetti can use the identified threats to produce an internal cohesion that will drive the IRS to new levels of cooperation and morale.

Of Gods and Devils

Religion uses the economic concept of conflict very openly. If there weren't a devil or a hell, there would be little need for religion. Church leaders get their flock to follow narrowly prescribed behavior patterns to fend off the enemy. Without a threat, both cults and more traditional churches would lack the tools to manage the behavior of their congregants. This begins to sound like a section on religious cults instead of the main subject, corporate cults. However, the same technique is used in both: the threat of unfavorable consequences if member behavior does not conform.

Collective Narcissism

Narcissism is love of self, and corporate cults love themselves. It's easy to adopt the advice to "start a fight" because the cult is always the good guy. All that's necessary to start a fight is to find a reasonably qualified bad guy. There are lots of them, and corporate cult leaders find them.

Good and bad exist only relative to others, so the mission of the corporate cult leader is to simply find a group that is, in some measurable way, worse than the corporate cult. This kind of collective narcissism is rampant in religious cults, where leaders righteously claim to have the *only* connection to God. Corporate cult leaders aren't much different. In management circles, we trot around to the latest guru who has made a pile of money and try to find her or his secret of life, or at least secret of management success. A thorough study of America's richest man, Bill Gates, reveals that he did many things right, but that he also was extremely fortunate to have so many circumstances fall into place at exactly the right time. I'm not denigrating effective organizational management, because I teach it. I'm only saying that perhaps organizational humility should be more admired than organizational narcissism. There's nothing humble about cult leaders or corporate cult leaders.

Good and Bad Icebergs

The iceberg in Figure 7-1 represents a metaphor for the two worlds in which humans exist: the *concept* world below the water and the *construct* world above the water. Constructs can be subjected to scientific investigation. We can observe the top part of the iceberg and make replicable measures. (Replicable means that you and I can both make the same measurements.) We cannot, however, scientifically measure the bottom part of the iceberg, because it is obscured to us beneath the water. That's where the intangibles lie, which in social science we call concepts. We all agree that concepts exist, but they cannot be submitted to scientific measurement because replicable observations cannot be made.

This applies to corporate cults in the following way: People with a healthy ego think of themselves as good people. Good is a

Figure 7-1. The Iceberg of Social Science

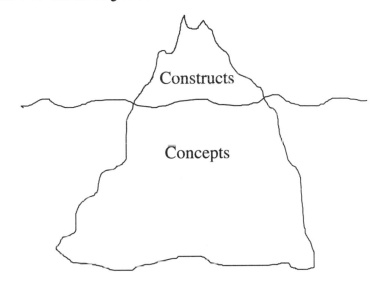

below-the-water concept that cannot be measured. The only way in which people can obtain a verifiable sense of their self-worth is relative to others. That measurement must be made above the water because that's the only place the judgment can be made. Good exists only relative to bad. Thus, as individuals, we must find others who are in some measurable way worse than we are. To compare ourselves to thousands of individuals would be too difficult. We use a convenient shorthand by comparing *our group* to some other group. My teenagers make a quick application of this methodology when they assume that the students in *their* high school are better than those in the neighboring high school.

Leaders of corporate cults simply extend this rather juvenile, heuristic method to encourage the idea that people in their organization are better than those outside the organization. This is a thought pattern that employees easily buy into, because it satisfies their search for meaning and explanation in their lives. Once they find these things in a corporate cult leader, their preconceptions about themselves are validated. The new member had low self-esteem *outside* the organization and has high self-esteem *within* it. Given those simple facts, staying in the corporate cult is an easy decision.

The Five Sources of Power

French and Raven say that there are five sources of power that contribute to leadership: legitimate, reward, coercive, expert, and referent.[7] It's important to know which of these types are used in
corporate cults.

Legitimate power comes from the position held by the leader.
It's called legitimate because it comes from a source other than
the leader. The corporation puts this mantle of leadership on an
individual by giving him or her a title that grants power. This type
of power is not very important in corporate cults. People are not
sentenced to corporate cult membership; they enter of their own
volition.

Legitimate lines of hierarchical power are not respected in corporate cults, because corporate cult leaders gain their power from
claiming not to have it at all. That's the elegance and the paradox
of corporate cults: People willingly join the corporate cult because
they want the empowerment promised by the leader. Titles aren't
important at corporate cults, so legitimate power is not an issue.

Reward power is the leader's ability to grant rewards such as
pay and promotion. Pay in corporate cults is often low relative to
that in other corporations of comparable size in the same industry.
Thus, reward power is not used in corporate cults. People who
respond to reward power self-select to a collection of specialists,
where the rewards are better. Employees join specialist collections
for affiliation and fellowship, not for rewards.

Coercive power is the leader's authority to punish or recommend punishment. Leaders use this power when they wield the
right to fire or demote and to withhold raises or promotions. Coercive power is used in corporate cults, but not in the traditional
manner. Corporate cult members are punished not by withholding
rewards or promotions, but by withholding the affiliation that is
so important to them. Being with people is important to corporate
cult members, so isolation is punishment. Thus, corporate cult
leaders use coercive power to control their members by threatening
to move them to a socially less attractive work setting. Or the leader
may threaten to withhold the invitation to a training session, corporate celebration, or some other culture-building event.

Expert power comes from the leader's knowledge of the task being performed. When a leader is a true expert, people follow because of task qualifications. This is not used in corporate cults. One of the building blocks of the corporate cult paradigm is the self-selection of employees to a specialist collection. People are collected not for their task specialization, but for their people skills. In a people-oriented organization, tasks are not highly valued. Thus, expert power is not used in corporate cults.

Referent power comes from the leader's personality characteristics that are respected and admired. People follow a referent leader because they wish to emulate that leader. Referent power depends on the leader's characteristics rather than on his or her formal title or position and is often called charismatic leadership. This is the power base that corporate cult leaders use widely. It's a leadership style that appeals to the emotions of the followers. Often, followers are not even sure *why* they follow. It just *feels* like the right thing to do.

A former member of a traditional cult explained the high compliment he received from his cult leader, "John, you have become the white paper."[8] The white paper was the study guide for the cult group. The leader meant that John was becoming less like himself and more what the cult leader wanted him to be.

In corporate cults, the leader is often a workaholic, good looking, and suave, and/or has a famous reputation for business acumen. The halo of those characteristics floods over the corporate cult member, so that she or he wants to become more like the leader. It attracts members at the emotional level.

Leader-Follower Relations in a Corporate Cult

Corporate cult leaders are like religious cult leaders in that they don't consciously submit their members to cult techniques, it just comes naturally. The leader doesn't have to map out a plan for culting members, he or she simply goes about leading and growing the organization in the manner that makes sense to him or her, and it works!

"Personal space" is an important concept in developing individual identity. Corporate cult leaders know instinctively that depriving members of this personal space is an important first step in the culting process. Everything, including personal identity, must be subordinated to the larger group membership. In traditional cults as well as corporate cults, the group is more important than individuals. What is the source of this leadership thinking?

Corporate cult members typically grew up in an environment in which a strong leader ruled the family unit. This strong leadership usually involved a violation of the individual's personal space. In this situation, the person learns early in life the idea of subordinating her or his need for personal space to the larger family unit. From that point, it is easy to transfer those personal identity deprivations to the corporate cult.

In the corporate cult, the leader takes the role of parent, and interacts with the organizational members the same way their parents did. The members are accustomed to having personal space violated by the biological family, so they accept the same personal space violation from the corporate cult leader.

Corporate cult members are devoted to the organization and view their leader as charismatic. Chapter 8 is about the last element of the definition: separation from community.

Notes

1. Jennifer Steinhauer, "When a Boss Is Out of Line, What's the Legal Boundary?" *The New York Times*, March 27, 1997.
2. John Edmiston, *How Cults Manipulate People*, Internet site ultra.net, December 1996.
3. Josh McDowell, speech at Lake Pointe Baptist Church, Rockwall, TX, May 1998.
4. Greg Brown, "Anecdotes from Corporate Cults," Paper for Organizational Behavior class, Dallas Baptist University, Fall 1997.
5. Amy Harmon, "Microsofties Say They're Right as Rain," *The New York Times*, May 26, 1998.
6. Colin Powell, speech to Southwest Human Resources Meeting, Fort Worth, Texas, October 10, 1996.

7. J. P. R. French and B. Raven, "The Bases of Social Power," a chapter in *Studies in Social Power* by D. Cartwright (ed.) (Ann Arbor, Mich.: University of Michigan Press, 1959).
8. John Goldhammer, *Under the Influence* (Amherst, N.Y.: Prometheus Books, 1996).

Chapter 8
Separation From Community

*A*n employee can be devoted to an organization that has a charismatic leader, but still not be culted. However, when "work becomes life," the individual is in a cult.

A warden at a state bureau of prisons said, "The only people I associate with are bureau people," he says. "After they move you five times in twelve years, you don't know anyone else."[1] After getting a very high score on the separation-from-community portion of the cult test, he became very interested in finding out more about corporate cults.

At-work day care, auto repairs, bookstores, exercise facilities, and parties all bring the employee closer to the organization—and further from the community. These fringe benefits begin as inducements to make the employees' life easier, which they do. The unintended effect is that they separate the workers from traditional community relationships and replace them with work relationships as the workplace becomes the only community the employee has.

Cults remove themselves from the rest of the community. This happens incrementally, through actions that are intended to make life easier for the employee. That's the paradox of cutting the corporation off from the rest of the community: It *does* make life easier for the employee, but corporate cults do it because it's good for the corporation and bad for the individual.

Loss of Community

American culture no longer fosters a sense of community.[2] This produces a decrease in family unity. While it may be easier to see an opposite causal relationship—that the loss in family vitality decreases the sense of community—this book is not concerned with the causality at that level of analysis. It makes no difference which way the causality flows. I am happy to concede that the loss of identity at both the family and the community levels contributes to workers' need to find those affiliation and emotional elements at the workplace, often at corporate cults. At the individual level, which is the level of analysis used in this book, it's sufficient simply to determine that employees are finding more community at work and less community in their traditional home communities, defined by geographic boundaries.

Transportation efficiency is responsible for much of the loss in the sense of shared community. Whether the suburbs brought the cars or cars brought the suburbs, together they have had a negative effect on community. Pre-World War II towns had a sense of community, a sense of place. Inexpensive automobiles allowed growing families of the baby-boom generation to buy larger houses on larger tracts of land farther from the city. The effect was the loss of community.

The New York Islanders won the National Hockey League's Stanley Cup four years in a row, from 1980 to 1983. Sadly, they had no place to celebrate. Nassau County exemplifies the growth of the postwar suburbs with efficient cookie-cutter houses in master planned communities. Nassau County is a community with no *sense* of community. Thus, the victorious Islanders had no place to celebrate. For a victory parade, they drove around the Nassau Coliseum parking lot to the cheers of their adoring fans. Somehow, the circular parade did not have the intensity of driving through New York City's Times Square or Paris' Arc de Triomphe.

Nassau County doesn't have a city center in the terms of a traditional Main Street. The Islanders had a *reason* to celebrate, but no *place* to do it. So, they celebrated at work. They practice at Nassau Coliseum; they play their games at Nassau Coliseum; they celebrate their victories at Nassau Coliseum.[3]

The postwar suburbanization of America removed the sense of community from communities. Developed as low-density, cheap alternatives to traditional towns, suburbs without a Main Street lack heart. They have no central core, no sense of place that residents can lean on, take pride in, or turn to in times of celebration.

The economics of cheap land and systematized house building that drove families to the suburbs drove the sense of belonging from their lives. Intellectuals, church leaders, TV and radio commentators, and suburban residents are calling for a return of the sense of community that was lost in the suburban sprawl.

Having realized that Main Street is more than a place to shop, some communities are trying to fix the problem. Valencia, California, is a planned community thirty miles north of Los Angeles known mostly as the home of Magic Mountain amusement park. A project underway at the main cross streets will create a half-mile-long pedestrian-oriented Main Street called Town Center Drive. It is hoped that the tree-lined streets and friendly mix of retail and restaurants will attract people, creating a common meeting place that can be considered the heart of the community.[4]

Schaumburg, Illinois, sprouted from the prairie near O'Hare airport in the 1970s. Like most economically driven suburbs, it lacks a central meeting place. The city has cleared a twenty-nine-acre site to create a town square. The project will be anchored by the Schaumburg Township Library and a Dominick's supermarket. It is hoped that the combination of these two attractions will create a "people space" that will define the center of what currently is suburban sprawl.[5]

Perhaps the most interesting part of Schaumburg's town square is the focal point: a large clock tower. Clock towers have traditionally been the center of town and the heart of a community. But they were originally installed not to create a sense of community, but to control workers. The wristwatch is a very recent invention. Even standard wall clocks were not common in the 1800s. European towns and cities erected clock towers so that they could standardize the workday.

Clock towers were a significant element in the crushing social experiment called the Industrial Revolution. In the agrarian and craft society that preceded the Industrial Age, people worked at shifting clusters of tasks as the season and crop development demanded.[6] Workers were "controlled" largely by the seasons, not by managers. It was the development of industrial settings, in which workers could be submitted to control and the laws of efficiency, that created the environment for corporate cults. Clock towers were a vital piece of the industrial movement. So it's quite ironic that cities like Schaumburg are attempting to create community with a clock tower, which is a symbol of worker control.

Celebration is a planned community owned by the Walt Disney Company as part of its mammoth Disney World complex near Orlando. Would you want to *live* at Disney World? The housing development is not that different from the park itself—every detail is planned, right down to garden hose holders with a Mickey emblem. It is a strange mix of Magic Kingdom and suburban sprawl. The objective is to create a "perfect" community, in which the culture is meticulously designed.

Tree-lined streets and parks with band gazebos create a feeling of a Norman Rockwell picture brought to life. The popularity of Celebration is indicative of people's need for community. So many suburbs lack community that home buyers are willing to pay a premium to have Disney create it for them.

Community streets used to be a place of life. They knit neighborhoods together through a system of sidewalks, porches, picnics, and other family activities that produced community. When the purpose of streets became to convey automobiles, they changed from a place that *gave* life to a place that *took* life. Streets now take people to other places for their activities: organized soccer, band, and dance practices for the kids; movies and the mall for teenagers; business and the symphony for adults.

People now *sleep* in their houses. They used to *live* in their neighborhoods. A neighborhood used to be an end; it existed as a community. It is now a means, a stopping-off place between work and entertainment excursions.

"Community is what we've most destroyed in the U.S.," says architectural historian Vincent Scully, "and community is what we need to bring back."[7]

The movie *The Truman Show* featured a perfect community in which the life of the lead character, played by Jim Carrey, was transmitted to the world via television. The movie was shot in the planned community of Seaside, Florida. It's about as perfect as life gets, with color-coordinated houses, picket fences, and trees trimmed with microscopic precision.

This pressure to conform to the stringent community standards exemplified by Seaside prepares people for life in the work-place community, where conformity is just as narrowly defined. While corporate cults talk a lot about creativity and "doing your own thing," casual observation indicates that the people in corporate cults are as cloned as the perfectly coordinated planned communities in which they live.

A Close-to-Home Example

My own suburb of Rowlett, Texas, is a good example. I moved here twelve years ago in order to get a less expensive house on a larger lot. Apparently, my fellow citizens did the same. We are a bedroom community to Garland, a city of 200,000, which could be considered a bedroom community for the one million population center of Dallas. Rowlett lacks a central business district, a central park area, a central anything.

This small town has been through three stages of development, all caused by changes in transportation. During the first stage, a cluster of six shops was built facing the railroad tracks. The popularization of the automobile marked the second stage, in which the fronts and rears of the shops were switched so that they faced Main Street. We're now in the third stage, in which the stores are mostly ignored, having been replaced by grocery superstores that sit on massive concrete parking lots on a major highway just a few blocks away.

Logically responding to economic pressures, retail establishments have appeared along the highway that streaks through the geographic center of town. Last year a beautiful new high school was erected at the end of Main Street. A four-lane road connects the high school to the rest of the world. The old downtown Main Street remains neglected. There has been some talk of creating a retro shopping and restaurant district. Without the economics to drive it, it won't happen. If the Rowlett Eagles High School athletic teams win any championships, they—like the New York Islanders—will be without a place to celebrate.

As communities lose their sense of community, people increasingly find it at work. The citizens of Nassau County, Schaumburg, Rowlett, and thousands of other suburban sprawl cities and towns find no community in their community. But there is a *need* for community, so people find it at work.

The Corporation as Community

It's easy to find community at Eastman Chemical's plant in Kingsport, Tennessee. This paternalistic plant virtually controls the small city. Employees can vacation at company-owned campgrounds, square dance in the company gymnasium, and go to free movies at the company theater. The Recreation Club serves as the meeting place for nineteen different hobby clubs, from hiking to computers. It also offers a wide variety of sports activities like basketball and softball.[8] As neighborhoods and towns relinquish the job of providing community, the workplace happily takes it over. Here's how.

Some services that separate the worker from the community are day care, exercise facilities, banking, laundry services, and bookstores.

Day Care

You won't find many complaints about corporations that offer child day care. On the contrary, corporate day care allows the children to spend drive time with parents, the parents are available for consultation when needed, and the parent is a greater part of the child's life. However, corporate day care is a major element of creeping cultedness, because the family that uses it removes itself from a major portion of the community it could be attached to. Without corporate day care, the family would have to be connected with a community-based day care center, a church or synagogue, or a neighbor or family member who might care for the child.

Are children important? Of course they are. Doesn't anyone have a problem with turning over their most valued possession to a corporation? Not in corporate cults. Okay, it's only for a few hours five days a week. But the message is cultic in nature. Children become aware that the corporation provides many things in their lives, in addition to their parents' jobs. Who does the child play with at corporate day care? Children of other employees. This unwittingly sets up the same hierarchy in day care that exists in the corporation. The old, "My dad can beat your dad," becomes "My dad beat your dad" to a promotion, project funding, etc. Or, even worse, "Let me have that toy. If you don't, my dad will fire your dad." If you think that *wouldn't* happen, you haven't spent enough time around preschoolers.

A Sioux Falls, South Dakota school board member is proud that her school district has placed a kindergarten on the campus of the city's largest employer, Citibank.[9] Makes you wonder if the Federal Reserve Bank discount rate is printed on the message board in the cafeteria. The students probably study amortization tables in math class.

Miami International Airport is another of about seventy-five businesses nationwide that have installed public school units in the workplace.[10]

Day care and schools at the corporation, while convenient, effectively separate the employee from the community. Not only is the worker cut off from the community, the child is cut off as well. The employee increasingly socializes only with other workers who are parents of children in corporate day care. The child knows only the children of other workers. Whatever cultural stereotype exists in the corporation is magnified in the children. All the programs aimed at diversifying society by integrating people from different ethnic and racial backgrounds are turned on their head by corporate day care. Oh, yes, the children may be from different ethnic and racial groups, but the day care is *creating* another group: the corporate identity, which is as threatening to healthy diversity as ethnic and racial separation.

Exercise Facilities

The goal of the organization is to further the organization's objective. Exercise facilities are utilitarian for the corporation because they increase the level of employees' physical health, which decreases absenteeism and health care claims. And what's wrong with a healthy body? Doesn't everyone want one? And if the corporation provides the facility at low or no cost, who should complain. This is another example of an employee benefit that *seems* to benefit both the organization and the employee. However, while doing so, it separates employees from their community.

Hewlett-Packard's manufacturing facility in Boise, Idaho, features a jogging track, softball and soccer fields, basketball courts and tennis courts. When a visitor asked about the seemingly lavish athletic facilities, he was informed that there is also an indoor swimming pool, a gymnasium, and racquetball courts. Many of the HP employees do not have specific work hours, so they break up their tedious or concentration-intensive work with periods of recreation.

On the surface, this seems like a nice thing for HP to do for its employees. In reality, it separates the employees from the community, where they would have the opportunity to associate with non-HP employees.[11]

Allow me to use my own exercise regime as an example. I am a college professor. Since I live forty miles from the university, I try to limit my long commutes to campus. That means that while I am on campus, I am pretty focused on getting my business done, so I seldom take the time to exercise there. However, I thoroughly enjoy the exceptions when I do. A few times a year I play pickup basketball games with an interesting mix of students, faculty, and staff. Each time, I leave the gym with a few new friends and a greater understanding of the makeup of our student body and administrative staff. It's a good thing.

A few times a year I run with a staff member from another department within the university. His wife is a faculty member, and both of them have been at the university longer than I have. So, through our discussions, I always gain some insight into the culture and politics of the university. This is also a good thing.

But most of my exercising is done in the suburb in which I live. A few days a week, I jog around the neighborhood. I have met two fellow runners in the neighborhood. When we happen to be out at the same time, we run together and talk about the school system, their kids, my kids, traffic on our street, and other neighborhood news.

About once a week, I play basketball at the middle school gym. The group is mostly middle school coaches. Frankly, we don't talk much, but they are great basketball players. The key for me, is this: These are the coaches and teachers of my kids. By knowing these coaches, I have a direct line into which are the good kids and which are the bad kids. Are my kids in the right group? Are my kids coming to class? Are they doing their work?

I don't mean to set myself up as a righteous example. I just want to make the point that exercise facilities at work are a key element in separating the worker from the community. There is a lot of good to be gained from exercising in your community rather than at work. The only thing to be gained from exercising at work is membership in a corporate cult.

Banking

Sure, it's convenient to have banking on the corporate premises. All policies that separate the employee from the community are convenient. It's just that they are convenient for the corporation *because* they separate employees from their community.

In corporate day care, the employee commits her or his children to the corporation's control. Via the exercise facility, the body is committed. Banking allows corporate cult members to commit their money as well.

Because corporate banking is so convenient, it's easy to overlook the opportunity costs. Not the opportunity costs of the money, but those of the time and relationships that can be built with another entity and another set of individuals outside the organization. Perhaps calling for a return to the old bank on the corner is sentimental nostalgia. However, if you bank closer to home, you are likely to get acquainted with the parent of one of your children's friends. If you borrow money for your new car from your community bank, you are more likely to be recognized the next time your car runs out of gas or breaks down.

Silly examples, sure. But we all have choices about how to live our lives, and living them tied to the umbilical cord of the corporation is not a good way to live.

Laundry Services

Clothing is an indication of cultedness. The more clothes with the company logo a person owns, the more culted that person is. (Work uniforms are exempted from the count.) I suggest that clothing is an indication of cultedness for two reasons: First, clothes are worn on our bodies, so they are a highly personal item. Second, they are a message about who we are.

Clothes are a personal item. Recently, it became popular to ask famous people about their choice of undergarments. This trend exemplifies the need for increasingly more personal exploration of the lives of the famous. What we wear on our bodies is highly personal. We learned that President Clinton wore briefs, while then Senator Dole wore boxers. The media tried to justify such an intensely personal question by arguing that it contributed to some kind of weird character analysis. Hogwash! The reporters were simply testing the limits of personal investigation. I can almost hear the press corps ruminating about which question to ask: "Do you think he will answer this one?" they wonder delightedly.

The Importance of Uniforms

Military personnel wear uniforms because they provide standardization. The uniform identifies them as members of the organization. In the process, some personal identity is forfeited. The wearer of a uniform cannot totally be herself because she has forfeited part of her identity to the organization represented by the uniform.

To be more involved in the lives of my teenage children, I substitute teach at their high school on my days off. It's amazing what you can learn at the teachers' lunch table. Substitute teachers are often at a great disadvantage in managing the students because the students know more about the modus operandi than the substitute. On one particular day, while trying to catch up with the M.O. for the day, I found out a great deal about the girls' drill team. "Will someone volunteer to take roll for me?" I asked. A girl in a drill team uniform jumped up. "Yes, sir, I will." A few minutes later, I asked, "Does anyone know where your teacher keeps the stapler?" "Here, I'll staple it for you," responded another girl in a drill team uniform, taking the papers from my hand. "Will someone take this report to the office for me?" I asked. A third drill team member volunteered.

It was clear that these girls had been told that as members of the drill team, they were to be school leaders. They volunteered not as individuals, but as members of the organization they represented. It was no coincidence that I asked for three volunteers and got three who were wearing uniforms. They represented the drill team that day because they wore the uniform. In this example, the uniform had a positive consequence. Most cultic actions have some positive consequence.

There are many stories of a young, misguided youth whose life was turned around by military service. A Nike ad featured a devoted basketball fan trying to convince Michael Jordan that his athletic prowess was due to the shoes he wore: "The shoes, Mikey, it's the shoes!" The military answer is, "The uniform, it's the uniform." Clothes tell the world what group we belong to, who we are in a corporate sense.

That's why laundry service at work is another contributor to the corporate cult syndrome. Workers bring some of their most personal possessions, clothes, to work. The corporation takes care of these highly personal objects for the worker. By exposing personal clothing at the workplace, the employee voluntarily gives up a portion of his or her identity that was once held private. When this becomes public knowledge, the individual exchanges part of his or her private identity for corporate identity. This lowers the employee's guard and allows the corporation to take ownership of another element of the worker's life.

Laundry at work separates the individual from the community because it enables the individual to cut yet another tie with the community in which she or he lives. The corporate cult becomes the community.

Bookstores

Descartes said, "I think, therefore I am." Philosophers have debated this important thought extensively. Much of how we think is derived from what we read. I'm not Machiavellian enough to think that corporate managers stock the corporate bookstore with titles that brainwash their employees. I suppose the usual routine is that someone in the corporate hierarchy becomes enchanted with a certain book and suggests that others read it as well. Obviously, there is a great deal of inherent peer pressure to read the book, so that the employee will know the lingo used by corporate leadership.

Corporate bookstores, like other cultic techniques, are innocent attempts to help the employees fully develop themselves. In the process, they help the employees develop in ways that fit into the narrow cultural constraints of the corporation. They make organizations into corporate cults.

Multiple studies have shown that diverse groups make better decisions than homogeneous ones.[12] Yet the corporate bookstore encourages members of the corporation to think alike, because they are affected by the same writers. While there is nothing wrong with cultural continuity, there *is* something wrong with cultural homogeneity. A corporation filled with like-thinking employees is not a collection of individuals at all. It is a collection of automatons—"yes-men" who groupthink the corporation down the path to destruction.

A few years ago, I did a series of book reviews for Barnes & Noble bookstores in Dallas. I divided the business section of the Barnes & Noble bookstore into twelve major subject headings. My long-term goal was to provide twelve sessions, one on each of the subject headings. During a one-hour session, I would review all of Barnes & Noble's books on that subject.

The sessions were very enlightening for me—and, I hope, for the Barnes & Noble customers as well. Two years later, I still turn to these book reviews when I teach graduate classes on these subjects.

My thinking was expanded by reviewing all the writers on a particular subject at the same time. This provided a framework for contrast and comparison of these writers and thinkers. It provided a "tree" upon which to hang theories in the subject field. While I was a Ph.D. candidate at the University of Texas at Arlington, I was privileged to attend a two-semester colloquium on strategy research. The entire strategy research field was broken into twenty-eight streams, and we studied one each week. The course was team-taught by three excellent strategy researchers.

About the third week, a fellow student voiced the frustration I was feeling. "This class is great," he began. "I feel as though each week we meet, I am given a box of Christmas ornaments. They are glittering and beautiful and very attractive. But I am beginning to wonder," he concluded, "what the tree looks like." He was asking for a framework, a guide to help him compare and contrast the research he was absorbing in this important class. Each of the three team-teaching professors refused to answer the question. "That's the purpose of the course," they answered. "Build your own tree."

And we did. After twenty-eight weeks of study, each of us had built a mental framework that was slightly different from those of the other class members. My tree related strategy research to international issues, and my dissertation was on U.S.–Russian joint ventures. A fellow class member continually looked at the research as it related to small business, and that led to his dissertation. We had a wonderfully fruitful seminar, because the professors taught us how to think but declined to tell us *what* to think.

The professors did exactly the opposite of what corporate cult leaders do. They allowed each individual to design his or her own mental framework. Even though we were reading the same material, we developed different ways of looking at the subject. This is the great advantage of academic institutions: Free and innovative thinking are encouraged. Corporate cults do the opposite. They discourage free and innovative thinking. If the corporate cult leader claims to encourage such free thinking, this usually means, "Think innovatively, as long as it is the *kind* of innovative thinking that is approved at this corporation."

Corporate bookstores promote a narrowly homogeneous way of thinking, and thereby contribute to corporate cultism. But corporate bookstores make a more consequential contribution to corporate cults through the fact that an employee who has a bookstore available at the office ceases to associate with fellow shoppers at public bookstores. For many, the social atmosphere that has been created by Barnes & Noble and Borders provides a retreat to the innovative and free-thinking atmosphere that is the hallmark of the university experience. There is also the serendipity that is produced when you happen upon a book review, such as the one I was offering, or a book signing by an author, or some other type of expanded learning experience that is not available at the corporate bookstore.

Corporate bookstores tell people how to think and what to think. Worse yet, they constrain the *way* in which people buy books. The medium—what people buy and how they buy it— becomes the message. The message is that company bookstores make an organization into a corporate cult.

The Community That Provides Everything

Where is the line between being nice to employees and culting them? Somewhere to the left of AlliedSignal, whose Morristown, New Jersey, corporate headquarters offers an on-site beauty salon, company store, post office, film processing, prescription services, dry cleaners, shoe repair, takeout food, and catering.[13]

Another example is Greenpages, a computer company in Kittery, Maine, that offers a traditional lobster bake for employees every Friday. That effectively separates the employees from their families and community lobster restaurants on Friday night. Andersen Consulting has joined the burgeoning ranks of companies that offer a concierge to perform such personal tasks as arranging birthday parties, buying gifts, and picking up dry cleaning. Dorothy and her friends expected less from the Wizard of Oz.

A napping loft has become so popular at Berkeley, California–based consulting firm 42 IS that reservations are now necessary.[14]

Napping, birthday parties, gifts, dry cleaning, and dinner. Do these sound like activities that are best performed at home or at the workplace? When they are performed at the workplace, it's a corporate cult.

Cult Members Are Happy!

Remember this truth as you study and think about cults of any kind: *Cult members don't complain.*

Richard Schlesinger interviewed me for a segment of the CBS program *48 Hours* that explored the culture of Southwest Airlines. I am one of the few contrarians about the seemingly wonderful culture at the airline. "The people at Southwest Airlines are *happy* working there. How could a business professor complain about that?" queried Schlesinger. I overstated my case, but still, I was right. "Three years ago, I could have taken you to the Branch Davidian compound near Waco to interview the cult members living there," I responded. "When asked why they were there, they would have answered, 'I love it here, this is my family, I feel valuable here, this is my home.' Have you heard those same phrases as you have interviewed employees at Southwest Airlines?"

Yes, he had heard those same phrases, and that's why he

sought me out, an unknown spokesperson on corporate culture, to appear on a national TV news program. I was the only person who had drawn a parallel between corporations and cults.

Office Romance

"Work is one of the few places available these days where you can get to know another person slowly and perhaps make a deep personal connection," says Mark Johonsson, director of leadership and team development at Damark International in Minneapolis, Minnesota. A 1994 survey by the American Management Association found that 30 percent of employees had been romantically involved with a coworker at some point in their career.[15]

Freud said that people have two major needs: love and work. They should not be found at the same place. Being romantically involved at work is the worst way for employees to separate themselves from their community. The romance will either succeed or fail, and in either case it will cause organizational trouble for the individuals involved.

If the romance succeeds, it causes multiple power relationship problems. Some people will argue that as long as the romantic partners are in different departments where they don't have much contact, no harm is done. If they didn't have much contact, how did the romance get started? Romantic relationships at work that succeed simply cause interorganizational problems and are a very effective medium for separating the employee from the community.

A failed romantic relationship at work produces the kind of individual-corporation separation that I support, but perhaps not in the way the employee wanted it. Often it results in one of the parties leaving the corporation. That's a separation that employees don't often enjoy.

While I sympathize with love-starved employees, we must examine the reason they are finding love at work. It's because *they don't have a life outside work.* If they were to find one, they would find the type of romantic relationship they are seeking. Thus, romantic relationships are part of the inward spiral of connectedness to a corporation. The employee spends so much time at work that she or he doesn't mingle in any other circles in which it would be possible to find a mate. Finding a mate at work further binds the employee to the corporation. It's a self-reinforcing spiral that separates employees from the community.

Micro-Softies

Microsoft's primary competitive strategy is to eliminate competitors. Its secondary strategy is to compete via corporate culture. The most visible aspect of its culture is the collection of buildings at the main headquarters. Its resemblance to a university causes the headquarters to be called a campus. Like university campuses, Microsoft provides all the amenities an employee could want: cafeteria, company store, athletic club, valet parking, and free bus passes. The refrigerators on every floor are stocked with free juice and soft drinks. There are Softie basketball and volleyball courts, softball and soccer fields. Bereavement counseling is provided at no cost to the employee. Employees work in identical cubicles throughout the company's campus. Their geographic seclusion (from the rest of the industry in Silicon Valley) helps explain Microsoft's sense of exclusion from mainstream computer culture. There is an unstated but verifiable summer uniform: sandals, shorts, and a T-shirt. The winter uniform is slightly modified to jeans, plaid shirt, and hiking boots.[16]

Every office has a window. (Perhaps it would be difficult to solve Windows-based problems without one.) Every project is considered developmental, so team cooperation is the ultimate dogma. Projects are assigned to teams, and peer pressure within groups is very evident.

Microsoft has a culture with very narrowly prescribed values and norms. The predominant value is that work is the most important thing in life. "Softies," or "Microserfs" as they are sometimes called, live, eat, breathe, and talk Microsoft. They also spend their recreational time—what little there is—with fellow Softies.

Following the belief that recruiters find others like themselves, Microsoft relies on current employees to find new ones. About 30 percent of new hires come with a recommendation from a current employee.

Microsoft University indoctrinates the new hire into the Microsoft way. The training program begins the building of alliances and bonding with other new Softies. After training, the employee is assigned to a project and is expected to begin making a contribution immediately.

Softies spend a great deal of time together, inside and outside of work. The referral system tends to find people with few outside interests, and what outside interests they do have are often shared by many other Softies. An employee with the mindset, "My job is just a job" will not last long at Microsoft. The people at Microsoft want to change the world, and anything less is considered unacceptable.

When the U.S. Department of Justice filed antitrust charges against Microsoft, it was seen on the Redmond campus as not so much a threat to the business as a challenge to the close-knit culture of the twenty-three-year-old company. "It heightened the awareness of the boundaries between those who have key-cards to the enclave campus and those who don't."[17]

Many of Microsoft's organizational procedures encourage cultish behavior among the employees. There is a great deal of devotion to the organization, charismatic leadership is practiced, and the employees are separated from the community.

Escape From a Seminar

Fred, a human resources consultant in Dallas, tells a story of a friend who paid a large fee to attend a weekend personal enrichment seminar that had been recommended by a work associate. When she arrived on Friday evening, it seemed like many other seminars she had attended. As the evening wore on, however, she noticed that cultic methods were being used. Most of them were related to dress.

"We're all going to relax and escape the up-tight corporate world in this seminar," announced the leader. "Men, take off the neckties that have been strangling you all week. Women, take off your restrictive shoes." The undressing did not reach an embarrassing or improper stage, but the seminar leader was practicing the cultic technique of self-disclosure. When you disclose something personal about yourself—like clothing choices—you give up a bit of your self-identity to the group. You no longer own that identity element after you pass it off to group ownership.

The woman began to feel uncomfortable about the seminar leader's instructions to "get comfortable." She bolted for the pay phone to call a friend to "rescue" her. A seminar associate cut her off and suggested that if she had *any* outside contact at this point, it would ruin what was certain to become a highly meaningful weekend for her. Also, it would significantly decrease her chances of upward corporate mobility, which had obviously been achieved by other seminar graduates. She persisted, made it to the phone, and called a friend with an urgent plea to rescue her. While she waited for her friend, the seminar associate used even stronger language in urging the woman to stay. As the rescuer's car pulled into the driveway, she ran to the car, clutching her shoes and jacket. She absolutely insists that she "escaped."

But the seminar was extremely successful. So I asked Fred, "Why did the other attendees stay, enjoy the weekend, enroll for advanced sessions, and recommend it to their friends?" "It provides family and community for them," Fred answered. "The seminar plays to the need for comfort, emotional support, and the chance to 'be yourself' for a weekend."[18] This type of cultic seminar is further evidence of people's need for family and community. They will find it somewhere, and often they find it in a corporate cult.

People who operate rationally in all three circles—work, family and community—have the opportunity to experience different sides of their being. To some extent, they are different at work from the people they are at home, and they are somewhat different again in their community endeavors. However, corporate cult members don't have the other two experiences. They need the weekend seminar because it becomes their family and community.

People like the seminar associate who tried to talk the woman back into the seminar are often referred to as "guards" because they guard against any escape from the group. Group cohesion is very important. Just like Libby Sartain at Southwest Airlines, who invoked the pledge to do whatever attendees were told to do for the rest of the day, the guards know that there is a possibility for early "escapees." If a critical mass were to escape, the entire seminar crowd could see that "the emperor has no clothes," which, of course, would ruin the seminar and end the cultic technique.

The seminar operators know that the greatest freeing agent in the legendary Milgram shock experiments was a fellow shocker. In the early stages of culting, it is critical that no one break rank, because a small hole in the dike could cause a flood of defections. At later stages in the culting process, individuals can be trusted not to bolt, but in the early stages, bolting is a great concern. People want to exercise their right to leave. They stay because of the promise of great benefits. Later on, when the person is more highly culted, the benefits don't have to be so great, because the person has escalated her or his commitment to the cause, and is less likely to leave.

Company Housing

You would have thought that company housing ended with the demise of company towns. But there are still small pockets of company housing in some industries. Hudson Foods, in Noel, Missouri, pays workers an average of $16,000 a year to process chickens. There is a small amount of company housing, which is in such demand that employees have to earn it through a clean work record, a low absentee rate, and long service. In addition to the traditional concern about company control over the lives of employees, the union has complained that a worker who is injured gets evicted from the housing unit, so the worker loses his or her job and housing—work and community—at the same time.

The Opryland Hotel just north of Nashville, Tennessee, has converted a Days Inn to company housing. Employees have allowed the corporation to provide another of the vital elements of their life. Worship services are conducted on-site, which makes one wonder if the corporation is trying to affect its workers' spiritual lives as well.[19]

Civic Organizations

In recent years, membership in the PTA, the League of Women Voters, the Red Cross, the Boy Scouts, the Lions Club, the Elks, the Jaycees, the Masons, and most other major civic organizations has fallen.[20] This has happened because those civic organizations are competing with the workplace for the employee's time. Employees would rather spend time at work than volunteer in civic organizations.

Much of the credit for the public service performed by civic organizations accrues not to the individual, but to the employer. Corporations direct the time of their employees so carefully that controlling their at-work time is no longer sufficient; the corporation is controlling off-the-clock hours as well.

"Forced volunteering" is an oxymoron. The individual is not *volunteering* at all—she is *working*. But the volunteer aspect of the civic organization masks the work nature of the contribution the member is making. Once again, the employee has allowed the corporation to determine "who I am," this time as a volunteer. That's because the employee is volunteering as a member of the corporation, not as an individual. The corporation—"what I do"—further encroaches on "who I am."

The Time Bind talks about the link between employees' desire for escape and a company's desire for profit.[21] Employees want to escape from home, where they feel out of control, to work, where they feel in control. The carefully constructed "comfort zone" of the workplace has replaced the home as the center of a person's universe, according to Hochschild. This successfully cuts out the community, because there is no longer time for it.

There is another barrier to individuals' volunteering in civic organizations: There's no profit in it. People *do* respond to economic incentives, and these incentives are greater in the workplace than in civic organizations. A community of civic organizations as a place where values are shared and transmitted is dull compared with the excitement, interaction, and money to be made at the workplace.

Thus, there are two major reasons why corporations are incrementally taking over civic organizations: time and money. First, corporations can commit the time of the large labor force needed to perform large civic projects. Second, corporations have the money and are willing to spend it to buy a reputation as a good neighbor to the community.

The largest canned food drive in the United States is performed each year by the employees of Northrop's Grand Prairie, Texas, division. Defense contracting and giving food to hungry people find their nexus at the door of the political machine. The corporation commits the time of its workforce to buy a good community reputation. In a time of decreasing defense expenditures, a good reputation is valuable.

But don't expect a collection of specialists to take over civic duties, because it won't. Remember, these workers are there just for the bucks, so if they volunteer, it will be as individuals, not as an organization. Civic organizations are going to be taken over by specialist collections, whose members must continually prove to the corporation and to themselves that their contributions are valuable. By volunteering together, members of the specialist collection cut themselves off from the rest of the community, the third element of the definition of a cult.

Corporate cultism is an individual-level construct. Corporations serve their own interest by propagating cultish behavior, but I maintain that only the employee can make the corporation into a cult. It's an individual's decision to be devoted to their organization, to view the leader as charismatic, and to separate from the community. All three of those elements are measured by the corporate cult test in Chapter 9.

Notes

1. Interview with the author, August 12, 1997.
2. Mary Pipher, *Reviving Ophelia* (New York: Penguin Putnam, 1994).
3. Charles Lockwood, "Rebuilding a Sense of Community," *The Wall Street Journal*, August 29, 1997.
4. Ibid.
5. Ibid.
6. William Bridges, *Job Shift* (Reading, Mass.: Addison-Wesley, 1994).
7. Stephen Budiansky, *Community Instead of Kitsch, U. S. Excellence Through Diversity* (Boston: Harvard Business School Press, 1994).
8. Fred Bleakley, "A Bastion of Paternalism Fights Against Change," *The Wall Street Journal*, January 16, 1997.
9. Interview with the author.
10. ABC News, July 1997.
11. Bret Hammonds, unpublished paper for Management Theory class, Dallas Baptist University, Fall 1997.
12. Mary Gentile, *Differences in Work: Organizational Excellence Through Diversity* (Boston: Harvard Business School Press, 1994).

13. Chris Coats, "Fringe Binge," *Dallas Morning News*, June 4, 1998.
14. Ibid.
15. Carol Hymowitz, "Drawing the Line on Budding Romances in Your Workplace," *The Wall Street Journal*, November 18, 1997.
16. Amy Harmon, "Microsofties Say They're Right as Rain," *The New York Times*, May 26, 1998.
17. Ibid.
18. Author interview with Fred Bedford, October 1997.
19. Andrea Gerlin, "Pluses and Pitfalls of Company Housing," *The Wall Street Journal*, 1997.
20. Arlie Russell Hochschild, *The Time Bind* (New York, Metropolitan Books, 1997).
21. Ibid

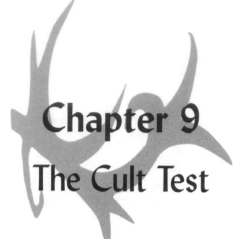

Chapter 9

The Cult Test

*Y*ou've probably been wondering where you are relative to other employees on the cultedness scale. The results of the corporate cult test in this chapter place individuals along a continuum from culted to unculted. Only twenty questions are necessary to measure the cultedness of an employee with his or her organization. This chapter explains the genesis of the three sections of the cult test, which measure devotion, charismatic leadership, and separation from community. It also explains the development of individual questions and their meaning. Finally, there are instructions for completing the test and analyzing the results.

Measuring Organizational Culture

Organizational culture is an intangible concept. Since it can't be seen or touched, it's difficult to examine or quantify precisely. All social science concepts are hard to measure, but organizational culture is more so than many.

Culture is usually defined as the deep-seated values, beliefs, and principles of those within the organization.[1] This keeps the focus at the individual level of analysis. Culture exists at three levels:

1. Observable artifacts
2. Values
3. Basic underlying assumptions[2]

This book focuses on the third level of culture—a pattern of basic assumptions that employees use to guide their behavior in the organizational setting.

In its deepest and most important sense, culture exists at a preconscious level. This makes it distinguishable from organizational *climate,* which is easier to measure because it is more readily visible. Climate, however, is merely an outward expression of the deeper constructs of values and culture.[3]

Several different types of research methodology exist to measure organizational culture. By far the most popular is the use of surveys like the Organizational Culture Inventory[4] and the Kilman-Saxon Culture-Gap Survey.[5] With this technique, the analyst uses questionnaires to present a series of items that are assumed to be relevant to the theme of an organization's culture. This method of quantifying and measuring a firm's culture is the one I have used to develop the cult test.

A major advantage of the survey method is that it is less subjective than qualitative measurement devices like direct observation and ethnography, which are sometimes used. The survey method also lends itself to comparisons within and between organizations. Qualitative measures present serious problems for the researcher. Qualitative research produces a very rich, complex collection of observations, but it is highly reliant upon the observer's biased interpretation of an organization's stories, rites, rituals, and symbolic manifestations.

Because this research is subjective in nature, findings from observational and descriptive studies cannot be used for systematic comparison. Also, in larger organizations in which subcultures exist, comparing different departments within the same organization using qualitative measures presents difficulties. The survey method was chosen for the cult test because it is a robust, reliable, and valid instrument for this type of study.[6] Quantifying organizational culture can be a frustrating task because the concept is pervasive and the examination of an employee's level of cultedness requires an all-encompassing view of the organization—including both its psychological and its structural elements. In order to resolve the rather nebulous nature of measuring organizational culture, researchers in the social sciences have conveniently operationalized culture in much the same way as personality—

using types and dimensions. Examples of these paradigms include the strong culture, the adaptive culture, and the learning culture. It is in this vein that this book creates a new paradigm: corporate cults.

It's an Index, Not a Dichotomous Measure

People's feelings are often hurt when they perceive that I am calling their organization a cult. There are three reasons I am careful not to do that:

1. A corporate cult is an individual-level construct. Only individuals can make their corporation into a cult.

2. All organizations have some level of cultish behavior; it's just that some have more than others.

3. Those who live in glass houses shouldn't throw stones. I am a professor at Dallas Baptist University, where we have our own set of cultish behaviors. We are allied with the Southern Baptist Convention, so most of us are devoted to the same religion, if not to the same workplace. Our president, Dr. Gary Cook, is a charismatic leader. The campus is physically separated from the community of Dallas. It sits alone on a hill, surrounded only by mesquite trees and a lake, an eight-minute drive from downtown. There is absolutely no development around the university. There is not even a convenience store within walking distance of the university. So to some degree we are separated from the rest of community.

Corporate cultism is not a dichotomous measure, as it often is assumed to be. Every person who joins an organization takes on some degree of cultedness, but some are more culted than others. It's a fine-grained ordinal index, not a dichotomous measure.

Are Higher-Level Employees More Culted?

Yes, there is a relationship between an employee's level in the hierarchy and his or her level of cultedness. The higher an employee's status, the more culted that person is. Organizations reward cultedness, so, in general, promotions go to employees whose values are collinear with those of the corporation. Contribution is often collinear with devotion, following the charismatic leader, and working so many hours that the employee is separated from the rest of the community.

There remains the causality question, however: Does cultedness cause promotions, or do promotions cause cultedness? I tend to think that cultedness comes first, but it's really not important in my analysis. If you look at the highest levels of management in your company, you are likely to observe this very noticeable correlation between cultedness and position level.

The Three Traits of a Cult

In order to measure cultedness, it is important to identify the defining characteristics of a culted employee. The previous chapters have established that corporate cult members display three traits:

1. Devotion
2. Charismatic leadership
3. Separation from community

These traits combine together to determine the level of cultedness an employee has with the corporation. Individuals who rate high on all three traits relative to other test takers are considered more culted. Those who rate low on all three traits are considered less culted. We would expect to see about half the employees in the middle range and the remaining test takers at either extreme. One of the premises of this book, however, is that employees are moving from the middle to either extreme in level of cultedness.

It's an Individual-Level Construct

The corporate cult test measures how the individual employee views the cultedness of the organization. Since cultedness is an individual-level construct, there will be great variations in cult test scores among individuals within the same organization. Even in what is described as a highly culted environment, there will be individuals who are extremely independent of the organization.

Scores can vary for other reasons as well. Departmental function and physical location will skew scores high or low on the cult test. Employees' scores will vary with the department or division in which the employees work. Some departments are older than others, and thus are likely to be more culted. The finance and accounting functions usually operate under tighter external scrutiny, because they have to follow CPA board rules and FASB requirements. For some employees, this external commitment decreases the degree of cultedness with their corporation.

Marketing and sales divisions are highly dependent on the products and services of the corporation for survival, so a case could be made for their being more culted. Also, they are encouraged to believe in the product or service they are selling, and that could create a closer bonding to the corporation. However, people in marketing and sales are generally more independent than employees in other functions, which might reduce their level of cultedness. Employees in operations functions spend most of their time in the workplace with their hands on the product or service that is being delivered. This could cause them to be more culted to the organization, simply because how employees spend their time is a great predictor of cultedness.

Physical location in the company affects scoring. Employees who work at company headquarters with top-level management tend to be more highly culted than those who work in a branch location. That's because the employees at headquarters have more contact with the leader of the organization. Closer contact heightens the perceived charisma of the leader. Employees who work in a remote office location or from home have their attention diverted from the corporation more easily, so they will maintain outside interests that prevent culting. This also affects the degree to which employees feel that work is the center of everything they do or the degree to which they feel separated from others outside of work.

Development of the Test

The cult test helps employees understand their level of cultedness with their organization. There are two major parts of test development. The first is conceptualization of questions that tap into the constructs under investigation, and the second is testing of the scale to determine how it holds up under statistical scrutiny.

To produce an overall measure of cultedness, scales for the

three traits—devotion, charismatic leadership, and separation—were adopted from existing research literature sources when they existed. This test marks the first time the indices have been accumulated to measure corporate cultedness.

In the first step of the research phase, more than seventy measurement items were considered and presented to several focus group of business leaders at a leadership seminar I was conducting. Participants were asked to choose the items that best corresponded to the topics devotion, charismatic leadership, and separateness. After we discussed these items and the rationale behind an organizational cult had been thoroughly explained, these groups were able to narrow the seventy questions to twenty.

Devotion

The twenty surviving items come from three main sources. What I call devotion in this book, researchers call commitment. To determine the level of an employee's devotion, items from Cooke and Walls' measure of organizational commitment were used.[7] This measure examines what it means to be a member of an organization. The items that were retained from the focus group interviews centered on the area of loyalty to the organization. According to Cooke and Walls, some people feel they are nothing more than an employee who works. Other employees feel more personally involved and devoted to the organization. According to the corporate cult definition, those who are more devoted are more culted.

Charismatic Leadership

The questions measuring charismatic leadership were adopted from Behling and McFillen's Charismatic Leadership Follower Belief Questionnaire.[8] Several items were used to measure the employee's feelings about the charismatic nature of leadership in her or his organization. The items that were retained for the measure of cultedness relate to the leader's ability to inspire followers and the followers' feeling of awe for the leader.

Separation from Community

Separation from community was measured by questions that relate to the importance of work for the employee and the employee's work-centeredness. Several items from Aryee and Luk's Work-Family Conflict Scale were used.[9] These items tap into the degree to which an employee's job and work environment are an important part of his or her life and sense of fulfillment. To further measure the degree of separation from community, I developed some additional questions, since questions on this topic did not seem to exist in the literature. These items measure the importance of work relationships in the employee's life. Included were items measuring the number of social events an organization sponsors for its employees, how much the individual enjoys being with others at work, and the involvement of other workers in the employee's life.

The Cult Test

The preceding research and testing produced a final test of corporate cultedness consisting of twenty questions. The test is found in Figure 9-1.

Taking the Test

To determine the level of your cultedness with your organization, answer each of the twenty questions on a scale from strongly agree (1) to strongly disagree (5).

The test measures three separate constructs. Scores from questions 1 through 8 should be totaled to produce a devotion score. The same procedure with items 9 through 12 produces a charismatic leadership score. The scores from questions 13 through 20 should be totaled to produce a measure of separation from community.

Figure 9-2 (see page 170) shows the score interpretation. Scores on the devotion scale, questions 1 through 8, range from 8 to 40. If your score is between 8 and 14, you have a high level of devotion to your organization. The mid-range for people who have taken this test is 15 to 19; such people have a medium level of devotion to their organization. If your score is between 20 and 40, you are a maverick because you have a very low level of devotion for your organization.

Scores on the charismatic leadership section, questions 9

Figure 9-1. Work Relationship Survey

1. I feel a strong sense of loyalty toward this company.
2. Even if the firm were not doing well financially, I would be reluctant to change to another employer.
3. The offer of a bit more money with another employer would not seriously make me think of changing my job.
4. Based on what I know now and what I believe I can expect, I would be quite willing to spend the rest of my career with this company.
5. I believe in the work my organization/unit does.
6. I feel that I am working for a cause that is greater than just earning a living.
7. My work serves a good cause.
8. The work of my organization/unit benefits society.
9. I have faith in the leader even when things go wrong.
10. I admire the leader.
11. It would be hard to find someone who could lead this organization better than the leader.
12. I trust the leader's decisions.
13. The major satisfactions in my life come from my work.
14. The most important things that happen to me involve my work.
15. My life goals are mainly work-oriented.
16. My work is a large part of who I am.
17. Many of my close personal friends work at this company.
18. The organization where I work is always planning social events for its employees.
19. I look forward to being with members of my immediate work group each day.
20. The people in my immediate work group take a personal interest in what I do.

Adapted from Cooke and T. Walls, "New Work Attitude Measures of Trust, Organizational Commitment and Need Fulfillment," *Journal of Occupational Psychology* 53 (1980): 39–52; O. Behling and J. M. McFillen, "A Syncretical Model of Charismatic Transformational Leadership," *Group Organization Management* 21 (1990): 163–192; and S. Aryee and V. Luk, "Balancing Two Major Parts of Adult Life Experience: Work and Family Identity Among Dual-Earner Couples," *Human Relations* 49 (1996): 465–488.

through 12, range from 4 to 20. If your score is in the 4 to 10 range, you think your organizational leader is very charismatic. If your score is between 11 and 13, you are in the midrange. If your score is between 14 and 20, you think your organizational leader is not charismatic at all.

Scores on the separation from community section, questions 13 through 20, range from 8 to 40. If your score is between 8 and 23, you have a high level of work-centeredness, meaning that your work may separate you from other activities outside your work environment. The midrange is 24 to 29. Respondents in that range have a mid-level amount of separation from their community. If your score is between 30 and 40, you have low work-centeredness and are probably highly involved in organizations and activities outside work.

Figure 9-2. Scores on the Individual Constructs of Corporate Cultedness

	High	Medium	Low
Devotion	8–14	15–19	20–40
Charismatic Leadership	4–10	11–13	14–20
Separation From Community	8–23	24–29	30–40

Devotion, charismatic leadership, and separation from community are three separate constructs, and they are more meaningful when kept separate. That's why I initially instruct respondents to keep the scores separate. However, when the entire test is considered, it produces an overall measure of corporate cultedness.

I'm sure you're interested in your overall score, so I encourage you to produce a total score for all twenty questions. In doing this, you should understand that this provides a valid statistical measure of corporate cultedness, but that the combination of the three measures is not as meaningful as the three separate scores. To cite an example, a soccer test that independently measures dribbling, shooting, and passing abilities is more accurate than an overall test of soccer-playing ability.

Figure 9-3 indicates that if your total score on all twenty items is in the first quartile, between 20 and 39, you are highly culted according to the test. You are devoted to the organization, you view your leader as charismatic, and you are separated from the com-

Figure 9-3. Scores on the Combined Constructs of Corporate Cultedness

20–39	First quartile	Highly culted
40–59	Second quartile	Somewhat culted
60–79	Third quartile	Pretty independent
80–100	Fourth quartile	Maverick

munity. If your score is in this category, you probably will want to take some action to change your lifestyle to one that is less culted. There are suggestions for those actions in Chapter 12, "How to Avoid a Corporate Cult Next Time."

If your score is in the second quartile, between 40 and 59, you have one foot in a cult and one foot in the independent world. You may be on your way into a cult. This score should get your attention, and you will want to consult the advice in Chapter 12.

If your score is in the third quartile, between 60 and 79, you have some cultish tendencies, but probably no more than are necessary for organizational survival. Everyone who belongs to an organization has some level of cultedness. You're not in a cult, so you don't have to change your workstyle or lifestyle significantly. However, you will want to look at the three individual constructs to find your lowest score, indicating the area in which you are the most culted.

If your score is in the fourth quartile, from 80 and 100, you are quite a maverick, because the test shows you are extremely unculted. While this independent attitude is to be admired, you might consider whether working in an organizational environment is a good fit for you. Perhaps you would be more successful in a collection of specialists where you have a great deal of freedom to do your own thing.

Explaining the Questions

The previous section explained that the cult test questions were derived from an extensive literature search of previously validated survey items. My contribution is to combine the three elements under the definition of a corporate cult. Now for a more in-depth analysis of what the questions mean individually.

The Devotion Questions

Items 1 through 8 measure an employee's level of commitment to the organization. Question 1 taps into the loyalty an employee feels toward the company as a way of determining an employee's level of obedience to the organization. How far will the employee go for the organization? Obedience is an important value that all organizations want to cultivate in their employees. It's also indicative of cultish behavior because loyalty is an important antecedent of corporate cult membership.

Questions 2, 3, and 4 also measure the employee's loyalty to the organization. Many employees display a type of commitment called *continuance commitment*. They are committed as long as they perceive the rewards to have a higher value than what is offered by a competing organization. In corporate cults, these rewards often take the form of emotional and affiliational rewards, rather than financial rewards. Thus, corporate cults develop a deeper type of commitment—one based more on emotions than on money. This is called *affective commitment*, and it leads to low employee turnover and a high number of organizational citizenship behaviors that the member conducts above and beyond normally expected job assignments.[10]

Questions 5 through 8 measure the degree to which an employee identifies with the organization. "Believing in the work of the organization," doing something "greater than just earning a living," working for a "good cause," and working in an organization that "benefits society" are all important to the emotional commitment an employee feels toward the company.

This construct is similar to loyalty and is not a negative. Employees should *want* to work for an organization that fosters a sense of significance for the individual. In corporate cults, however, the organization claims the individual's sense of significance in order to further its goals at the cost of individual goals.

The Charismatic Leadership Questions

Items 9 through 12 measure the level of charismatic leadership in the organization. Corporate cults have a charismatic leader at their core, as explained in Chapter 7. These questions specifically tap into the employee's level of awe for the leader. Awe can be defined as the follower's unreasoned faith in the leader's abilities.

Like affective commitment, charismatic leadership engenders several behaviors in followers: exceptionally high levels of effort, unusually high commitment, and willingness to take risks for the organization.

The Separation From Community Questions

The remaining items, 13 through 20, measure separation from the community, which is often termed *work-centeredness*. Questions 13 through 16 tap into the importance of work in a person's life. These questions determine the contribution of work to a person's overall satisfaction, life goals, and sense of accomplishment. These questions come from the work/family literature stream, which studies the degree of segregation or integration of an employee's work life and family life. These particular questions measure the level of an employee's involvement in work activities.

Items 17 through 20 were developed specifically to measure other aspects of work-centeredness that are common to corporate cults. Questions 17 and 20 measure an employee's level of intimacy with coworkers. Question 20 was purposely written as value-neutral so that it could measure the level of intimacy whether the employee likes or dislikes it. The employee may not like the fact that coworkers take a personal interest in her or his actions, but this is still an important measure of corporate cultedness because it indicates a blurring of the line between the employee's work life and personal life.

Question 18 measures the degree to which an organization provides for the social needs of the employee. As explained in Chapter 4, a corporate cult becomes a surrogate family that meets the emotional and psychological needs of its members. Question 19 measures the employee's level of anticipation of being with members of the work group. It is an indication of the centrality and importance of emotional involvement with fellow group members.

Testing the Test

The term *corporate cults* did not appear anywhere on the test, because I wanted to limit the bias of the respondents. *Cult* is often viewed as an incendiary term, and using it might have motivated respondents to try to obtain a more independent score that would not be a true indication of their cultedness. Instead, the questionnaire was labeled "Work Relationship Survey." Respondents were told that its purpose was to gain a better understanding of individuals' feelings about the organization, their supervisors, their job, themselves, and their coworkers.

After being pretested with several small groups, the cult test was distributed to a group of middle-level managers from a wide variety of companies and industries. In this segment of the study, 118 surveys were returned and analyzed. After the data were collected, the validity of the test was determined.

Validity is a gauge of how well the test measures the dimensions it was intended to measure. In this case, the test has validity if it measures the three discrete aspects of cultedness. Results from the survey show that it has a high level of validity. If the measurement items had been correlated in a way that had not been predicted, then the validity of the twenty-item measure would not have been supported.

Statistical measures of validity show that the items measuring the three dimensions of cultedness—devotion, charismatic leadership, and separation from community—fall into distinct groups, as I predicted. In addition, the items for the three dimensions of cultedness were highly correlated with one another, but still fairly independent. This implies that the three dimensions are separate and distinct from one another and are actually measuring different dimensions of organizational culture. Only one of the items appears to be disappointing—question 20, measuring the degree to which people in the immediate work group take a personal interest in the respondent. While this question could be omitted because of its statistical weakness relative to the other items, I retained it because I believe this is a very important dimension of the construct.

As anticipated, the three constructs measure the defined dimensions of a corporate cult quite successfully. Now that you know your level of cultedness, you probably want to do something about it. That's why the subject of Chapter 10 is independence. It tells corporate cult members how to become "the captain of your soul."

Notes

1. Andrew Pettigrew, "On Studying Organizational Cultures," *Administrative Science Quarterly* 24 (1979): 570–581.
2. Edgar Schein, *Organizational Culture and Leadership* (San Francisco: Jossey-Bass, 1985).
3. R. E. Kopelman, A. P. Brief, and R. A. Guzzo, "The Role of Climate and Culture in Productivity," in *Organizational Climate and Culture*, (ed.) B. Schneider (San Francisco: Jossey-Bass, 1990).
4. R. A. Cooke and D. M. Rousseau, "Behavioral Norms and Expectations: A Quantitative Approach to the Measurement of Organizational Culture," *Group & Organizational Studies* 13 (1988), 245–273.
5. R. H. Kilman and M. J. Saxon, *The Kilman-Saxon Culture-Gap Survey* (Pittsburgh: Organizational Design Consultants, 1983).
6. S. Lahiry, "Building Commitment Through Organizational Culture," *Training & Development* 48 (1994): 50–52.
7. J. Cooke and T. Walls, "New Work Attitude Measures of Trust, Organizational Commitment and Need Fulfillment," *Journal of Occupational Psychology* 53 (1980): 39–52.
8. O. Behling and J. M. McFillen, "A Syncretical Model of Charismatic Transformational Leadership," *Group & Organization Management* 21 (1990): 163–192.
9. S. Aryee and V. Luk, "Balancing Two Major Parts of Adult Life Experience: Work and Family Identity Among Dual-Earner Couples," *Human Relations* 49 (1996): 465–488.
10. R. T. Mowaday, R. M. Steers, and L. W. Porter, *Employee Organization Linkages: The Psychology of Commitment, Absenteeism and Turnover* (New York: Academic Press, 1979).

Chapter 10
Independence

*A*s director of operations, Sherri Hutcheon did many things that made her job at the Dallas Mavericks into a cult. She was just out of college and full of energy, and she loved her job. When she married Jeff, however, she took a job selling advertising for Dallas Cowboys radio broadcasts. The less stressful job allowed time for her marriage. When she was pregnant with her first child, she started The Home Base, a sports advertising consultancy that she operates from home. Sherri's career path exemplifies more than making good choices of family over career. It also shows the independence to separate "who I am" from "what I do."

Independence From Organizational Life

Norma Warner was a teacher and administrator for the USDA Graduate School, a recently privatized business that provides training for federal employees. She was excited as we walked out of a corporate cults presentation. "I really enjoyed your presentation," she said. I thanked her. "I'm quitting my job," she said emphatically.

I was stunned. Congratulating me on a good speech was one thing. Her quitting her job was something I was not ready to accept responsibility for. "Is it because of something I said?" I asked.

"I have been thinking about it," she answered. "I really enjoy teaching, but I don't enjoy the administration they make me do. I'm quitting on May 31," she said again, this time even more definitely, totally convinced that this was the right thing to do.

I was surprised that the discussion of organizational cults had moved her to make such a definite decision about her career. However, it was *her* decision. She had obviously been thinking about her career, and the discussion of corporate cults brought her to the realization that she needed more independence than her current employment allowed. Norma needed more control over her life, and quitting her job was the way to obtain it. She quit her job, but not her profession. She now serves as an adjunct teacher for the graduate school, doing more of what she likes—teaching—and less of what she doesn't like—administration. Her ability to quit her job indicated a great deal of independence from organizational life. The following story tells of a young girl and her friends who expected much more.

The Oz Principle

Dorothy and Toto wanted to get back to Kansas. The scarecrow wanted a brain, the tin man wanted a heart, and the lion wanted courage. That's quite an impressive list of wishes to present to a single person. But Dorothy and her friends were confident that they could get all those things, and more, from just one person: the Wizard of Oz. The Wizard of Oz is an effective metaphor for the great expectations employees have for their workplace.[1]

Employees of corporate cults expect to receive money, vacation, status, friends, encouragement, medical benefits, and professional esteem from the corporation. They would be well advised to remember the end of Dorothy's trip down the yellow brick road. A crushing reality descends upon them when Toto pulls back the curtain to reveal a mortal man *acting* as a wizard. "Pay no attention to the man behind the curtain," he bellows over the superamplified speakers. But it was too late. Dorothy and her crew had discovered the truth: There is no wizard.

However, Dorothy and her friends *did* get what they wanted—by clicking *their own* heels. That's the message of the Wizard of Oz: Don't look to your workplace for all the rewards of life; click your own heels. Employees who have such high expectations for the organization and expect their needs and wants to be fulfilled by the workplace are as naïve as Dorothy and her band marching down the yellow brick road. Corporate cults like the dependence, because it binds the employee closer to the organization for financial and emotional support.

An interview subject in *The Time Bind* explained why she was back at work soon after giving birth: "That was six weeks I didn't have anybody to talk to. My friends are at work. The things that interest me are at work. My stimulation is at work. I am delighted to come back."[2] This employee had just given birth to a new life, but she needed to find one herself! Get a life! Somewhere else, please! This is even further evidence of the swaddling concept from Chapter 4. Are employees so dependent on their corporation that they can't find fulfillment elsewhere?

Let's look closely at this quote. This woman is finding more at work than Dorothy and her friends hoped to get from the Wizard of Oz. This employee has found someone to talk to, friends, interest, and stimulation. Work was more stimulating to her than caring for her new child! This person suffers from a serious case of dependence. Since the workplace is dependent on her fanatically committed lifestyle, the two are codependent. Unfortunately, the codependence is with the corporation, her corporate cult. She could take some good advice from the people portrayed in the next section.

Success vs. Significance

A growing number of workers are beginning to feel less obsessed with organizational success. They have a sense that they can achieve greater fulfillment outside their narrow workplace. This causes them to ask themselves why they should give so much to the corporations they work for. Baby Boomers who were once workaholics have come to realize that there are more important things in life.[3]

These workers populate the collection of specialist organizations described in Chapter 3. As old organizations from the middle of the competitive advantage selection model downsize, many of the downsized employees with this attitude are migrating to organizations on this end of the model.

This has been a typical life-stage development for all generations. In the book *Half Time*, Bob Buford encourages readers to shift gears from "success" to "significance." Buford says that people spend the first half of their professional life seeking success, and the enlightened spend the other half seeking significance. His book shies away from telling others what success is, but instead describes the process for self-discovery of it.[4]

Buford implies that success has to do with position, power, and money, which are gained through the corporation. Significance is an entirely different set of characteristics and includes the emotional and relational benefits gained from family and community involvement. Following Buford's advice demands a break from corporate cults that honor the workaholic dysfunction that is inherent in so many employees.

Honoring Dysfunction

American business honors dysfunction. There is a direct correlation between cultedness and organizational success. The higher the person gets in the company, the more culted he or she is. Organizations thrive on dysfunctional workaholics. Culted employees have a "hole in their soul" that they satisfy by work. Their definition of "who I am" is totally answered by "what I do" at work.

My seminar attendees often point out the correlation between commitment and success in organizations. I challenge my college students to write their own definition of success, for two reasons:

1. It is easier to achieve.
2. You will feel more gratified when you have achieved it.

People who chase after *society's* definition of success will never reach it. It's a self-perpetuating problem. Individuals seek society's definition of success (status and money), but as they gain more of both, they still feel unsatisfied. So they seek still more status and money by working harder and longer. The organization loves this kind of dysfunctional activity. The workers are never fulfilled, because they are seeking society's definition of success instead of their own.

Many of those unsatisfied people go to see my brother, who is a personal counselor. I guess the system takes care of itself; this is what happens to people:

1. They seek status and money by working hard.
2. They feel unfulfilled.
3. They work harder.
4. They remain unfulfilled.
5. They go to see my brother, and he tells them how to feel fulfilled.

The system supports itself, because through their dedicated work, they have earned enough money to pay my brother $150 an hour to tell them why they're unhappy. Some people think power brings happiness, but we all have plenty of it.

Power

Adults do whatever they want every second of their lives. I often challenge university students to tell me something they *have* to do that they don't want to do. "Pay taxes," is a common response. "You don't have to pay taxes," I answer. "Work," says another. "You don't have to work," I say. "Attend this class," says an outspoken (and brave) student. "You don't have to come to this class, and you can stand up and leave anytime you want," I insist. They soon figure out that they really *are* doing what they want.

Our lives are a continual series of choices and consequences. We pay taxes because we don't want to suffer the consequences of not paying. We work because we want the consequences of that choice—i.e., we want the things that money buys. Corporate cult members work because they want the emotional support of the workplace.

Many of my students don't like the responsibility that comes with the choices. If they *have* to go to class, they can blame someone else: their parents, me, or the university administration. They don't like having the freedom to make decisions, because that means that they are responsible for those decisions. They feel more comfortable if they have someone else to blame.

I must add one small caveat to the fiercely independent ideal of the previous paragraphs, just in case my teenagers read this section: That concept is limited to adults. Underage people often are forced to do things they don't want to.

No Person Can Tell Another What to Do

If people do whatever they want, then organizational power, as normally defined, does not exist. In the movie *Dances With Wolves,* there is a great scene after the Native Americans first see the character played by Kevin Costner living alone on the plains. They conduct a council meeting to decide what to do about this unusual circumstance. There is a split within the council as to what action should be taken. One group sees him as an instrument for forging peace treaties with whites. Another suggests that he may have spiritual powers. A third suggests that he is a threat, and logically proposes a test of his spiritual powers. "Let's go shoot some arrows into him," says a brazen warrior. "If he has powers, he will live; if he doesn't, he will die." The shaman finds a middle ground: "No man can tell another what to do."[5]

The shaman is correct: No person can tell another what to do. When it is defined as the ability to make another person do something he or she doesn't want to, *power does not exist.* What *does* exist is organizational authority. Authority is granted by the organization to apply consequences to choices. When people don't pay taxes, a governmental organization has the authority to put them in jail. People who don't work don't have the money to buy the things they want. Students who don't attend university classes won't earn a college degree. Those who stand up and leave in the middle of class will pay a visit to the dean of students.

My mother studies genealogy, and she likes to remind me of ancestors who were French Huguenots. Huguenots who did not pledge allegiance to the state church were burned at the stake. Many would say that the state had the *power* to make the Huguenots convert. If that were the case, there would have been no burnings at the stake—but there were. The state could not make the Huguenots convert; it could only take their lives if they didn't.

If power existed, there would be no crime. Governmental organizations would use their power to prevent it. No one has *power* over you. They only have organizational authority to assign consequences to your choices.

Some Good Choices

Anne Mulcahy is a Xerox vice president with two young sons who finds success in the work-life continuum by stiff-arming the corporation once in a while. "You always have to be in control of your boundaries," she says. "The minute you let any company, any manager, try to set them for you, you've lost it." She agrees with me that the "you-can-have-it-all" promise is a myth. "I am no more than two-dimensional," she says. "I do work, and I do family. When it comes to writing down hobbies on résumés, I make them up." She says she envies people who have time for community service.[6]

While I wish Mulcahy could find time for some community involvement, I truly admire her clear understanding of the dimensions of her life. She has made conscious choices to divide her time between work and family. Furthermore, she has control over those decisions. She credits Xerox for its favorable family policies and understanding of her work-family choices. Can you "have it all"? No, but it's more important to have the independence to make choices about what you *will* have and what you *won't*, as Mulcahy has.

After I gave a speech in Albuquerque, New Mexico, an attendee introduced himself to me by saying, "I know your boss." "That's interesting," I responded. "I didn't think I had one." University professors can be highly independent.

"I served on the city council of Waco, Texas, with your university president, Gary Cook," he continued. When I researched the issue, I found that Dr. Cook had, in fact, served on the city council. At age 32, he was in line to be the youngest mayor in the history of Waco when he suddenly and unexpectedly resigned from the council. "I did a lot of thinking and decided I wanted to spend more time with my wife and son," he said. "It would have been exciting to be mayor, but that would have required even more of my time."[7]

He then accepted the presidency of Dallas Baptist University and worked long, difficult days to resurrect it from the brink of closure. As the university was turning the corner to success, he raised the funds to build a president's home on campus. While that presents separation from community issues, it certainly confirms the importance of family in his life. Much like Mulcahy, he has found a satisfying balance between a passion for work and a passion for family.

"Invictus"

Independence is the theme of "Invictus," by W. E. Henley:

Out of the night that covers me,
Black as the Pit from pole to pole,
I thank whatever gods may be
For my unconquerable soul.

In the fell clutch of circumstance
I have not winced nor cried aloud.
Under the bludgeonings of chance
My head is bloody, but unbowed.

Beyond this place of wrath and tears
Looms but the Horror of the shade
And yet the menace of the years,
Finds, and shall find, me unafraid.

It matters not how strait the gate
How charged with punishments the scroll,
I am the master of my fate;
I am the captain of my soul.[8]

In "Invictus," Henley is stating that even the greatest being ever conceived of—God—cannot take away an individual's soul. It belongs to the individual, and only the individual can give it away. The individual is in control, as the students in the following anecdote indicate.

Is There Life Outside Work?

Intel conducted 2,500 prescreening employment interviews on fifty campuses in 1996 and found a marked increase in life balance questions from potential recruits. College recruiting manager Mike Foster says that fully 50 percent of the interviewees asked questions about life outside the company and whether Intel was going to allow them to have one. Only 20 percent asked those questions just five years earlier.[9]

The real question is whether this increase in lifestyle questions affects job performance. GTE finds that recruits who ask lifestyle questions in the prehire interviews end up being top performers in their jobs. Other corporate recruiters have also found that passion is a thread that flows through the person's life. Candidates who ask corporate lifestyle questions in preemployment interviews are passionate about both their personal and their professional lives.[10]

I have always liked Generation X, and this is why. The college students mentioned in these interviews already have the ability at their young age to see the balance of the three life circles: work, community, and family. They are going to make contributions in all three and maintain a balanced life. Students who ask these questions are much less likely to become members of corporate cults. They are also likely to work fewer hours, as explained in the next section.

Working Smarter, Not Harder

Continuing to be a member in good standing of a corporate cult means putting in face time at the office. Since corporate cults hire people for who they are, not what they do, the measure of success is being who you are at the office and spending a lot of time there. In this sense, corporate cults are one era behind. In the Industrial Age, output was highly correlated with the number of hours worked, but in the Information Age, it is not. Noncult companies measure success by output, not face time.

In many industries, the best performers actually spend *less* time at work than the average.[11] An individual makes the greatest contribution to an organization by finding the critical path and staying on it, without interference from company norms. These star performers have interesting and rich lives outside the work-place.

These star performers use many shortcuts that would be considered terrible indiscretions at corporate cults, such as skipping boring meetings so that they can get work done. This breed of no-nonsense workers is easily frustrated by stifling bureaucracy and inefficient work processes and will leave the organization quickly when the satisfaction that comes with task completion is not provided.[12]

The "stars" that are explained in this conceptual analysis obviously do not fit into the people-oriented specialist collection. They are much better suited for the collection of specialists, where they are allowed the freedom to operate as they choose outside the corporate cult environment. Their independence also means that they like to continually upgrade their education.

Educate, Educate, Educate

I have spent most of my academic career educating adults. Dallas Baptist University has one of the most highly developed and respected degree completion programs in the country. The typical student is in his or her mid-thirties with fifteen years of professional experience. The program is based on the assumption that in those fifteen years, a student has done *something* that was valuable enough to justify college credit. Students go through a rigorous class in which they write a voluminous portfolio explaining why they should receive university-level credit for practical workplace experience. The lengthy and detailed portfolio is analyzed by two evaluators, one internal to the university and one external, to determine the level and amount of credit the student should receive.

After this lengthy and rigorous course of study, students register for the management classes I teach. They are truly an independent lot. In the first place, the portfolio class has placed a chip on their shoulder. Their attitude is, "I wrote a 100-page portfolio. There's nothing you can ask me to do in this class that is tougher than that!" As a general rule, they are very good students.

These students' sponsoring corporations have made them independent as well. On many occasions we have discussed the wisdom of the corporation paying for part or all of students' degree completion. It's good for the students, because they complete their degrees. It's not always good for the corporation, because employees often leave to take a better job offer after completing the degree. Some have to commit to stay with the corporation for a few years after graduation. However, students and their sponsoring corporations continue to believe that the investment is worthwhile, even if some of the recent graduates leave the employer shortly after graduation. It's very difficult for the corporation to encult such workers. Yes, the employee may feel some loyalty because the corporation funded the degree, but the predominant outcome is that the student-employee has learned a great deal in seeking the degree, and is anxious to use it. This often means that she or he has to leave the sponsoring corporation to take a job elsewhere that fulfills the need to contribute.

The philosophy is supported by Carolyn Corbin of the Center for the Twenty-First Century, "If you want to create conditions that will motivate the best people to stay, you have to help them develop the skills and allow them the freedoms that will enable them to leave."[13] Healthy corporations, like healthy families, teach choice and independence. Corporate cults don't.

The continuing education program could also be viewed from the corporate point of view: "Is the corporation better off with the tuition support program, or without it?" These corporations have continued to believe that if they did not have the tuition support program, they would lose good people sooner, rather than later. When they are paying tuition, at least they keep the employee during the educational process. Good people are hard to find, and good people want to continue to educate themselves for a constantly changing future. Thus, corporations that provide tuition assistance for education at a university of the employee's choice are not corporate cults. Those that educate their own employees are more likely to be cultish in nature.

Education and Corporation Cults

The way corporate cults treat continuing education is the exact opposite to the attitude of the degree completion students who enter my classes. Corporate cults don't let their employees go elsewhere for education. They keep them at *home*.

Corporate cults are afraid that employees who go elsewhere for education might be indoctrinated with foreign ideas or values. They feel much more comfortable keeping their employees in educational programs that are designed and delivered by company staff.

These "corporate trainer" posts are highly sought-after positions within the corporation, and are usually held by employees who have been with the company for a long time. There is obviously a direct correlation between tenure and cultedness. Thus, company trainers must be the most culted, so that management can be confident of their ability to pass along company dogma in the educational setting. Corporate cults would shudder at the thought of their employees sitting in a classroom under the tutelage of a professor who might be teaching something other than the company line.

Of course, corporate cults don't come out and say directly that they don't want their employees going outside the company for education. They couch it in terms that are more covert. "It's less expensive for us to do our own education" is one good excuse. Remember, corporate cults are always trying to satisfy the employee, at least on the surface. So they will blame their in-house training program on convenience, stating, "It's more convenient to provide in-house training. That way, our employees don't have to run across town to your campus."

Off-site education separates employees from the corporation. On-site education separates employees from the community, which is something that corporate cults want to do. The after-hours bonding that takes place in on-site educational programs builds teams that are good for the corporation and bad for the employee's home and community life.

Temping in the Year 2000

Temporary work has come a long way since the Kelly Girl image of the 1960s. Manpower Temporaries, the nation's largest temp agency, has joined with outplacement specialist Drake Beam Morin to find temporary positions for white-collar workers.[14] Some choose the temp solution as a means of protecting time with their family. Some just dislike the elbowing that takes place in the climb up the corporate ladder. Most are people who don't need the family security of the specialist collection and just want the money that accrues from doing a task well in a collection of specialists. "Employees have changed," says Jeff Joerres, senior vice president of marketing at Milwaukee-based Manpower. "They are increasingly interested in a specific *project*, rather than a specific *company*. They are interested in getting more skills and moving on to the next project."[15]

Those who enjoy the freedom of this type of collection of specialists say they see no need to "go captive," their phrase for employment at a specialist collection. They are typical of employees who see work as simply one-third of the three-part equation that includes family and community. Working on temporary projects allows the employee to concentrate on family life and get involved in the community.

The U.S. Department of Labor estimates that the number of temporary employees will increase from 2.25 million to 3.6 million in the ten years from 1995 to 2005. These are workers whose high level of independence will prevent them from being easily culted.[16]

Making a Commitment to Family Life

Lori Perry Peterson is independent enough to separate her family life from her work life as an administrator for the Dallas city auditor's office. She describes her commitment to her family: "My husband and I both had parents who were married to their jobs. It allowed us to see firsthand that money is not what makes you happy. We saw our parents ignoring their families and trying to keep up with the corporate American rat race. Yes, they did get rich. But they were not happy, and, what was worse, we as their children were not the beneficiaries of their time, a better education, or greater opportunities because of our parents' riches. They were too busy making money to spend the time with us that was necessary to assure that we received a good education or that our athletic potential was fostered. Both of our families had beautiful fruit hanging from their trees, and they just let it fall to the ground and rot. My husband and I have dedicated our lives 100 percent to our children. We sit down and do homework with them at night, we sign them up for sporting teams, we attend each practice and game, we practice with them on the weekends, and we take them and include them in every aspect of our lives. This is our treasure, three small fruit trees that we spend our time with, manicuring, watering, and nurturing. This is a legacy that has the potential to be carried on through many generations. If we don't dedicate our lives to our kids, if our jobs mean more to us than our children's development and future, how are they to believe that anyone else in the world will see value in them? Parents are the first line of defense against a child's loss of self-esteem. Children will believe in themselves if first their parents believe in them and show them they have worth."[17]

Lori and her family represent the kind of independence that will keep their family out of corporate cults. Middle management may not be as fortunate.

Goodbye to Middle Management

Middle management is being replaced by a strong corporate ethos at corporate cults. There are at least three reasons for this:

1. *Job losses.* Although middle managers make up 5 to 8 percent of the workforce, they account for 15 to 20 percent of job losses, according to an American Management Association survey.

2. *Disgruntled employees.* Subordinates don't like middle managers. They get low marks for mentoring, discipline, and making work fun, according to a report by Interim Services.

3. *Low morale.* Middle managers are less likely than other managers to say they have the resources they need to perform their jobs.[18]

As an antagonist of corporate cults, I think this reduction in middle management is good. At the university level, we find many students preparing themselves to be task and industry specialists, which will keep them out of corporate cults. They obtain their degree for *skills* security, not *job* security. They are preparing themselves to work for many different companies, but to perform within a relatively narrow functional niche where they can provide value to these different companies.

Those industry-level consultants cannot be culted into a corporation because they will continually move among and between corporations throughout their career. The following anecdote exemplifies another way to avoid the clutches of a corporate cult.

"Way to Go, Brenda!"

The departure of Brenda Barnes from PepsiCo made headlines in the business press. When Barnes gave up the title of president and chief executive officer of Pepsi-Cola North America in late 1997, she was one of the highest-ranking women in corporate America. She quit to spend more time with her family. After years of hectic travel, dinner meetings, missing children's birthdays, and even living in separate cities from her husband, Barnes decided that she had made enough sacrifices for her employer, and that it was time to choose family over work.

She seems to share my attitude about the individual-corporate relationship: The business of business is business, and the business of family is not. It's a family, not a business. Clear on her decisions, Barnes says of corporate pressure, "If you want to be president and CEO, that's a choice you have to make," indicating that she clearly understood her choice to honor the corporation for many years and was clearly confident of her new decision to spend more time with her husband and preadolescent children.[19]

She won't be culted. That kind of independent spirit is what keeps corporate cults from taking over American business. The lie of having it all—career, marriage, home, children—is trashed by Barnes's clear economic thinking.

Sharing the Workplace

Job sharing is a bright spot as an antidote to corporate cults. Ann Sedita and Carlene Swensson share a job selling advertising at radio station KLIF in Dallas. Both women wanted more time with their kids, but didn't want to quit the business. They share a cubicle that's adorned with sales awards earned together.

The "twins," as they are called around the radio station, sit back to back in their cramped cubicle only on Wednesday, which they call the hand-off day. Swensson works the first three days of the week, Sedita the last three. They are on commission, so everybody wins by their impressive performance except competing radio stations. They're 30 percent over their sales goal for the year.

They use the same phone mail. Each half of the twins carries a cell phone when she is not at work. They like job sharing because it gives them the job they want in the company they want, and they have confidence that the job is being done effectively when they're not there.[20]

When independent-minded employees realize the cultedness

of their organizations, they flee traditional work settings for the kind of freedom exemplified by job sharing. The twins in this example have the best of both worlds: a rewarding job and a rewarding family life. Since they are on commission, their pay is limited only by their performance. These job sharers have taken responsibility for their lives, both personal and professional. The following section describes some who haven't.

Blame It on the Corporate Cult

Many corporate cult members are looking for someone or something to blame their decisions on. They really dislike making decisions, and would like someone else to make them.

In the small, conservative religion in which I grew up, we weren't allowed to attend movies at the theater. When my childhood friends were surprised by this, my response was, "My church won't let me." Children do well under such rules. Adults don't, unless they are in a corporate cult.

Corporate cult members have many of their most important decisions made for them, and they appreciate it. Picture a religious cult; you probably envision mindless automatons stumbling around in matching uniforms, doing the bidding of the cult leader. Now open your eyes and take a look at your workplace. Scary, isn't it?

The intervening factor that separates your workplace from the cult you have just envisioned is *choice*. Cult members choose to join the organization because the cult is offering something that is missing in their lives. The commitment slowly escalates until the member forfeits control of his or her life to the cult.

You probably know someone who would like to change jobs, or even totally change industries, but can't because he is trapped in his job or industry. The problem is caused by his escalation of commitment to his functional profession or company. Such people become proficient and knowledgeable about the function they are performing, and their salary slowly increases until they are worth so much more in their functional specialization than they would be outside it that they can't leave. They are trapped. Control has slowly shifted from the individuals to the organization, and they have lost their independence.

The best way to prevent this is to remain independent of the organization. The trick is to be a member of the organization, yet retain individual identity. A periodic reanalysis of "who's in charge, me or the organization?" provides a healthy dose of prevention. The woman in the following story has answered the question very successfully.

Job Hopping

Employees tend to stay put at specialist collections, where corporate cults are common. At the other end of the spectrum, job hopping—from one collection of specialists to another—is becoming fashionable. Paul Smith is the site general manager for Fidelity Investments in Covington, Kentucky, where the staff has grown from 300 to 2,800 in just five years. In looking over a lot of résumés, he has begun to notice that it's common for candidates in their late twenties to have already had three jobs. "Ten years ago someone with three jobs was a job hopper. Today, someone who is 30 and has had 10 years with one company, you ask if they are too conservative."[21] No, they're not too conservative; they simply spent ten years in a specialist collection working for a corporate cult.

The experience of twenty-six-year-old Jodi Strassberg is a good example. She worked in three different international shipping companies in short order (probably collections of specialists) before jumping out of her industry to find a "home" at Englehard Corporation in Iselin, New Jersey. There, she was paired with a "buddy" who inculcated her with the corporate culture. "I got along with people right away," says Strassberg "The buddy program makes me feel wanted, which in turn makes me want to stay and do a really good job."[22]

That's because she's found the type of specialist collection that satisfies her need for family. This is an archetypal case of a person transferring through four companies in five years until she self-selects to the type of organizational culture (corporate cult) in which she feels at home. She will probably stay a long time. She seems to have corporate cult tendencies that are hard to break. Her employer has become the instrument through which she receives emotional support, as explained in the next section.

The "Organon"

The word *organization* has its genesis in the Greek word *organon*, which means an instrument. I like that definition, because it indicates that the organization is not an end in itself, it is a means to an end.

People are ends and organizations are means. Organizations are used as a means to achieve ends for the people in them. A musical instrument is admired not for its inherent beauty, but for the beauty of the music it produces. It's an instrument that is designed for producing something. A Stradivarius violin looks much like other violins; its special characteristic is its ability to produce beautiful music.

Musicians don't make the mistake of admiring the instrument more than its product, so why do so many organizational members make the mistake of honoring the corporation when it's simply an "organon" for getting something done?

They do so because corporations have produced so many valuable things for us. They have enriched our lives with material goods. Just as Dorothy and her friends believed in the Wizard of Oz, corporate cult members have become enchanted by the instrument and have confused the organon with its product. That's when the organization becomes a corporate cult.

The Most Independent Generation Yet: X

It was established in an earlier chapter that Gen Xers are extremely independent. In theory, this should help keep them out of corporate cults. However, *Rocking the Ages* offers exactly the opposite prediction. The book states, "Generation Xers feel that having a career means giving up a life, but just having a job means boredom." Gen Xers separated work into two neat bundles: A corporate cult contains a career and excitement; noncults contain a job, a life, and boredom.[23]

This analysis seems to say that Gen-Xers make the tough choice between an exciting life in a corporate cult and a dull life in a regular job. My hope has been that this generation would use its well-known independence to find a satisfying mix of work, family, and community. However, the opposite seems to be happening.

Its members seem to be polarized at opposite ends of the work commitment continuum. One group is clustering in the collection of specialist type organizations, and the other is clustering at the specialist collection end of the conceptual framework. This generation will divide between those who want career and excitement in a specialist collection and those who want a job, a life, and boredom in a collection of specialists.

Making Your Hobby Your Job

Dale Winfrey is about as unculted a man as you could ever find. He is the archetypal Baby Boomer individualist. During his career, he was a salesman for a medical supply company, several computer firms, and a printing company.

He worked under many different leaders, but he never considered any of them charismatic. He performed his sales function successfully and was paid accordingly. In his late fifties, he quit his job to pursue a lifelong dream: to become a black bass fishing guide. Dale not only refused to be culted by the many corporations he worked for, he finally left to make his hobby his job. He successfully maintained his individual identity throughout his life. Perhaps he should worry about losing it in death.

FDR Chose His Own Identity

A Washington, D.C., statue of Franklin Roosevelt that was unveiled in 1997 showed the former president sitting in a chair, a cape discreetly cloaking the wheelchair that he was compelled to use for the last years of his presidency. When he was alive, Roosevelt chose to hide his disability. Of the thousands of photographs of him as president, only two show him in a wheelchair.

However, disability-rights activists protested the statue until President Clinton announced that he would back legislation to produce a statue of FDR in a wheelchair. It's sad that a U.S. president who was so in control of his destiny when he was alive, lost control of his legacy in death.

A magazine writer took on the disability-rights activists:

> There's considerable evidence that Roosevelt derived psychological strength from *not* identifying with his disabil-

ity—in fact, by denying it. The idea that one can live truthfully only by identifying with one's physical self is a very unappealing part of the current drift toward group-rights thinking. Our identities, formed by any number of factors—race, gender, class, family—are subject to our will. This freedom of choice is one of the things that most define America. It's a freedom worth preserving.[24]

Roosevelt was a great example of independent thinking. He literally developed his own vision of who he was, separate from his obvious physical impairment. While he could be accused of being in denial, it was his choice to be in denial about a physical characteristic that belonged to him, not to the group.

First Lady Eleanor Roosevelt apparently was as independent-minded as her husband. "You not only have the right to be an individual," she said, "you have the obligation to be one. You cannot make a meaningful contribution to life unless you do this." She was right, as Dorothy and her friends found: People must be individuals. They must be individuals who don't rely on organizations for emotional support.

Employees in corporate cults can take a lesson from the Roosevelts. Even the most obvious characteristics of your personal identity are not predetermined for you. *You* have the ability to determine who *you* are. Groups would like to do this for you, and they will if you let them. The only reason the disability-rights activists succeeded in co-opting Roosevelt is that he's dead. If he were alive, he wouldn't stand for it, and you shouldn't either. You can have an identity separate from the physical characteristics you were born with, and you can certainly have an identity separate from corporate cults. Some people are finding that separate identity by downshifting.

Downshifting

It was almost predictable that when the consumer-crazed Baby Boomers reached middle age, a movement of this type would occur. Baby Boomers have done most things differently from the way the generations that preceded them did, and they have also mellowed differently.

This movement is called "downshifting," and it's indicative of the escape from corporate cults. A downshifter is someone who has decided that in one's career, more isn't always better.[25] This concept seems to be a nice blend of civic responsibility and individual choice. Downshifters haven't dropped *out* of life, they've dropped *into* it. They trade eighty-hour weeks for jobs with less stress and less pay. It's a difficult step to take for corporate cult members, who measure success by level in the organization.

Corporate cults sternly disapprove of downshifters and are likely to spurn them. But taking control of your life is going to cost you something, as all lifestyle changes do. You don't have to downshift to escape a corporate cult, but some will. Just as traditional cult members have to be deprogrammed and some addicts can only quit cold turkey, some corporate cult escapees will choose the downshifting option as a way out.

Exactly *how* people remain independent of corporate cults is largely determined by the individual's personality.

That's the subject of Chapter 11.

Notes

1. Roger Connors, Tom Smith, and Craig Hickman, *The Oz Principle* (Englewood Cliffs, N.J.: Prentice Hall, 1994).
2. Arlie Russell Hochschild, *The Time Bind* (New York: Metropolitan Books, 1997).
3. Carolyn Corbin, *Strategies 2000* (Austin, Tex.: Eakin Press, 1991).
4. Bob Buford, *Halftime* (Grand Rapids, Mich.: Zondervon, 1994).
5. Michael Blake, *Dances with Wolves* (New York: New Market Press, 1988).
6. Sue Shellenbarger, "Some Top Executives Are Finding a Balance Between Job and Home," *The Wall Street Journal*, April 23, 1997.
7. Sheila Pimpler, "Waco Councilman Not to Run in '84," *Waco Lariat*, September 2, 1983.
8. William Ernest Henley, *The Works of W. E. Henley* (New York: AMS Press, 1970).
9. Sue Shellenbarger, "New Job Hunters Ask Recruiters, 'Is There a Life After Work?'" *The Wall Street Journal*, January 29, 1997.
10. Ibid.

11. Robert E. Kelley, *How to Be a Star at Work: 9 Breakthrough Strategies to Help* (New York: Times Books, 1996).
12. Sue Shellenbarger, "You Don't Have to Be Chained to Your Desk to Be a Star Performer," *Wall Street Journal*, August 14, 1998.
13. Carolyn Corbin, *Strategies 2000* (Austin, Tex.: Eakin Press, 1991).
14. Vincent Schodolski, "Temporary Phenomenon," *Chicago Tribune*, July 8, 1996.
15. Ibid.
16. Ibid.
17. Interview with the author, February 1997.
18. Stephanie Armour, "Management Loses Its Allure," *USA Today*, October 10, 1997.
19. Nikhil Deogun, "Top PepsiCo Executive Picks Family Over Job," *Wall Street Journal*, September 24, 1997.
20. Diane Kunde, "Job Sharing Can Give Clients, Employers Double Benefits," *Dallas Morning News*, September 3, 1997.
21. Joann Lublin and Joseph White, "Throwing Off Angst, Workers Are Feeling in Control of Careers," *Wall Street Journal*, September 11, 1997.
22. Ibid.
23. J. Walker Smith and Ann Clurman, *Rocking the Ages* (New York: HarperBusiness, 1997).
24. Paul Glastris, "Spoiling a Proper Memorial," *U.S. News & World Report*, May 5, 1997.
25. Hal Lancaster, "Downshifters Find More Balance in Life by Shrinking Careers," *Wall Street Journal*, January 20, 1998.

Chapter 11

Is It My Personality, or Just Bad Timing?

*I*t's both. Some personalities have a greater predilection to cult membership, but *everyone* is susceptible to cult membership at certain times in life. This chapter explains the personality characteristics and timing circumstances that are associated with corporate cult membership.

Personality

A surveyor with the Forest Service in Utah said to me, "There definitely is a personality type that works in the Forest Service," he says. "If people don't have it when they join, they get it pretty soon."[1]

Same Place as Last Year

Corporate cult members get so accustomed to the security of cult membership that they even begin to enjoy the negatives of membership. The idea of enjoying faults is exemplified in the following story about two hunters and their pilot.

The bush pilot shook his head in disgust as he landed his little plane on the smooth waters of the secluded lake in the outback of Alaska to pick up two hunters he had left a week earlier. He related his frustration when he reached their camp: "Fellas, I told you last week when I left you, this plane can carry one pilot, two hunters with gear, and one elk. I see you have killed and dressed out two elk, so you're going to have to leave one of them."

The hunters responded emphatically, "We hunted this very spot last year and were transported by a plane exactly like yours, in which we carried two elk." The hunters continued to tell the pilot of the engine power and thrust, of the wing lift and the air pressure at that elevation. They explained carefully and accurately the height of the mountain range they needed to cross. The key to their story was that the pilot would be correct with a full load of fuel, but that in the trip *to* the lake, he had burned the exact weight of fuel that the extra elk carcass represents. Thus, they *could* take two elk home with them.

The pilot listened carefully and verified that, yes, all their data were correct. "Ok," agreed the pilot. "Load up and let's go home."

They loaded their gear, the elk, the hunters, and the pilot into the plane and took off. They almost made it over the mountain range, but they crashed just near the crest. Fortunately, they crashed into some soft underbrush, and no one was killed. But the mountainside was a mess of guns, gear, hunters, and elk parts. As they emerged from the bushes, one hunter asked the other, "Where in the world are we?" The other hunter responded, "I think we're about 100 yards from where we crashed last year."

That's where people with corporate cult syndrome usually end up. That's because the need for emotional support never goes away. Employees who have found this familial support in an organizational family will become accustomed to finding it there. Even if they leave one corporate cult, they are likely to stumble into another. That's why, instead of escaping the clutches of a corporate cult, many members simply migrate from one to another, and end up crashing about a hundred yards from where they did the last time.

Internal and External Locus of Control

There are many instruments for determining personality. The Myers-Briggs Type Indicator is the most popular. Based on the answers to several questions, the MBTI dichotomizes each individual's personality on four different measures. Thus, there are sixteen different personality types. Another test categorizes personality by shapes: squares, circles, rectangles, and triangles. Another categorizes people by animal types: lions, otters, etc. A fourth test uses colors: red, yellow, blue, etc. Each of these tests has a degree of accuracy and acceptability, but I have come to believe that the greatest *single* determinant of personality is locus of control.

People who have a strong internal locus of control believe that they are in charge of their environment. People who have an eternal locus of control believe that the environment—fate—is in control.[2]

The Broadway musical *Camelot* is about internal and external locus of control. The play begins with an external locus of control: Fate is in control. As a squire to his cousin, Arthur is sent to retrieve a forgotten sword. He decides it would be more convenient to "borrow" a sword from what appears to be a city monument. As he pulls the sword from the stone, he is cheered as the new king, because it is Excalibur. Fate made him king.

The play switches to internal locus of control when Arthur meets Guinevere and makes an emotional pledge to her: "I didn't want to be king, and I have been uncomfortable since becoming king—until seeing you just now. Now that I have seen you, I want to be the grandest king to ever sit on a throne." Guinevere inspires King Arthur to create the Round Table, where "might is *not* right, might is *for* right." The Round Table exemplifies internal locus of control; Arthur has taken control of his environment.

External locus of control rears its head again when Lancelot and Guinevere *fall* in love. They don't *step* into love, they fall. They can't stay apart; fate pushes them together. The Round Table is dissolved, and the kingdom falls. The play returns control to an external force. The environment—fate—is again in control. Thus the play moves from eternal to internal and then back to external control.

Obviously, internal and external locus of control are not as discrete as this explanation suggests. All personalities have some combination of internal and external locus of control. However, if we could line up everyone's personality along a continuum, we could see the degree of internal vs. external locus of control of each individual.

Relative to the cultures of other countries, U.S. culture has a strong internal locus of control. We tend to think *we* are in control of our environment. Old River, Louisiana, is a point just north of Baton Rouge where the Mississippi River comes within a few hundred yards of the much smaller Atchafalaya. At this point, the Atchafalaya is thirty-five feet lower than the Mississippi. From Old River to the sea through the New Orleans, the Mississippi travels 450 miles. The distance via the Atchafalaya is only 220 miles. Gravity continually impels the Mississippi to break through the levees and run down the Atchafalaya. If it were not for the heroic efforts of the U.S. Army Corps of Engineers in building levees, the Mississippi today would be running down the Atchafalaya, and New Orleans would have ceased to be a river city sometime in the late 1960s.

Even the Corps of Engineers employees who operate the pumps and maintain the levees agree that someday the environment will win and the Mississippi will run down the Atchafalaya. They are just delaying the forces of nature for a few—or a few hundred—years.

A nation that thinks it can change the route of one of the world's greatest rivers is consumed with internal locus of control thinking.

The conclusion from the study of locus of control is this: People with an internal locus of control run their own lives and are much less likely to join corporate cults. People with an external locus of control not only are more likely to become culted, but fully expect some stroke of fate to throw them into an organization in which all their needs are met. They welcome corporate cult membership because they want an external force—in this case the organization—to have control over their lives. Some people with an external locus of control look to TV to run their lives.

The End of Seinfeld

In May 1998 the country celebrated—or bemoaned—the last episode of the *Seinfeld* show. "Who shall we now look to for advice about how to live?" asked one TV critic.

"How about yourself, how about your family, how about your neighbors?" I would ask. Those who looked to *Seinfeld* for advice about lifestyle are extreme external-locus-of-control individuals who can't make decisions for themselves.

Corporate cult members do the same. With no one else to tell them how to live their lives, they rely on the corporation. And the corporation is only too happy to tell them. We shouldn't be surprised when a corporation tells its members to live their lives to satisfy the corporation, considering the source of the advice.

"The business of business is business," said Milton Friedman.[3] And I don't disagree with him. The corporation *should* take care of itself and encourage employees to work for it whatever the cost to themselves. It's the individual's responsibility to refuse. Some can't refuse because their personality won't allow them to. Some can't refuse because it's just the wrong time in their life.

Just Bad Timing

Intuitively, you would think that differences in personality type would make some people more susceptible to corporate cult membership than others. While this is a contributing factor, timing is important as well. I assumed that personality was the only factor until I asked Fred, who is a former personal counselor and who now runs a human resources consulting business. He understands both the personal and the organizational sides of the corporate cult relationship. "Do employees make their corporation into a cult because of personality characteristics, or does it happen just because of bad timing in their life stage?" I asked. His unhesitating answer surprised me.

"Everyone is susceptible to corporate cult membership at some point in his or her life," Fred answered. "Even you." As I thought about it, I had to admit that he was right. When I first got out of college, I worked for the Association of Tennis Professionals. I was twenty-one years old and was flying around the world with Jimmy Connors and Bjorn Borg. I was very dedicated to the organization and to Executive Director Bob Briner who had "given" me the job. I use the word *given* because I was not qualified, and I knew it. I worked very hard and showed great dedication to him and the organization to make up for my lack of qualifications.

I was a prime candidate for corporate cult membership. However, fortunately for me, Briner allowed a great deal of independence, so I was about as far from culted as an employee can get. I still worked until 2:00 A.M. a few times and traveled for three weeks at a stretch during the busy season, but I was definitely not culted. I was ripe for cultedness, but he refused to take advantage of my willingness.

Figure 11-1 lists many situations in which people are susceptible to corporate cult membership. I encourage you to compare your personal circumstance with those situations to see when you have been susceptible.

System Gaps

A corporate cult is a surrogate family for its members. Why does this happen? Because there is a gap in systems. First, let me explain gaps.

The Roman Era was just two thousand years ago, a very brief time period in evolutionary terms. During the Roman Era, women had to conceive nine times just to maintain the population. Since the drive to perpetuate the species is very strong, women living during the Roman Era got pregnant as soon as they were fertile, and stayed pregnant a good deal of their adult lives. Women in the year 2000 still have this drive to procreate as soon as they become fertile. Improved health and nutrition are pushing the fertility age lower while pushing life expectancy higher.

This drive clashes with the social system of our age, which states that women shouldn't get pregnant until they're married. The biological system tells women to get pregnant at fourteen, whereas the social system tells them to wait until they are twenty-six, the average marriage age for U.S. women. This creates a period

Figure 11-1. Situations in Which People Are Susceptible to Corporate Cult Membership

- When they are new to the corporation
- When they are young
- After the death of a spouse
- Upon moving away from family
- When changing industries
- Upon leaving a church or synagogue
- After a divorce

of about twelve years in the lives of young women in which two systems are in conflict.

A similar clash between two ideological systems produces gaps that encourage membership in corporate cults. In the agrarian era, just over a hundred years ago, families were forced to work together for economic survival. People spent their entire lives near their nuclear families, so the social need for familial support and the economic imperative for survival could both be satisfied.

The explosion of the factory system around the turn of the century drove workers from the farm to the city. It also drove them away from their families. This conflict between economic and family systems was an entirely new element in socioeconomic relations. People living away from their families for an extended period of time had been unheard of in the agrarian era. Now it was becoming commonplace.

Henry Ford brags in his autobiography that he paid his workers the princely sum of five dollars a day so that they could afford to buy the product they were making. Other sources tell a more accurate story. Ford continually raised the wage to combat an astronomically high turnover rate. It was about 375 percent a year when he began to raise wages. He had to raise wages, because workers hated the conditions! Many of them had come from an agricultural setting, where even though the work was hard, they had the independence to do the work and the goal satisfaction that comes with a job well done.

In Ford's plants, workers had to stand in the same spot all day and perform boring, regimented work. They hated it. They left in droves, which forced Ford to raise the wages to a level that "bought off" their values. In essence, the workers finally said, "We still hate the work, but for five dollars a day, you can buy our unhappiness."

The system gap between family and financial needs was finally won by the factory system, which offered enough financial incentives to overcome the family support system. Workers moved to the industrialized cities and "sold their souls" for five dollars a day.

Odysseus was perhaps the first person who encountered this gap. He wanted to explore—that is, to be about his work—but he wanted to be home as well. Work won out for Odysseus as he continually traveled from one place to another at the expense of his home life.

The gap between the desire to make money and the desire to be near family still exists. Financial considerations are still winning. People regularly move away from their families to seek financial gains. These people are perfect candidates for corporate cult membership. They move away from their biological family and find a new family in the corporation. After all, the drive for family affection and support is a need, not a want. By definition, then, it has to be filled. People will find family someplace, somewhere, somehow.

The system gap—between financial and family concerns—has produced the formula for corporate cults. Even though the gap is just over a hundred years old, there aren't enough anecdotes about life before the Industrial Age to remind us of what society was like before industrial organizations changed it. Corporations have discovered that individuals are increasingly finding family at work. This is good for corporations and bad for individuals.

Unconditional Acceptance

Some corporations promise unconditional acceptance in the form of lifetime employment or a no-layoff policy. Such promises are valid only for the lifetime of the corporation and are based on policies that can change. No organization can guarantee a lifetime employment contract or a no layoff policy.

Figure 11-2 shows the relationship of individuals to organizations. Organizational concepts are on the left side of the diagram. Behaviors on this side—"what I do"—produce self-confidence and support the organization's well-being.

The individual-level concepts are on the right side of the diagram. Those are values that produce self-esteem and support the individual's well-being.

The problem comes when there is a significant level of crossover. As the diagram shows, helpful organizational behavior produces self-righteous or cocky behavior that gives the individual value. The problem with this is that self-righteousness is gained from a relative point of view. The individual is gaining value not from "who I am" but from "what I do." As long as the person

Figure 11-2. Unconditional Acceptance Model

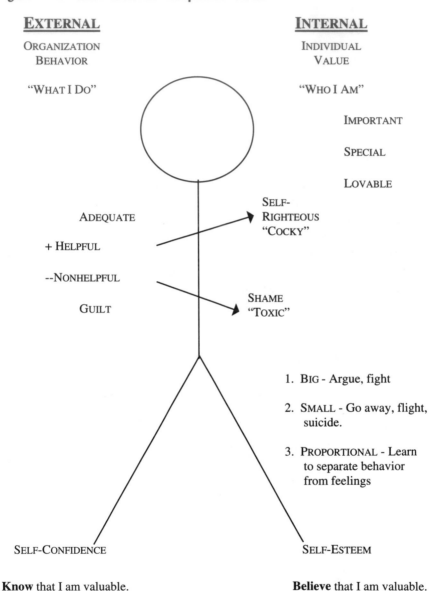

EXTERNAL

ORGANIZATION
BEHAVIOR

"WHAT I DO"

ADEQUATE

+ HELPFUL

--NONHELPFUL

GUILT

SELF-CONFIDENCE

Know that I am valuable.

INTERNAL

INDIVIDUAL
VALUE

"WHO I AM"

IMPORTANT

SPECIAL

LOVABLE

SELF-
RIGHTEOUS
"COCKY"

SHAME
"TOXIC"

1. BIG - Argue, fight

2. SMALL - Go away, flight,
   suicide.

3. PROPORTIONAL - Learn
   to separate behavior
   from feelings

SELF-ESTEEM

Believe that I am valuable.

© Dean Arnott, used by permission.

continues to behave in the way the organization desires, she has positive value. When she stops behaving in that manner, she loses personal value. Corporate cults love this. The employee becomes a puppet on a string. Whatever the corporation demands, the worker must do, or lose her value as a person. This is the strongest of all cultism. The person has no value as an individual and finds value only as a member of the organization.

Nonhelpful organizational behavior can have the same effect of tying the individual to the organization. The employee feels guilty about nonapproved organizational conduct and feels toxic shame. This toxic shame reinforces organizationally sanctioned "correct" behavior until the employee returns to being the model corporate citizen the corporation wants.

This toxic shame manifests itself in three different responses from the individual. The "big" response is to argue and fight against the shame. In fight-or-flight terms, this is the fight response. This is not acceptable in corporate cults. Arguing indicates that the individual's needs are not being met in some way. This is antithetical to the corporate cult purpose. When cult members see arguing and fighting, there is an immediate and urgent desire to brand one of the parties "right" and one of them "wrong". The basis of this branding, of course, is which member is conducting himself in closer concert with the mores of the corporation.

The "good" fighter is awarded a higher place in the corporate cult, and the "bad" fighter is either demoted or, in classic Greek fashion, "banished into the woods" in order to keep the cult pure.

The second response is to be "small". In fight-or-flight terms, this is the flight response. In corporate cults this is an acceptable response, because the needs of the corporation are viewed as superior to the needs of the individual. The individual is merely a mechanism to serve the needs of the corporation. When the individual becomes "small", he retreats, asks forgiveness, and goes back to his assigned place in the corporation.

Psychological counselors tell of people losing weight to literally *become* small because they feel small. They feel they don't deserve many rewards, so they consume less of the world's goods. When this includes food, it leads to their becoming physically smaller, so they consume less space. Then they feel more comfortable with their place in the world.

The most severe form of becoming small is to commit suicide. While this is an extreme response, it does happen in some organizations. However, the more common response in corporate cults is to commit organizational suicide by leaving the corporation.

Expulsion of nonconforming members is important to corporate cults because it maintains a feeling of separateness or righteousness in the corporation. It perpetuates the us-them dialectic in which insiders are seen as righteous and outsiders are seen as unrighteous. In gangs this takes the form of secret handshakes, tattoos, clothing, and other signs that bond the individual to the organization. Surviving behavioral conflicts is an important part of corporate cult membership for employees, because it enables them to differentiate between behaviors that are acceptable and those that are unacceptable.

In this model, self-confidence is derived from "what I do" in the corporation. When self-confidence totally determines self-esteem—when "what I do" totally defines "who I am"—the employee is in a corporate cult.

The healthiest relationship between organizational behavior and individual value is a proportional response. A person's value is somewhat derived from actions, but not totally derived from it.

When I work with University level athletes this is a delicate issue. Those who have a total and direct connection between performance on the left side and value on the right side are exhilarated by success and dashed by defeat. That connection makes great athletes and lousy people because their value is totally driven by their athletic performance. I encourage them to decrease their value response to their on-field performance.

But there is a danger: If the connection is totally broken, they don't care if they win or lose. A total lack of connection between behavior and feelings makes lousy athletes and great individuals. That's why a proportional response is so important.

A proportional response is also important for members of business organizations. If you gain too much individual value from what you do on the left side, you are a prime candidate for cult membership. If you derive too little value, you have no organizational relationships, because you don't care about your performance.

A proportional response is the best answer. Proportional individuals learn to develop a healthy separation of their behavior from their feelings.

The greater the degree to which the two sides of the diagram are separate, the healthier the individual-organizational relationship. The greater the degree to which the left side ("what I do") determines the right side ("who I am"), the less healthy the relationship. The following is an example of healthy self-esteem.

What a Lovely Baby!

There was a great deal of excitement when you were born. Your parents called all the family members to enthusiastically announce, "We have a baby! It's a girl, she weighs eight pounds, she's nineteen inches long with dark hair, ten fingers, and ten toes. We've named her Phyllis!"

If you had been self-conscious at the time, your esteem level would have been very high. Why? Because you had done nothing! Your high self-esteem would have been totally dependent upon "who I am" and would have in no way been related to "what I do," because you hadn't done anything. So why is it that twenty to fifty years later you have low self-esteem? It's because over the years, you have allowed "what I do" to replace "who I am." You have allowed those around you, particularly those in corporations, to convince you that your self-esteem should be based on what you do, not who you are.

But there's hope! You are still a good person. You still are a girl. You might weigh more than eight pounds and be longer than nineteen inches, but you still have ten fingers and ten toes. You are still a worthy person—even if you never do another thing in your life.

Perhaps that's why Richard Schlessinger of CBS News had trouble understanding my statement to him in the interview aired on the CBS news program *48 hours*. "I love teaching and I think being a college professor is the most important work I can do in my life," I said. "But if I never teach another class, I will still have worth and value, because my value comes from who I am, which never changes, instead of what I do, which *does* change."

Corporate cults want "what I do" to define "who I am." Don't fall into the organization's trap. You're much more than what you do.

Conflict in Corporate Cults

In healthy organizations, conflict centers on actions and behavior, not on personalities. In corporate cults, conflict is attributed to the personality of the combatants. After all, they were hired into the specialist collection because of "who I am," and their conforming to that prescribed organizational culture is seen as critical to the survival of the organization. Thus, when conflict arises, it must be because of who the person is, not what he or she has done.

This flies in the face of all reasonable advice about limiting conflict in organizations, which typically advises exactly the opposite: Concentrate on the behavior, not the person. However, concentrating on the person works in corporate cults because membership is based on defending "who I am" for each person in the organization. Conflict is an indication that a member has ceased to be "who she is" and caused a conflict. Thus, the *person*, not the *behavior*, is out of line. The belief in corporate cults is that when the person is brought into alignment with the rest of the organization, behavior will follow.

In the negotiation book *Getting to Yes*, Roger Fisher and William Ury provide four rules for negotiating reasonably.[4] Not many are followed in corporate cults:

1. Separate personalities from problems.
2. Focus on common interests, not polarized positions.
3. Explore as many options as possible in attempting to reach mutually acceptable solutions.
4. Use objective criteria, not subjective feelings, to make determinations.

Corporate cults cannot separate personalities from problems, because personalities are critical to the success of the organization. The strength of personalities is what runs the corporate cult; it's what gives it identity and competitive advantage. Disagreements in corporate cults often center on personalities. The deciding question for the combatants is whether the opponent has the *right* personality. That's because the personalities of corporate cult members are in constant and incremental change from their individual personality to the corporate personality.

Conflict resolution is often based on Fisher and Ury's second rule: Focus on common interests. In corporate cults, individuals subjugate their own interests to the interest of the whole. The greater good is served by doing what's best for the organization, not for individuals. The social science term for this concept is "superordinate goals," i.e., finding a higher-level goal upon which the arguing parties can agree. Once this level of agreement is found, the parties can more successfully work on their disagreements. This is easily done in corporate cults, because individuals have already agreed to subordinate their own personal interests to those of the corporate cult.

The third rule is to explore many options. This is done in corporate cults, but only within the narrowly defined culture of the organization. This is the paradox of corporate cults. They will worship at the altar of multiple choices, yet when the choices are analyzed, they all have their roots in the narrowly defined cultures of the corporate cult.

The fourth rule is to use objective rather than subjective criteria to make determinations. In corporate cults, subjective criteria are favored because "who I am" is a subjective determination. If the employees used objective criteria for decision making, they would be throwing out the very reason they were selected for organizational membership in the first place.

I could make a good argument for the nonexistence of objective measures, because all data are colored by the way in which we find them. However, for purposes of conflict resolution, it is easy enough to postulate that some measures are clearly more objective than others. When both objective and subjective measures exist, corporate cults are more likely to select the subjective measures, because they have more personalized meaning for employees than objective measures do.

Employees become corporate cult members because of both their personalities and because they are at a place or time in their lives when they are susceptible to being culted. But corporate cult membership can be avoided, as explained in Chapter 12.

Notes

1. Interview with the author.
2. B. Spector, "Behavior in Organizations as a Function of Employees' Locus of Control," *Psychological Bulletin* 91 (1982): 482–497.
3. Milton Friedman, "The Social Responsibility of Business Is to Increase Its Profits," *New York Times Magazine*, September 13, 1970.
4. Roger Fisher and William Ury, *Getting to Yes: Negotiating Agreement Without Giving In* (New York: Viking Penguin, 1991).

Chapter 12
How to Avoid a Corporate Cult Next Time

*I*f the previous chapters have explained your workplace, then your really need this chapter. Up to this point, the book has described corporate cults, and it's very likely that you found a good deal of yourself and your organization reflected in those sections. Now it's time for some *prescription* about how to avoid corporate cult membership in the future.

Write Your Own Definition of Success

As mentioned in Chapter 10, I tell my college students to write their own definition of success. People would be better off if they would write their own definition of success and save themselves some frustration.

The frustration comes from trying to live out someone else's dream, which often has organizational success as a big part of the formula. Organizations love this, because it gives them an ample supply of dedicated workers to do their bidding. All other things being equal, a person with a balanced life will be at a disadvantage when compared to the employee who is unbalanced toward the corporation. Employees who suffer this imbalance would be well served by a better understanding of social economics.

Economics is the study of the distribution of scarce resources. Time is clearly a scarce resource. There are only twenty-four hours in a day, and they aren't planning to make any more. Applying this economic understanding of time to relationships produces a well-balanced individual who will gladly accept setbacks in some parts of life because he or she is aware of the concomitant gains in other parts.

I can afford almost *anything* but not *everything*. When I buy economic goods, I can no longer buy others. This simple principle of financial economics can also be applied to social economics. I can have just about *any* relationship I want, but I can't have *all* the relationships I want.

Employees who are unbalanced toward the corporation have made the choice to have a closer corporate relationship at the expense of other relationships. The model in Chapter 4 categorizes these relationships as work, family, and community. Gaining a closer work relationship means a decrease in the intensity of family or community relationships.

Advertising and popular culture encourage people to "have it all," which runs directly counter to the assumption of social economics. Social economics demands that tough choices be made in life. Understanding that gaining one thing means giving up another is an important lesson that many corporate cult members have not learned. Making informed choices that are aligned with your own definition of success can help you avoid a corporate cult next time.

Avoid Corporate Cults by Being Your Own Person

A Gatorade TV commercial featuring Michael Jordan encourages young people to "be like Mike." I encourage young people to be like a lot of *different* people. In doing so, you will become *you*. I try to find one admirable trait in each person I come in contact with. I then try to incorporate more of that trait into my life. However, there is a very important limitation to that process. The key is finding only one such trait in each person. Admiring another person for *one* trait is healthy. Admiring someone for *all* his or her traits is hero worship.

Corporate cult members who try to emulate the total bundle of characteristics of the charismatic leader lose themselves in the process. Individuals can make the contribution in life that they are uniquely qualified to make only by being themselves, not by being someone else.

In *Conquering Corporate Codependence,* Carolyn Corbin says that employees need to develop "Indipreneurship," a mix of independence and entrepreneurship.[1] Independence is an internal way of looking at the world and being self-sufficient and valuable—with or without membership in a work organization. Entrepreneurship is an outward expression of independent feelings that leads to transacting business in a way that provides degree of separation from organizations as well.

Developing this mix prevents corporate cult membership, because the individual is not devoted to the organization, there is no charismatic leader, and there is no group to separate the employee from the rest of the community. The biggest generational cohort has trouble taking this advice.

It's a Long and Winding Road

Authors J. Walter Smith and Ann Clurman say that Baby Boomers will not retire, because when they reach traditional retirement age, they will still be looking for meaning and fulfillment. Throughout their lives, they have been fulfilled by the financial and affiliative rewards that work have provided for them. There's good reason to believe will continue to seek it in work rather than retire.[2]

Boomers are by far the most likely to cite work as the primary means for expressing their personal creativity. Work will always be important to them. Boomers expect their careers to bring fulfillment, and that lofty expectation is not likely to change. Like Dorothy and her friends trudging down the yellow brick road, they have not yet figured out that the answers aren't at Oz. They will keep looking, hoping that just a few more years of work will satisfy them.

Their hope is that the next organization they become culted with will give them the satisfaction they have craved. After all, they have known other workers who were satisfied with their company. The Baby Boomers are trying to figure out why some of their counterparts have been so deliriously happy at work while they have been only mildly satisfied. The truth is that many of those deliri-

ously happy people have been working in corporate cults their entire careers.

The sad thing is that the Baby Boomer could find more meaning by *avoiding* corporate cults than by *joining* them. By their very
structure and nature, organizations must take before they can give
back. So, individuals who find complete fulfillment from their
work must remain aware that the organization was fulfilled first,
which was done by taking from it's workers. Satisfaction is found
as much in your family and in your community as in work. If
you're looking for total fulfillment from work, you're in the same
group with Dorothy and her friends, seeking the perfect life at Oz.
You should reevaluate every once in a while.

Periodic Reevaluations Are Good

Michael Adams is a forty-two-year-old executive for Cytyc Corporation in Foxborough, Massachusetts. He is in high demand as a
regulatory affairs officer, so he gets weekly calls from headhunters.
These have led him to reevaluate his potential market value. "It's
hard to gauge yourself unless you go through something like
that," he summarized. The experience gave him an increased sense
of his marketability.[3]

Adams may be going through the transformation from being
a member of a corporate cult to being unculted. When corporate
cult members talk about reevaluation, they are talking about a reevaluation of how the employee's values coalign with those of the
corporation. They will not escape the corporate cult until they lis-
ten to a job offer from another organization.

However, the paradox is that corporate cult members don't
look elsewhere, because to do so would be considered treason.
Thus, one way to avoid corporate cults is to periodically reevaluate
yourself relative to *other* corporations, not to the corporate cult
you're currently in. Some people simply move from cult to cult
because they can't control the urge to merge.

Controlling the Urge to Merge

In explaining his escape from a more traditional cult, John Goldhammer asks a key question, "How do we control the urge to

merge?" How does one hold the tension between the collective and the individual in a manner that adds richness, vitality, and meaning to both? He answers the question by suggesting that the only way to live what he calls an "authentic life" is to see things as they really are, from the individual's point of view looking out, not from that of the collective organization looking in. It's *your* view of the world that counts, not the collective view.[4]

There isn't a single, definable collective view. The collective view is merely a collection of individual views. Organizations cannot derive meaning and purpose in and of themselves, because the group viewpoint is merely a mathematical average of individual group members' viewpoints. Only individuals can give meaning to their own lives. Organizations have the *appearance* of meaning and purpose, but that meaning and purpose becomes action only through the lives of individual group members.

People join groups because they provide a temporary sense of purpose. Membership in a corporate cult gives employees a feeling of being okay, but it's a transitory, relativistic feeling because it is premised on the success of the group. Corporate cult members feel good about themselves only as long as they follow group norms and mores. When they stop following the rules, the false feeling of okay evaporates, leaving the individual with a feeling of low self-worth. Corporate cult memberships are false and fleeting. Don't count on them for ego satisfaction and self-worth. Those feelings are more successfully and sustainably found in families. A way to limit devotion to the organizational workplace is to change jobs.

Change Jobs—A Few Times!

One of the most intriguing e-mail forces that traveled the medium recently was a speech supposedly given by Kurt Vonnegut to the MIT graduating class. It was a fake, but it contained some good advice. "Don't feel guilty if you don't know what you want to do with your life," the speech said. "The most interesting people I know didn't know at the age of twenty-two what they wanted to do with their lives. Some of the most interesting forty-year-olds I know still don't."

Whoever the hidden author was, he or she offered some good advice for avoiding corporate cults, which is to change jobs, even change careers—a few times! It is estimated that our university graduates this year will have seven different jobs in the course of their careers. That will contribute to their avoidance of corporate cults.

I hesitate to use my own experience as an example, but at forty-four I am in my sixth job and third career. Not always by choice, I might add. I have been laid off, fired, and quit jobs—and my life got better each time! Change *is* good, especially in careers and jobs.

Trying to Replace a Corporate Cult

After eight intensive years as a public relations staffer for U.S. Robotics, Karen Nowak took a golden parachute. She discovered that the culture of her old company was more important to her than she had realized. She was bored at home and sought the comfort of the "family" she had left at U.S. Robotics. She looked for a U.S. Robotics look-alike: a high-tech start-up with a tight-knit family of managers who do good work and have fun. "I got very attached to the people at Robotics," she commented. "I didn't realize how strong the bond was." She soon recognized that such camaraderie is hard to replace.

Nowak had clearly been involved in some level of corporate cultedness at U.S. Robotics. The key words are *family, bond,* and *camaraderie.* At last report, she had been away from the workplace for eight months and had not yet found the fun culture she was seeking.[5] She would be well advised to analyze her previous organizational relationship for elements of corporate cultedness and determine whether she really wants to return to the same workstyle again. She could also take a good lesson from the following case study.

An Independent "Skygirl"

Early in 1930, Ellen Church visited the San Francisco office of United Airlines Director of Operations Steve Stimpson. She was a pilot and desperately wanted to fly, but she was pragmatic enough to realize that the airline was not going to put a woman at the controls in 1930. She pitched him on another plan for getting above the clouds. "Why don't you hire flight attendants?" she asked. Stimpson was intrigued and interested, mostly because he had had the same idea himself but hadn't been sure how to do it.

Church's urging gave him the impetus to follow through. By May 15, she had hired seven of her fellow nurses; they became known in air transport lore as "the Original Eight." The last surviving member of the Original Eight died in November 1995. She was my great-aunt, Margaret Arnott.

I knew my Aunt Margaret had lived an interesting life, in and out of the airlines, so in March of 1995 I interviewed her for a biography that is still on my to-do list.

I asked why she quit the airline after less than two years. Her first answer was that many women flew for a short time period. The "Skygirls," as they were called, had to be single, so that shortened many careers, but not hers. Her second answer astounded me. "I wasn't doing what I was trained to do," she said emphatically. "I was trained to be a nurse, to care for people. Not to hand out cold chicken and pour coffee."

"But Aunt Margaret," I insisted, "you were starting a whole new industry."

"Someone else could do it," she answered. "I went back to where I was valuable, where I could help people," she continued humbly.

"But you were a poor farm girl, suddenly thrust into the limelight of flying around the country with rich and powerful people. How could you give up such an opportunity?"

"It wasn't for me," she answered simply.

The life story of Margaret Arnott is laced with the themes of fierce independence and humility. She was the only woman in her high school science and math classes in the late 1920s, although she didn't see anything unusual about it. "I liked the subjects," she explained. She leapt into the limelight with United, and then just as quickly disappeared, to spend the rest of her life as a nurse to a family doctor in the small mountain hamlet of Del Norte, Colorado.

Caring for little Indian babies was more rewarding to her than pouring coffee for corporate presidents because it was what she was *trained* to do and what she *wanted* to do. She found value in it.

You should do the same: Find something that's valuable to *you*, not to others who may be in a corporate cult.

A Native American proverb says, "Do not follow where the path may lead, but go where there is no path and leave a trail."[6] Only those who avoid corporate cults can follow this advice. They also adhere to the next saying.

Don't Put All Your Eggs in One Basket

Your mother probably told you this proverb. You should abide by it when designing your social life. An emotionally healthy person has "eggs" in three distinctly separate baskets: work, family, and community.

This proverb has been turned around in strategic management to identify a very successful corporate strategy, "Put all your eggs in one basket, then watch that basket very closely." That's good advice at the *corporate* level, but bad advice at the *individual* level. But that's what corporate cult members do: They put all their relationships in one basket, the corporate basket, and watch it very closely. Don't do it. Life is too short to spend it watching a basket—any basket.

One of the most effective ways to avoid codependence with any system is to maintain a diversity of relationships. People become codependent when they become too reliant on an institution. An organization cannot fulfill a person's needs. People who think it can are vulnerable to a wide variety of addictive behaviors, including corporate cults.[7] It's a struggle for all of us, especially professors.

Professors and the Cognitive Elite

Okay, I'll make an admission. I have my own little enclave. I am more comfortable within my enclave than I am outside of it. I teach management in the College of Business, and I have a Ph.D. in the subject. Through my education, I have gained a research framework for analyzing the world that mentally stimulates me. I would much rather have a conversation with one of my professional colleagues, Abdul, Rusty, or Mary Jane, than with someone outside my discipline.

I had to step out of my enclave recently when the city of Dallas was considering a new tax that would be used to build a sports arena. I teach professional sports management, so I got involved in the issue. I was totally frustrated by the inane arguments put forth by the city council members. I could barely sit through the video-taping of a PBS show hosted by Dennis McCuistion because the arguments offered by his guests, state senators and a former mayor, were theoretical mush.

The friends in my adult Bible fellowship class drive me crazy with their armchair sociological musings. Even my brother tried to explain the benefits of just-in-time production at a family reunion last summer. I was kind enough *not* to tell him it's a twenty-year-old concept.

I get frustrated with people outside my discipline because they don't speak the research language I prefer. I feel enriched by those inside my discipline. I am sure engineers, lawyers, psychologists, and theologians also get frustrated when the uninitiated toss around the concepts of their disciplines.

But don't miss the point: It is *good* for me to have those out-of-discipline experiences—frustrating, but good. Without those wider community connections, I would become separated from the community—the third element of the cult definition.

The default setting is to separate. It takes energy and motivation to be inclusive with those outside your patterned way of thinking. But it's good for you. It keeps you out of corporate cults. Dialectic thinking keeps employees out of corporate cults also.

Either-Or vs. Dialectic Thinking

Children have a black-and-white way of thinking that I call "either-or" reasoning. This concrete rationalization enables them to see everything in their little lives as exclusively good or bad; there are no shades of gray. Most movie plots are mired in this mode, which features distinct and discrete good guys and bad guys. Good and bad are seldom mixed in a single character. Through years of conditioning, children learn to understand their world in those simplistic terms. This system works very effectively for them until they reach adolescence and are faced with shades of gray.

My own childhood is an example. My either-or thinking was so strong that it affected the products I bought as a young adult. Advertisers believe that early brand affiliations can last a lifetime, so there is quite a battle for the hearts and minds of young people. In my case, my dad spent most of his professional life working for Standard Oil. My either-or thinking told me quite clearly that Standard Oil sold good gas and its competitors sold bad gas. This way of thinking was so strong that when I was a young adult, I had pangs of guilt when I bought gas from a competing company. I got over it.

Members of corporate cults don't get over it. They continue to think that good and bad are separable constructs, and that issues are black and white with no gray areas. A strong either-or thinker has no problem pledging loyalty to a corporate cult. The leader simply portrays the corporate cult as good and the rest of the world as bad. This fits very nicely into the narrow, programmed thinking of the member.

The opposite of either-or thinking is dialectic thinking. Dialectics is the mental positioning of a thesis against an antithesis for the purposes of determining a synthesis. It recognizes ambiguities and contradictions and shows increasing tolerance of them.[8]

I have lived in Dallas for twenty-two of the thirty-six years since the assassination of John F. Kennedy, so I have heard many of the complicated conspiracy theories. While I was seeking a degree at the University of Texas at Arlington, a professor taught a course on the subject that was guaranteed to convince the students of a conspiracy. While I am not an expert in the subject, I reviewed many of the stories and theories. My very brief conclusion is that Oswald acted alone; there was no conspiracy. However, if you ask me about the grassy knoll, I would say there was a second gunman there.

Contradictory? Only if you think in either-or terms. There is good evidence for both theories, and I believe both. Which is right? Both. How can that be? Don't the theories contradict each other? Not when you think in dialectic terms. The purpose of dialectics is to produce a synthesis, but I'm not frustrated by the absence of one. People who think in dialectic terms are hardly ever culted.

They see shades of gray in the black and white and realize that there are few absolutely right and wrong situations. I *do* believe there is a God who has declared absolute right and wrong, but we humans do a poor job of interpreting it.

Economic Exchanges and Riches

Economics is the study of the distribution of scarce resources. Each time you make a transaction, like buying a soft drink, you exchange one scarce resource for another. In essence, you are saying, "I am willing to trade this scarce resource (maybe it's seventy-five cents) for the scarce resource in the soft drink machine." You actually think the soft drink is worth more than seventy-five cents, or you wouldn't make the trade. Each transaction makes you economically richer.

You are *financially* poorer by seventy-five cents but *economically* richer by one soft drink, which improves your economic riches. People often confuse the terms financial and economic. Money is a financial good that is distributed by economic means. If you think the soft drink is worth exactly seventy-five cents, you are on the indifference curve. In this situation, you won't bother to make the transaction, because it won't make you economically richer. Rational people make only transactions that make them richer.

By most gauges, Bill Gates is rich: His personal worth is estimated at $61.7 billion. He got rich by making others rich, that is, he conducted a lot of transactions. If I buy his Windows 98 software program for $100, I am making the statement that the program will make me more than $100 richer. And it surely will. It makes writing easier and more efficient, so it improves my productivity. That makes me economically richer by enabling me to produce more writing material in a shorter time period.

In case you are about to grab your credit cards and sprint to the mall to make yourself "richer" by buying, remember that you can be involved on either side of the transaction—buying or selling. When you "sell" your time and skills to your employer or a client, you are indicating that the scarce resources you contribute (time and skill) are worth less to you than the scarce resource (money) you receive as payment. That has to be so, because if you weren't getting richer, you wouldn't make the transaction. People only make transactions that make them richer.

It's a simple matter of exchanging economic resources. Whenever you make a trade, you become richer. That is so because the choices we make in a free market system are just that, choices. We are not coerced to buy any particular product. The Sherman Antitrust Act and the Clayton Act were written to prevent monopolies that could produce forced transactions. With very few exceptions, all choices we make are free-market exchanges. Each free-market exchange makes *both* parties richer.

How does this affect corporate cults? Employees make many economic exchange decisions every day when they exchange time and skill for an economic good. In unculted organizations, like a collection of specialists, employees are motivated by the economic good called money. In corporate cults, members are also paid money as well, but they are motivated by a non-economic good: affiliation with the corporation.

Whether an exchange is an ethical, arms-length, free-market transaction is determined by the answer to the question, "Who gets richer?" In unculted organizations, both parties get richer. In corporate cults, the organization gets richer while the employee gets poorer. That's because the corporate cult is gaining an economic good (skill and time) and exchanging a noneconomic good (affiliation). Affiliation is noneconomic because it's not scarce.

Corporate cults enrich themselves at the expense of their members. This is not an arms-length transaction. It is not a win-win situation. The organization wins, and the individual loses control over her life. Employees stay in corporate cults because they are comfortable there.

Comfort Zones

People remain in corporate cults because they are happy with the affiliational rewards that they receive: family, friendships, camaraderie, status, and company reputation. Or, they may be staying because of the absence of a motivation to leave, i.e.: They're not *un*happy enough to leave. This story has been repeated many times: A frog will immediately leap out of hot water, but when the temperature of cold water is slowly raised, the frog will stay until it is cooked to death. Does this sound like anyone you know? At work maybe?

This is often called, "The devil I know is better than the one I don't know." That means the corporate cult member stays not because he is happy, but because of his fear of the unknown. This is a great fear, and cultivating it is an important technique for member retention in corporate cults.

James Belsco, in the book *Teaching the Elephant to Dance*, has a wonderful metaphor for organizational inertia. It seems that to teach elephants to stand still, the trainer chains one leg of a young elephant to a very stout stake. The young elephant pulls and pulls but cannot dislodge the stake. As a result, adult elephants can be tethered to a very weak stake. The elephant is conditioned to associate the chain around its leg with staking and assumes it cannot move. Belsco advises organizations to start a fire big enough to frighten the elephant so that it returns to its instincts and runs, but small enough that it doesn't burn down the circus tent.[9]

Corporate cult members often have a long history of culted behavior. Breaking that behavior pattern takes a pretty good-sized fire. Many successful escapes are more a result of environmental fires—downsizing and layoffs—than of introspection and individual willpower.

The Self-Fulfilling Prophecy

My dad and his brother raised their families in the same small town in South Dakota. When I was young, my parents told me that I was smart and I could accomplish anything I wanted in life. As an adult, I am and I do. When my cousins were young, my uncle told them that they were stupid and couldn't do anything. As adults, they are and they can't.

This is called the Pygmalion effect, named for the sculptor who created a beautiful statue and then fell in love with it. He willed the statue to life by his great desire for her. The animation of the statue was a self-fulfilling prophecy. The artisan's prophecy was fulfilled by the statue's actions.

Corporate cult members can fail to fulfill the prophecy for their lives, but it's a difficult process that demands a strong will to succeed. The following is an encouraging anecdote about a group of people who didn't have to change, because they were never in corporate cults.

Happy as a Firefighter

The graduate school of the USDA sends me around the country to deliver leadership and management seminars when I am not teaching at the university. It's rewarding, because I get to meet a wide variety of people. One of my favorite seminar questions is, "What's the best job you've ever had, and why?" The highest percentage of attendees who answered "this job" was a group of forest firefighters in Prescott, Arizona. They were the most contented group I have ever done a seminar with.

They don't make much money. Some of them drove beat-up old cars and trucks; some of them didn't even own cars, so they hitched rides to and from the seminar. They didn't seem to have any of the typical signs of material wealth. To a great degree they were held-over hippies from the 1970s, with simple clothing and a counterculture attitude. The women wore boots and no makeup. Many of the men had long hair.

They are seasonal employees who work only during the fire season, from March to August. When I asked them individually what they did the rest of the year, there were a variety of answers. "I help my brother-in-law in construction," said one. Another said he manages groups of troubled youths to rebuild trails in national parks. It seemed strange to me that people without the security of a full-time permanent job would be so happy, but they were.

As I explored it further, I found two factors that predicted happiness for the firefighters. The first is control. They feel that they are in control of their destiny. They know when the fire season is, and as long as they manage their lives to be ready for the season, they can do what they want the rest of the year.

The second factor is having a meaningful job with short-term recognizable goals. They get a lot of praise and credit for their work. Preventing a forest from burning up saves the habitat of animals and protects national forests so that thousands of people can enjoy them. When a forest fire is raging, it's quite clear that the objective is to put it out. There is a great deal of personal and team satisfaction when the job is done. Since firefighting usually takes only a few days, it has a very short-term orientation that produces quick and obvious rewards.

I'm not worried about the firefighters becoming culted. They are about as far from culted as any group I have found. They are extremely independent, but they still have the ability to work closely together under close team supervision when fighting a fire. If you've been in a corporate cult, try to incorporate some of that firefighter independence into your life. It's a wonderful feeling to be in control of your destiny. The firefighters were very good at pleasing themselves, unlike the people discussed in the next section.

People Pleasers and Corporate Cults

People pleasers are likely to become corporate cult members. These people typically grew up in a home where the child was encouraged to follow the dictates of the family matriarch or patriarch. The paradox of trying to please the family leaders was that the leader would never be satisfied, no matter what the child did. Having never pleased the family leader, these individuals have a continuing need to please someone, so they self-select to a corporate cult, where they try to please the charismatic leader. They feel comfortable in the clutches of the corporate cult because it replicates the family hierarchy in which they grew up.

Corporate cult leaders thrive on people pleasers, because they will allow "who I am" to be replaced by "what I do." People pleasing is usually accompanied by low self-esteem. The person thinks her or his own needs and desires are less important than those of others. The same needs and desires that were sacrificed to family members early in life are sacrificed to the corporate cult as adults.

People pleasers can avoid a corporate cult in their next employment by identifying their own needs first. This is often more difficult than it sounds. It is especially hard for people who have subordinated personal needs for a lengthy period. Such people become very good at it, and not only survive but thrive on the satisfaction of people pleasing.

A needs and desires inventory is often a good exercise. Few people have a good enough self-understanding to perform this analysis without help, so professional counseling is often necessary. It's important to realize that your relationship with your organization has many of the same dynamics as your interpersonal and family relationships. It's amazing to me that people flock to all kinds of psychologists, counselors, self-help books, and seminars to solve their *interpersonal* relationship problems, but so few seek help with *individual-organizational* relationship problems. Perhaps that's because corporate cults offer so much relationship assistance at the workplace. When individual-organizational counseling is offered at the workplace, employees don't need to find it outside the organization.

The first step toward achieving good health—of any kind—is a realization that you don't have it. Corporate cult members often suffer from a lack of self-awareness, so they don't seek help for the organizational relationship in which "what I do" has replaced "who I am."

There Is More to Career Preparation Than Education

One of the few regrets I have in life is that I jumped into my career too fast. I quit playing college basketball after my sophomore year so that I could participate in a work-study project with the Association of Tennis Professionals in Dallas. The ATP was growing fast, so I was able to win a highly coveted job after my junior year in college. I went back to college that fall and packed twenty-one credit hours into a semester so that I could graduate a semester early.

I graduated, got married, moved, and went to work all in the same week, at the age of twenty-one. Those are cultish signs. My regret is that I didn't do something else between college and work. I should have ridden my bike across Europe, worked as a ski instructor, or volunteered with Habitat for Humanity for a few months—or done all three!

There is hope for the next generation. My nephew just graduated from college and is on a missions trip to Ireland. He was an honor student in the College of Business and has great potential. He wants to sell Hondas for a dealership in Seattle, because he likes the honesty and integrity of the dealership where he bought one as a college student.

He is much less likely to become a workaholic culted to his organization than I was. The experience he will gain in nonwork situations will show him the value of family and community, which I didn't understand at his age. To avoid corporate cults, keep your work, family, and community circles well nurtured.

"Do Something Else!"

The principal of the middle school in my neighborhood decided that he was dismissing too many students for bad behavior, so he instituted a last-chance program. He hired Walter Beard to be his enforcer. Students are sent to Beard's "in-building suspension" for one last dose of strict supervision before being kicked out. It's not a pretty place. A storage room was cleaned out for IBS. It has cement floors and block walls with no windows. The students sit all day in separate study carrels and are not allowed to talk. At lunchtime, they don't go to the cafeteria; they eat peanut butter sandwiches at their desks. When my son was a student at the school, he admitted to me, "I'm scared of Mr. Beard." "Good," I said.

As I got to know Walter Beard, I found that he was a living example of tough love. He's tough on the kids because he really cares about them. I was having lunch with him one day when a counselor sat across from us. "I need your advice on a student," he said. "Each time he misbehaves, we take away more of his freedom. His parents have cooperated, so that we have now removed so many freedoms that all he does in school is sit in IBS. All he does at home is sit in his room. He's not responding. What do we do?" pleaded Beard.

"I know what we're going to do," the counselor said confidently. I leaned forward, anxious to hear the expert's advice. I could feel Beard's anticipation as well.

"Something else," she said flatly. I wondered if Walter was as disappointed as I was. "Yea, like what?" he asked. "I don't know," she said, "but it's obvious that what you're doing isn't working." Such good advice, and so simple. Insanity has been defined as continuing to take the same action while expecting different results. If you're in a corporate cult, take the counselor's advice. The most important thing you can do is "something else," because what you're doing isn't working. Find an organization that is different from the corporate cult, by the measures found in the corporate cult test.

All organizations have some level of cultedness, because each member gives up some of "who I am" to become part of the organization. But you're the one in charge of how much you give up. Don't give up more than you want to. You will always be who you are no matter what you do.

Notes

1. Carolyn Corbin, *Conquering Corporate Codependence* (Englewood Cliffs, N.J.: Prentice-Hall, 1993).
2. J. Walter Smith and Ann Clurman, *Rocking the Ages* (New York: Harper Business, 1997).
3. Joann Lublin and Joseph White "Throwing off Angst, Workers Are Feeling in Control of Careers," *The Wall Street Journal,* September 11, 1997.
4. John Goldhammer, *Under the Influence* (Amherst, N.Y.: Prometheus Books, 1996).
5. Hal Lancaster, "Many Merger Victims Can Take Their Time to Look for Work," *The Wall Street Journal,* May 12, 1998.
6. Carolyn Corbin, *Conquering Corporate Codependence* (Englewood Cliffs, N.J.: Prentice-Hall, 1993).
7. Ibid.
8. K. F. Riegel, "Dialectic Operations: The Final Period of Cognitive Development," *Human Development* 16 (1973): 346–370.
9. James Belasco, *Teaching the Elephant to Dance* (New York: Plume, 1991).

Index